RRARVM ORBIS TABVLA. *Auctore* IOANNE BLAEV.

THE COMPACT TIMELINE HISTORY OF
THE WORLD

First published 2010 by Worth Press Ltd.,
Cambridge, England
info@worthpress.co.uk

British Library Cataloging in Publication Data
A catalog record for this book is available from the British
Library

ISBN: 978-1-903025-95-6

Publisher's Note Every effort has been made to
ensure the accuracy of the information presented in
this book. The publisher will not assume liability for
damages caused by inaccuracies in the data and makes
no warranty whatsoever expressed or implied. The
publisher welcomes comments and corrections from
readers, emailed to info@worthpress.co.uk, which will
be considered for incorporation in future editions. Every
effort has been made to trace copyright holders and seek
permission to use illustrative and other material. The
publisher wishes to apologize for any inadvertent errors
or omissions and would be glad to rectify these in future.

Consultant Editor: Meredith MacArdle
Design and layout: Arati Devasher

Editor: Nirad Grover
Picture research: Malini Saigal
Assistant designer: Arun Aggarwal
Cartography: Sachin Pradhan
Illustrations: Vijay Sharma

Printed and bound in Malaysia for Imago.

Features section: Provides information on various aspects of history.

Timeline section: Entries on significant events flow in chronological order.

THE COMPACT TIMELINE HISTORY OF
THE WORLD

ROSHEN DALAL

WORTH
PRESS

CONTENTS

Human evolution took place over several million years against the backdrop of the changing earth, climate, and vegetation. According to present knowledge, human and chimpanzee ancestor lineages split between eight and seven mya (million years ago), and hominids, walking on two legs, began to develop. By 2.5 mya, *Homo habilis* (Handy man), the first tool-making hominid, had developed in Africa, and by one mya, the more advanced *Homo erectus* was in many parts of Asia and Europe.

Theories of human evolution

Charles Darwin's (1809–82) theory of evolution through natural selection forms the basis for today's studies on evolution, though there have been many advances on his theory. Theodosius Dobzhansky (1900–75), in 1937, showed how new species could emerge through mutation, genetic variability, and isolation. In 1981, Lynn Margolis (b. 1938) elaborated on the theory of endosymbiosis, indicating that organisms

from different lineages could join together to create new ones. Stephen Jay Gould (1941–2002) referred to changes in regulatory genes affecting development, which could explain variation in evolution. In 1972, Gould and Niles Eldredge put forward the theory of episodic rather than gradual change. Random mutations, the study of DNA, genetic similarities, and the theory of genetic drift and genetic bottlenecks are also incorporated into theories of evolution. Generally, though all scientists agree that evolution took place, refining and explaining theories of evolution is an ongoing process.

A caricature of Darwin from the 1870s, lampooning evolutionary theory.

Up to 50,000 BCE

4600 MYA Earth is formed.

3500 MYA Life starts: Bacteria and algae.

145–65 MYA Present-day continents begin to form.

8–7 MYA Hominids evolve.

7.2–6.9 MYA *Sahelanthropus tchadensis* (discovered in Chad, 2001).

6.5–5.9 MYA *Orrorin tugenensis* (Kenya, 2000).

5.8–5.2 MYA *Ardipithecus kadabba* (Ethiopia, 1992).

3.9–2.9 MYA *Australopithecus afarensis* (nicknamed "Lucy," Ethiopia, 1974).

3–2 MYA Early homo species.

2.6–2.2 MYA *Paranthropus aethiopicus* (Kenya, 1985).

2.5 MYA *Homo habilis* (Tanzania, 1962).

• Pebble chopper tools found at Koobi Fora, Kenya; earliest type of stone tool.

2–1.5 MYA *Homo erectus* evolves.

1.9 MYA First evidence of building; a wall of piled stones at Olduvai Gorge, Tanzania.

1.7–1 MYA *Homo erectus* moves out of Africa, spreads to Asia and Europe.

Homo sapiens

The ancestors of modern humans, *Homo sapiens* perhaps originated in Africa and then spread to Europe and Asia. Another theory is that parallel evolution occurred in various parts of the world. The first evidence of *Homo sapiens sapiens*, modern humans, is from Africa (Ethiopia), and is dated to about 190,000 years ago. By around 40,000 BCE, they had spread all over Eurasia, and were present even in Australia.

Neanderthals

Homoneanderthalensis(Neanderthal), sometimes called *Homo sapiens neanderthalensis*, was named after the Neander valley in Germany, where their remains were first found. They lived in Europe and West Asia between about 250,000 and 28,000 years ago. Neanderthals had large brains, walked upright, and used tools. Evidence of skin scrapers from southern Russia, dated to about 33,000 BCE, suggests they wore clothes made from skins. Neanderthal burials have also been found. One such, in Samarkand, Uzbekistan, is the grave of a child buried in a ring of horns, possibly indicating some sort of a belief in an afterlife. There may have been a social support system, as the finding of a Neanderthal skeleton without a right arm—lost long before his death—suggests that he must have survived with help from others. Though caves and natural shelters were the norm, in some areas simple shelters were built. Neanderthals died out about 30,000 years ago.

Use of Fire

Fire was a major aspect of human development. There were three early stages: Use of natural or accidental fire; lighting fires from naturally caused ones (controlled or deliberate use); learning to make fire at will. It is impossible to say when fire was first deliberately used, but burnt animal bones date as far back as 1 to 1.5 mya (Swartkrans cave in Transvaal, Africa). Effective means of making fire were probably acquired only after 10,000 BCE.

Hominids to Humans

1 Australopithecus africanus   2 Homo habilis   3 Homo erectus   4 Homo sapiens neanderthalensis   5 Homo sapiens sapiens

---

1.5 MYA–200,000 YEARS AGO Acheulian industry, standardized method of making stone tools, particularly hand axes, found at several sites in Africa, Europe, and Asia.

500,000 YEARS AGO Archaic *Homo sapiens*, ancestors of *Homo sapiens sapiens*, modern humans, develop.

500,000–200,000 YEARS AGO A range of hominids species co-exist such as "Peking Man," Neanderthals, and Swanscombe man.

190,000 YEARS AGO–40,000 BCE *Homo sapiens sapiens*, modern humans, develop.

100,000–50,000 YEARS AGO Caves in Dordogne, France, occupied.

70,000 YEARS AGO Neanderthal man uses fire.

60,000 YEARS AGO–40,000 BCE Aboriginal ancestors reach Australia by sea.

50,000 YEARS AGO Humans begin to create art and construct burials; Shanidar cave, northern Iraq, is an important burial site.

HUNTERS AND GATHERERS

Neolithic
stone tool.

*H*omo sapiens began to spread across the world, walking long distances or traveling by sea until much of the world as we know it today was occupied. Neanderthal man died out around 30,000 BCE, and soon only *Homo sapiens sapiens* or modern humans existed in the last— and coldest—stages of the Ice Ages. Perhaps 10 million people populated the whole world by 20,000 BCE.

Lifestyle

*H*umans increasingly started building their own shelters, and living more settled lives. Though food still included that obtained by hunting and gathering, life began to grow more complex. Recent evidence suggests that wild cereal grains were processed and eaten as far back as 26,000 BCE.

Stone tools became more complex, and along with common stones such as flint and obsidian, a wider range of materials came into use, such as wood, bone, antler, and ivory. Small flint points were probably attached to weapons like spears, arrows, and harpoons. Some groups buried or cremated their dead with reverence. Beautiful paintings were made in dark caves.

THE STONE AGE
Referring to the period when all tools were made of stone, this term is convenient although controversial, since a culture cannot be characterised only by its tools. The dates are only indicative, as they vary across different areas of the world. For example, in areas such as New Guinea, the Paleolithic Age lasted into historic times.

STONE AGE DIVISIONS
Paleolithic Age (Old Stone Age)
Lower 2.5 mya–120,000 years ago
Middle 120,000 years ago–35,000 BCE
Upper 35,000–8000 BCE
Mesolithic Age (Intermediate Stone Age)
12,000–4000 BCE
Neolithic Age (New Stone Age)
10,000–c. 2000 BCE

LANGUAGE
An important part of human evolution, simple forms of language must have developed by 1 mya, although some scientists propose that early spoken language developed much later, perhaps around 30,000 BCE.

40,000–10,000 BCE

40,000 Modern humans have evolved.
40,000–6000 Rock art at Ubirr, Australia.
35,000 Counting device made from baboon bone in South Africa.
35,000–8000 First early modern humans in Europe (Cro-Magnon man).
34,000 Lesotho and Zambia in Africa occupied.
34,000–32,000 Horse figurine carved from mammoth ivory discovered at Vogelherd, Germany.

30,000 Female figurine carved from serpentine found at Galgenberg, Austria.
30,000–15,000 Bow and arrow invented.
30,000–13,000 Human migration into America across Bering Straits, or by sea.
28,000 Cro-Magnon carvings on bone, possibly representing phases of moon, found at Blanchard, France.
25,000–24,000 Cave paintings at Apollo site, Namibia, Africa.

Stencilled outline of hands in yellow, ochre, and green, executed between 13,000–9500 years ago, Cueva de las Manos, Rio Pinturas, Patagonia, Argentina.

Art

Palaeolithic art covered a wide range of forms and materials. In dark caves, paintings of animals, human figures, and hunting scenes were made with natural materials, perhaps as a type of "sympathetic magic," a visualization of a successful hunt. Another theory suggests links to shamanism. As artifical light was needed in the caves, some kind of a fire torch must have been used. Cave paintings have been found in France, Spain, Africa, India, and other places, dating back to 28,000 BCE.

From about 33,000 BCE other types of art included decorated and colored objects, even weapons, fashioned out of bone and ivory, as well as small figurines of stone, bone, terracotta, or clay.

CHAUVET CAVE

The earliest cave paintings found in Europe, the pictures in the 1,300-foot-long Chauvet cave in southern France depict an unusually large variety of animals: Lions, mammoths, rhinoceros, cave bears, horses, bison, ibex, reindeer, red deer, aurochs, megaceros deer, musk oxen, panthers, and owls. Radiocarbon dating reveals two periods of occupation: 30,000–28,000 BCE and 25,000–23,000 BCE. In addition, the cave contained fossilized remains of animals, while on the floor, footprints of both humans and animals are preserved.

Early hunters used arrows with flight feathers and flint arrowheads.

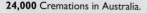

24,000 Cremations in Australia.
* Houses with clay roofs in Europe.
24,000–22,000 Female figurine known as "Venus of Willendorf" found at Willendorf village, Austria.
21,000 Ivory boomerang used for hunting in Poland.
18,000–11,000 Kutikina cave, southern Tasmania, occupied by users of stone tools.
17,000–15,000 Wadi Kubbaniya, Late Palaeolithic site in Upper Egypt.

16,000–10,000 Dwellings in Europe made of mammoth bones.
15,000–10,000 Cave paintings at Lascaux, France.
14,000–12,000 Cave paintings at Altamira, Spain.
13,000 Cave paintings at Bhimbetka, India.
* Terracotta figurines in Algeria.
12,000 Dog domesticated.
11,000 Chile, South America occupied.
* Cave dwellings in Fukui, Japan.
* Wheat cultivated in northern Mesopotamia.

10,000–5000 BCE

Although geological changes were still taking place, the topography of the earth was relatively stable by 9000 BCE. As the last Ice Age receded between 13,000 and 10,000 BCE, large amounts of water were released. The surface of the earth transformed, and the climate grew warmer. In some areas, regular rainfall made the land more fertile, and, although hunter-gatherer communities continued to exist, all over the world more communities began to grow crops and keep domestic animals, with the first major developments seen in West Asia around 9000 BCE. With crop cultivation, food storage began and settled villages emerged; by 6000 BCE, villages were widespread in the region and a few of these had developed into towns. Among these were Jericho and Catal Huyuk, both located near water sources.

Small farming communities in other parts of Asia, as well as in Europe, Africa, and the Americas developed distinctive styles of house building and craft production. Crops grown and animals domesticated varied according to the climate and region. Canal irrigation began in Mesopotamia. Painted pottery, along with other artifacts such as terracotta figurines, have been unearthed from several areas. Implements were made from bone and ivory, as well as stone, and towards the end of this period, copper began to be used. There was no writing at this time, but petroglyphs, signs that were possibly the precursor of writing, have been found at several sites.

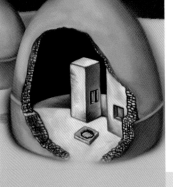

An artist's rendering of a Neolithic hut at Khirokitia, Cyprus.

KHIROKITIA

Village settlements began around 7000 BCE on the island of Cyprus, one of the earliest of which was Khirokitia, near the southern coast. Surrounded by a defensive wall, it had circular houses, usually with domed roofs. Dwelling walls were often of stone, and within were shelves, benches, and windows. Khirokitia's dead were buried beneath the floor of the house, and its people cultivated cereal crops, picked wild fruits, and domesticated sheep, goats, and pigs. Deer bones found here indicate hunting. At least 20 similar sites have been discovered across Cyprus, but Khirokitia was deserted by around 6000 BCE.

The ancient city of Jericho.

10,000–5000 BCE

10,000 Semi-permanent agricultural settlements begin in many parts of the world.

10,000–8200 Natufian people establish settlements in eastern Mediterranean; build houses, bury dead, and domesticate dogs.

10,000–6000 Cave art continues in Australia.

10,000–2000 Neolithic settlements in China.

10,000–300 Jomon culture flourishes in Japan.

9500–3000 Clovis culture at Blackwater Draw, North America.

9000 Cow's milk becomes part of human diet.

9000–3000 Rock paintings in caves, central India.

9000–2000 Cochise culture in North America.

8200 Stone engravings, Wonderwerk cave, South Africa.

8000 Clay tokens used in Mesopotamia.

• Sheep, goats domesticated at Ali Kosh, Iran.

• Shellfish eaten in European coastal areas.

8000–6000 Textiles woven, clay and plaster statues made at Jericho.

Above: A reconstructed Jomon village (10,000–300 BCE) in Japan.
Left: Neolithic carving of the Seated Goddess of Catal Huyuk, Turkey.

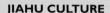

CATAL HUYUK

Catal Huyuk in Turkey, dated between 8000 and 6000 BCE, is estimated to have been inhabited by about 5000–10,000 people, living in mud-brick and plaster houses. The houses had no doors, and entrances were through the roofs. People grew cereals, kept herds of cattle, and made stone weapons and pottery. They also traded goods and performed rituals for the dead. Numerous figurines of females have been found, as well as shrines dedicated to a so-called Mother Goddess. Other finds include animal figurines, bone tools, wooden bowls, woven baskets, and pottery.

JIAHU CULTURE

Jiahu, located on the Huang (Yellow) river in China, was a complex Neolithic culture around 7000–5700 BCE. The whole site covered 592,000 sq ft (55,000 sq m), surrounded by a moat. Remains of houses, pottery, turquoise carvings, and tools from bone and stone have been discovered here. From the middle phase, there are markings carved on tortoise shells and bone, some of which are similar to characters in later Chinese writing. Some bone flutes found at the site are playable even today. Rice and millet were cultivated, and alcohol was brewed from fermented rice mixed with honey and hawthorn.

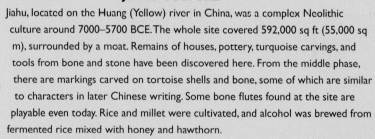

7000 Neolithic period begins in Europe; first farming communities.
• Fishing communities in the Sahara region.
7000–5700 Jiahu culture, Huang (Yellow) river, China.
7000–4500 Neolithic cultures in Egypt.
7000–4000 Cave painting depicting marching warriors at Cingle de la Molla, Spain.
6750 Pigs domesticated in Jarmo, Iraq.
6500 Copper objects made in Anatolia.
6000 Crops cultivated in several parts of the world.

• Canal irrigation in Mesopotamia.
• Drum used in Moravia.
• Cattle domesticated in Greece and Crete.
6000–5500 Halaf farming culture with polychrome pottery in north Mesopotamia, Syria.
6000–3000 Khartoum Mesolithic and Neolithic cultures in southern Nubia, Africa.
5900 Beer brewed in Sumer and Babylon.
5500–3500 Vinca copper culture in Balkans: Serbia, Romania, Bulgaria, Macedonia.

THE FIRST CIVILIZATIONS

Farming and the domestication of animals (such as cattle, pigs, camels, and dogs) became widespread. Advanced stone tools were used, along with copper and bronze tools and the potter's wheel. Art and building construction developed further, and urban centers continued to emerge. City civilizations dawned in Mesopotamia, Egypt, India and Pakistan, and the Mediterranean.

Mesopotamia

Upper part of the stele of Hammurabi's code of laws.

Broadly the region of modern Iraq, Mesopotamia lies between the valleys of the Tigris and Euphrates rivers. Its first cities were founded by c. 5000 BCE in Sumer, the name given to southern Mesopotamia, and developed into city states controlling the regions around them. Around 2500 BCE Sumerian culture was at its height, extending from the Zagros to the Taurus mountains, and from the Persian Gulf to the Mediterranean Sea. Crafts flourished; irrigation canals from rivers to villages and cities enabled crops of barley, wheat, millet, and sesame; and a system of writing was developed, first pictographic, and later stylized (cuneiform). These can be seen on the numerous stone seals and clay tablets that have been found in the region. The Sumerians worshiped a number of deities, and from 2200 to 500 BCE great temples on stepped towers known as ziggurats were built. The legendary Tower of Babel was probably the ziggurat of the temple of Marduk in Babylon.

Around 2334 BCE, Sargon I of Akkad, a so-far unidentified city in central Mesopotamia to the north of Sumer, conquered the Sumer region. The joint culture came to be known as Akkadian. Later, King Hammurabi of Babylon (1792–1750 BCE) conquered Sumer and Akkad, and created a strong empire. He is remembered for his code of law, engraved on stone pillars and clay tablets, the oldest such code known today. The Hittites, a people who spoke an Indo-European language, and had settled in Asia Minor around 1900 BCE, conquered Babylon in 1590 BCE.

THE EPIC OF GILGAMISH

Perhaps the oldest text in the world (the earliest version was written soon after 2000 BCE), the Epic describes a king who is said to have ruled at Uruk in Mesopotamia c. 2700–2650 BCE. Late versions include the story of a great flood and the building of an ark, which enabled one family to survive.

5000–3000 BCE

5200–4000 Several Neolithic farming cultures in Africa.
5000 First copper and gold metalwork in Europe.
- Cochise culture continues, North America.
- First cities in Sumer, West Asia.
- Farming and domestication of animals in Egypt.
- Copper used in Mesopotamia.
- Settled village cultures in China and India.
5000–4000 Gumelnitsa-Karanova culture in Romania, Bulgaria, and Thrace.

5000–3500 Corn cultivated in Mesoamerica.
5000–3000 Neolithic cultures in several parts of Europe.
5000–2800 Megaliths in various parts of Europe; earliest at Evora in Portugal.
4500–2000 Megaliths and menhirs constructed at Carnac, France.
4000 Farming in Sahara region, Africa.
- Crops cultivated in the British Isles.
- Grape cultivation in the Middle East.

Indus civilization

Another great civilization rose on the fertile plains of the Indus river on the Indian subcontinent. At its height during 2600–1800 BCE, the culture was dominated by large cities such as Harappa and Mohenjodaro in the Indus valley, Lothal and Dholavira in Gujarat, and Kalibangan in Rajasthan. The cities contained baked brick structures and an elaborate drainage system, and numerous objects have been found made of a range of materials—stone, metals, ivory, terracotta—as well as red pottery and stone seals that feature an undeciphered script.

Top: Steatite seal, Indus valley culture.
Above: Brick structures at Lothal, India.
Below: The Great Ziggurat at Ur (in present-day Iraq), built of mud bricks.

LOTHAL: A TRADING PORT

A major center of the Indus civilization, Lothal was located on the coast of Gujarat in India, and was probably involved in external trade. As well as the usual houses, streets, and drains, Lothal had a large warehouse, and a baked-brick structure that was possibly a dock for ships. This measures approximately 700 x 118 feet, and at high tide, ships could sail into it through a 40-foot gap. The whole city was enclosed by a massive defensive wall to resist floods.

- Horse domesticated.
4000–3200 Cernavoda culture succeeds Gumelnitsa in southeast Europe.
4000–3000 Funnelbeaker culture in Europe.
c. 3600 Chinese raise silkworms and weave silk.
c. 3500 City of Ur founded in Mesopotamia.
- Beans cultivated in Mesoamerica.
- Llama used for transport in Peru.
3200 Cuneiform script in Mesopotamia.
- Egyptian hieroglyphic writing begins.

- Newgrange passage grave in Ireland.
3100 Menes unites kingdoms of Upper and Lower Egypt.
- First stage of building at Stonehenge, England.
- Boats with sails in Egypt.
- City of Byblos founded on Mediterranean coast.
3000 Wheel used in Mesopotamia.
- Arched harp used in Egypt and Sumeria.
3000–2000 Beaker culture in Europe.
3000–1450 Minoan civilization.

THE FIRST CIVILIZATIONS

Egyptian civilization

Osiris was the king of the dead, and he, Isis, Nephthys, and Seth were part of a group of nine gods worshipped at Heliopolis, Egypt.

Some time after 4000 BCE, villages along the Nile river grouped into two kingdoms: Upper and Lower Egypt, which were united by King Menes around 3100 BCE. Thirty dynasties are said to have ruled between Menes's time and Alexander's conquest of Egypt in 332 BCE, mainly grouped together into the Old Kingdom, Middle Kingdom and New Kingdom, with some intermediate periods. Egyptian civilization included: An advanced system of government; irrigation works; magnificent buildings; the sciences of astronomy, mathematics, and medicine; a 365-day calendar; a hieroglyphic script used on monuments and a simpler hieratic script; and the invention of papyrus sheets for writing.

During the Old Kingdom, great pyramids, which were actually elaborate tombs, were developed. The dead were embalmed as mummies and buried inside, and large temple complexes were attached to the pyramids. The Egyptians worshipped many deities, including the important sun god Re, later Amon-Re. Both tombs and temple walls featured Egypt's naturalistic art.

The Nile's fertile plains allowed fruits, vegetables, and pulses to be grown, and the ancient Egyptians also indulged in wine and beer.

EGYPTIAN PYRAMIDS

About 80 pyramids have been found at various sites. Three of the greatest were built at Giza: Those of kings Khufu (2547–2524 BCE), Khafre (2516–2493 BCE), and Menkaure (2493–2475 BCE). The pyramid of Khufu (Cheops) is the largest in Egypt, with each of its base sides measuring 761 feet. It took 20 years and supposedly 100,000 men to build.

3000–1540 BCE

2925–2575 Early dynastic period (1st–3rd dynasties), Egypt.

2700 Tea known in China.

2600–1800 Indus civilization in northwest India and Pakistan at its peak.

2575–2130 Old Kingdom (4th–8th dynasties), Egypt

2547–2475 Great Pyramids built at Giza, Egypt.

c. 2543 Ur-Nanshe, 1st king of Lagash dynasty, begins rule in Mesopotamia.

2500 Potato grown in Peru.

c. 2400 Egyptians use papyrus to make writing material.

• City of Kerma, capital of kingdom later known as Kush, established in northeast Africa.

c. 2200–1700 Bactria-Margiana Archaeological Complex (culture), Central Asia.

c. 2200–1600 Kurgan grave culture, East Europe.

2130–1938 1st Intermediate period (9th–11th dynasties), Egypt.

Minoan civilization

This culture existed on the island of Crete, in Europe, during 3000–1450 BCE. Rich from sea trade, the Minoans built grand palaces such as Knossos. They created pottery, gold and bronze artifacts, and developed several types of writing.

The palace of Minos, Knossos, Crete.

Farming communities in Europe

In western Europe bronze technology was introduced and massive stone tombs were built, along with megalithic standing stones such as Stonehenge, in England. Several Neolithic cultures in southeast Europe show evidence of houses, cemeteries, cult objects, and the use of copper.

GUMELNITSA–KARANOVO CULTURE

Gumelnitsa in Romania and Karanovo in Bulgaria are sites typical of a copper-using, farming culture, dating to 4500–4000 BCE and extending from the Black Sea in the east to central Bulgaria in the west, and from the Danube river in the north to Thrace in the south. Amongst the many objects found in the region are female figurines.

SKARA BRAE

This well-preserved Neolithic village on Mainland, Orkney, Scotland dates to 3100–2500 BCE. With few trees on the island, houses and furniture were made of stone, including beds, shelves, tables and hearths, and an indoor toilet linked to a stream.

Left: Great Pyramid of Cheops, Giza, Egypt.
Right: Neolithic settlement of Skara Brae, Orkney Islands, Scotland.

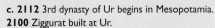

c. 2112 3rd dynasty of Ur begins in Mesopotamia.
2100 Ziggurat built at Ur.
c. 2000 Migrations of people speaking Indo-European languages across Europe and Asia.
• Inuits settle in the Arctic.
c. 2000–1900 Palace at Knossos, Crete built.
1938–1630 Middle Kingdom (12th and 13th dynasties), Egypt.
c. 1900–1350 Erlitou culture flourishes in China; known for its bronze work.

c. 1766–1520 Shang dynasty founded in China.
c. 1750 BCE Hierarchical village society develops in Soconusco region, Mexico.
1700 Hittite empire extends between Syria and Black Sea.
1700–1500 Kush kingdom on lower Nile becomes powerful.
1630–1540 2nd Intermediate period in Egypt.
1540 Hyksos invaders evicted from Egypt by Ahmose I.

Aspects of civilization such as urban centers, writing, the use of metals, large monuments, began to extend into new areas. Money began to be used and coins were made. Societies became more complex, with new philosophies and religions, monetary systems, and elaborate artifacts. At the same time there were wars and conquests as empires rose, and fell.

Egypt: the New Kingdom

One of Egypt's most prosperous periods, the New Kingdom was known for its monumental architecture and great art. Ahmose I began the period with the foundation of the 18th dynasty in 1540–39 BCE, and another notable king, Amenhotep IV (Akhenaten), founded a new cult of the sun god Aten and the new city of Akhetaten (Amarna) near Thebes. Probably the most famous pharaoh of all was Akhenaten's son, Tutankhamun, who died aged 19 in 1323 BCE. In the New Kingdom great buildings were constructed at Karnak and Luxor (Thebes), and at the Valley of the Kings near Luxor, many pharaohs, including Tutankhamun, were entombed in deep graves. Prosperity declined after the time of Rameses III (r. 1187–1156 BCE), with repeated invasions by the Libyans and sea-faring tribes.

Tutankhamen's solid gold mask, found placed over the mummy's head and shoulders, was evidently molded to mirror the pharaoh's facial characteristics. The vulture and cobra heads over the brow symbolize sovereignty over Upper and Lower Egypt.

THE PHOENICIANS

Also known as the Sea Peoples, the sea-trading Phoenicians flourished between 1200–800 BCE along the coastal regions of the eastern Mediterranean. Their port cities included Tyre and Sidon, as well as Berot (modern Beirut), Byblos, and Carthage.

A Phoenician coin.

TROY

Once thought to be a legend telling of the Greeks' rescue of Helen of Sparta, who had eloped with the Trojan warrior Paris, archaeologists now believe Troy is the mound of Hissarlik (Place of Fortresses) in Turkey, a site occupied from c. 3000–1260 BCE when it burnt down, the traditional date of its destruction by the Greeks.

Ruins at Hissarlik, Turkey.

1540–1000 BCE

1540–1075 New Kingdom (18–20th dynasties), Egypt.
1500 Civilization in China flourishes under Shang dynasty.
• Cuneiform script introduced in Asia Minor.
• Maya civilization founded in Mesoamerica.
1500–1200 Probable period within which the Prophet Zarathushtra (Zoroaster), founder of Zoroastrianism lived. in Iran.
1500–300 Olmec settlements in Mexico.

1493–c. 1482 Tuthmosis I is pharaoh of Egypt; makes the first underground tombs.
c. 1343–1333 Tutankhamun rules Egypt from Thebes.
1300 Ships sailing the eastern Mediterranean are capable of carrying more than 200 copper ingots.
c. 1260–1240 Probable date of destruction of Troy in the Trojan War.
1250 Lion Gate, Mycenae, constructed; elaborate lions guard outer gate of fortress palace.

The Shang dynasty

I n China, the Shang dynasty—known for its advanced bronze work—flourished in the valley of the Huang Ho (Yellow) river. Shang rulers practiced ancestor worship and divination, and were buried in massive grave chambers.

Oracle bones from the Shang dynasty.

The Vedic people

A n early text in Sanskrit, the *Rig Veda*, provides some information on life in northwest India between 1500 and 1000 BCE. The authors of the text refer to themselves as *arya* or noble, which has given rise to the colloquial name, "Aryans." The origin of these people remains controversial: Some scholars think they originated in India; others believe they were Indo-European speakers who migrated from the Caspian Sea region. Later, additional Vedas were composed, along with auxiliary texts including the *Upanishads*, containing deep philosophical thought.

A later manuscript of the *Rig Veda*.

CELTS

"Celtic" is a loose term that refers to people speaking a certain branch of Indo-European languages or to people of the Urnfield culture (1200–800 BCE) of north Germany and the Netherlands and their descendents, the rich Hallstatt culture of 800–500 BCE, which was known for its use of iron, including ploughshares and chariot wheels. By 500 BCE, Celtic culture had spread to Iberia, Ireland, and Britain. The mystical druids, priests proficient in magic and ritual, had an important role in Celtic society.

Celtic anklet.

c. 1225 Assyrians capture southern Mesopotamia and Babylon.
c. 1200 Exodus: Hebrews leave Egypt for Canaan.
1200 Mayas establish settlement of Chau Hiix in Belize.
1200–300 Chavin culture in Peru.
c. 1120 Mycenaean civilization ends after invasion of Dorian Greeks.
1100–1000 Iron weapons in Cyprus; soon spread across Aegean.

1075 New Kingdom in Egypt ends; period of turmoil follows.
c. 1050–479 *Wu Ching*, or five classics of Chinese literature, composed; includes *I-Ching*.
c. 1027 (traditional date 1122) Zhou dynasty founded in China.
c. 1000 King David captures Jerusalem and unites Israel.
• Iron used in Europe and Asia.
1000 Pen used by Chinese calligraphers.

EXTENSION OF CIVILIZATION

The Hebrews

The most prominent peoples in West Asia were the Hittites and Assyrians, but another important group was the Hebrews. As narrated in the Bible, they settled in Canaan (Palestine) under their leader Abraham.

Around 1500 BCE, famine forced one group to leave Canaan for Egypt, where they later became enslaved, escaping from Egypt at the time of Rameses II and returning to Canaan. They were also known as Israelites,

David being anointed king by Samuel (from a wood panel in the Dura Synagogue, Syria).

and later as Jews. Around the 11th century BCE, the dynasty of David was founded. His son, Solomon, built the first Temple at Jerusalem in c. 950 BCE, but after his death the kingdom divided into two: Israel in the north, and Judah in the south. The northern kingdom was destroyed by the Assyrians in 721 BCE, after which several Hebrew tribes migrated away and became the "Lost Tribes of Israel." The southern kingdom lasted until Nebuchadnezzar II of Babylon destroyed the Temple and deported most of the inhabitants to Babylon in 587–86 BCE.

Kush

Part of Nubia in Africa, the kingdom of Kush was influenced by Egypt, but from c. 770–671 BCE actually ruled Egypt until it was overthrown by the Assyrians.

Mycenaeans and the Greek states

The Mycenaeans from mainland Greece began to influence Crete's Minoan culture from around 1500 BCE. Greek city states began to emerge from around 800 BCE, each with its own governing body, military forces, and deities.

JUDAISM

Judaism, the Jewish religion, developed with the Hebrews or Israelites. Its main tenets are belief in one supreme god, Yahweh, and the Ten Commandments, which were revealed in about the 13th century BCE to Moses, who led the Exodus from Egypt to Canaan.

1000–500 BCE

1000–600 Neolithic and Megalithic cultures in south India.
- Vedic people in north India compose additional texts, expand to new areas.

c. 1000–450 City states develop in southern Arabia; Saba is the most powerful.

c. 1000–400 CE Paracas culture flourishes in Peru, South America.

c. 970–935 Solomon is king of Israel.

c. 928 Israel splits into Kingdoms of Israel and Judah.

900 Napata established as capital of Kush kingdom in Sudan.

c. 850–480 Greeks develop alphabet.

814 Carthage founded. by Phoenicians.

c. 800 Olmecs construct pyramid at La Venta.
- Etruscans found city-states in Italy.
- Hallstatt culture in Austria.

c. 800–700 Homer, Greek poet, is believed to have composed *Iliad* and *Odyssey*.

776 First Olympic Games, Greece.

ROMULUS AND REMUS

According to mythology, the twins Romulus and Remus, sons of Mars, the God of War, were abandoned after birth but were rescued and nursed by a she-wolf, and were later adopted by a shepherd. Romulus grew up to found the city of Rome in 753 BCE, while Remus was killed after a quarrel.

Sculpture of Romulus and Remus, with the she-wolf.

Etruscans

The Etruscans, whose origin is unclear, probably settled in parts of Italy between 1200–700 BCE, and maintained close relationships with the people who already occupied the site of Rome, though the Roman Republic was founded only in 509 BCE.

Olmecs

Known for its massive basalt heads and delicate jade figurines, the later Olmec civilization of Mexico and Central America was centered at La Venta, an urban site with several houses and a complex of temples around a tall pyramid.

A stone Olmec head.

Chavin culture

South America's Chavin culture centered around Chavin de Huantar in the Peruvian Andes. Remains include a stone temple complex and bas reliefs depicting gods, humans, and animals.

c. 700 Greek poet Hesiod's books include *Theogony* and *Works and Days*.
668–627 Ashurbanipal is Assyrian king; founds library in Nineveh.
c. 650 Beginning of Archaic period in Greek art; attention to human anatomy, depiction of scenes from epics.
612 Nineveh invaded by Babylonians and Medes, effectively ending the Assyrian Empire.
c. 610–580 Life of female Greek poet Sappho.

c. 605–561 Nebuchadnezzar II reigns in Babylon; **597** deports Jews from Judah to Babylon.
c. 563–483 Life of the Buddha, founder of Buddhism.
559 Cyrus II (the Great) founds the Achaemenid (Persian) empire; **539** captures Babylon, allows the people of Judah to return to Jerusalem and rebuild temple.
c. 540 Birth of Mahavira, 24th tirthankara (Great Guide) of Jainism and last of the present era.

CONQUESTS AND EMPIRES

This was an age of great battles and conquests, when vast empires were founded. At the same time, there were peaceful periods, and art, culture, and philosophy flourished.

The Empire of Darius I

Darius I (521–486 BCE) of Persia extended his empire to northwest India, Thrace, and Macedonia. The vast empire was reorganized into 20 satrapies or provinces, each under a governor. Darius lost the Battle of Marathon against the Greeks (490 BCE), and the Persian empire was brought to an end, finally, with Darius III's defeat by Alexander the Great at the Battle of Gaugamela (331 BCE).

Mosaic of Darius III in battle against Alexander, Pompeii, Italy.

ZOROASTRIANISM

Established by the Prophet Zarathushtra (Zoroaster in Greek) of what is now Iran, this religion holds that there is only one god, known as Ahura Mazda. The state religion of the Sasanian Persians, Zoroastrianism was thus the earliest monotheistic religion, influencing Judaism, Christianity, and Islam. In its later form, it saw the world in dualistic terms of opposing forces of good and evil.

Judah

Judah was ruled by Persians, Alexander the Great, Seleucid Greeks of Syria, and Jewish Hasmoneans, before it was taken over by Rome. In 37 BCE, Herod was made king of Judah, then known as Judea. Around 5 BCE Jesus Christ, the founder of Christianity, was born.

521–323 BCE

521–486 Darius I rules Persia.
c. 500 Zapotec culture at Mt Alban, in Oaxaca, Mexico; has a system of writing and calendar.
• Adena culture in Ohio, North America reaches its height.
• Nok culture in Nigeria.
500–200 Hindu Scripture Bhagavad Gita composed.
496–406 Life of Greek playwright Sophocles.
492–449 Greco-Persian Wars.

c. 485–221 Zhou kingdom in China breaks up into smaller states (Period of Warring States).
484–430 Life of Greek historian Herodotus.
c. 480 Admiral Hanno of Carthage voyages along the West African coast.
c. 478 Athens becomes powerful; forms the Delian League of Greek states.
460 Temple of Hera II (or Neptune) built at Paestum, Italy.
c. 451–450 Twelve Tables of Roman Law formulated.

The Parthenon temple, Athens, Greece, c. fifth century BCE.

Greek city-states

Some of the main Greek city states were Athens (leader of the Delian League), Sparta (head of the Peloponnesian League), Olympia, Corinth, and Argos. After the Greco-Persian Wars, Athens emerged as preeminent, and Greek culture reached its height there, with the introduction of democracy, monumental buildings including the temple to the goddess Athena at the Parthenon, and flourishing arts, science, and philosophy. Aeschylus, Sophocles, and Euripides were amongst the classical Athenian playwrights, while great sculptors included Phidias, Praxiteles, and Scopas. The Greek civilization declined following wars between Sparta and Athens, and in 338 BCE it was taken over by Philip II of Macedonia. His son Alexander became king in 336 BCE.

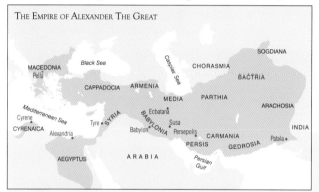

THE EMPIRE OF ALEXANDER THE GREAT

ALEXANDER THE GREAT

Extending control over Greece, Alexander defeated the Persians then conquered Syria, Tyre, Gaza, and Egypt. Next, he took Babylon, Susa, and Persepolis, and invaded northwest India. His troops refused to proceed further from here, forcing him to turn back. A great general, Alexander also valued learning, and had been a pupil of Aristotle.

431–421 Peloponnesian Wars between Athens and Sparta; end in Peace of Nicias.

430 Greek sculptor Phidias carves statue of Zeus at Olympia.

415–405 Peloponnesian Wars resume; Athens surrenders to Sparta.

405 Erecthium, temple of Goddess Athena, built on Acropolis at Athens, Greece.

c. 400 Farming settlements at Tiahuanaco, near Lake Titicaca, Bolivia.

• Olmec city of La Venta, Mexico declines.

384–322 Life of Greek sage Aristotle.

371 Sparta defeated by Thebes.

350 Sculpture of Hermes carrying infant Dionysus carved by Greek sculptor Praxiteles **(370–330)**.

337 Philip II of Macedonia defeats Athens and forms League of Corinth.

336 Alexander the Great becomes king of Macedonia; **332** conquers Egypt; **331** defeats Persia; **327–326** invades India; **323** dies at Babylon.

CONQUESTS AND EMPIRES

The Qin and the Han

A number of warring states existed in China until the ruler of the state of Qin created a united empire in 221 BCE, taking the name Qin Shi Huangdi, or "First Emperor of Qin." After his death in 210 BCE, Liu Bang or Liu Ji, an army officer, rose to power as emperor (202–195 BCE), and founded the Han dynasty. His strong imperial system, with Confucianism as the state ideology, was followed in essence for the next 2000 years.

QIN SHI HUANGDI'S TOMB

The famous Terracotta Army, life-sized models of more than 7,000 warriors along with charioteers and horses, is only part of Emperor Qin Shi Huangdi's grandiose monument that he began to build for himself early on in his reign. Near the city of Xian, the tomb also contained a replica of an imperial palace, and skeletons of humans and horses were discovered in the complex.

The terracotta army of Qin Shi Huangdi.

Ashoka

A shoka (r. 269–232 BCE), an emperor of India, belonged to the Mauryan dynasty whose capital was at Pataliputra (modern Patna). After seeing the suffering caused by his own wars of conquest, he turned to Buddhism and developed a philosophy of Dhamma (Sanskrit *dharma* or "right living") that included a model code of behavior such as respect for people of all classes and religions. He engraved his ideas on pillars and rocks across India.

Mauryan silver punch-marked coin.

326–166 BCE

326 Circus Maximus, a large stadium, constructed in Rome; later rebuilt and enlarged.

306 Greek philosopher Epicurus (341–271) founds a school, Ho Kepas (The Garden), in Athens; admits women.

305 Ptolemy founds a new dynasty in Egypt.

301 Macedonian generals fight for control of Alexander's empire in Battle of Ipsus; divide empire between themselves.

c. 300 Cuicuilco in Mexico gains importance; has large buildings and circular pyramids.

• Kush kingdom expands in Africa.

• Moche civilization begins in Peru.

c. 300 BCE–250 CE Yayoi civilization in Japan.

c. 294–284 Chares of Lyndus builds the Colossus of Rhodes, a bronze statue of the sun god Helios 105-feet high, to commemorate victory over Macedonian invaders.

Rome

Julius Caesar.

Gradually, Rome became the dominant state of the Western world. At first a kingdom, a popular uprising in 509 BCE saw the creation of the Roman Republic, which lasted to 27 BCE. Instead of a king at the helm, the Republic had two magistrates known as consuls, selected by the citizens and advised by the senate. A number of internal conflicts within the Republic ended when the politician-general Julius Caesar made himself dictator for life, but the senate was opposed to this, and Caesar was murdered by Longinus, Brutus, and other senators. There followed a period of transition before Octavius became the first emperor of Rome in 27 BCE.

The Romans eventually conquered a huge empire including: Syria; Macedonia; Greece; Spain; France; Pergamum in Asia Minor; and parts of North Africa, Germany, and Britain. Rome destroyed the North African state of Carthage, despite Carthaginian general Hannibal's expedition across the Alps to attack Rome with war elephants. After the conquest of Greece, Rome absorbed Greek culture, which became the foundation of its own culture.

The Roman empire, which lasted until 450 CE, was characterized by large houses, good roads, markets with rich produce, public baths, sports and games, as well as great literature, art, and culture: *The Aeneid*, composed by the poet Virgil (70-19 BCE), and the works of Horace (65-8 BCE) are Latin classics, while the senator Cicero (106-43 BCE) is remembered as Rome's greatest orator.

THE KUSH KINGDOM

In the Sudan region of Africa, the Kush kingdom, heavily influenced by Egypt, had its capital at Meroe, which became a trade center for northern Africa, the Middle East, and Europe. The Kush civilization was in decline by the first century CE.

Meroitic pyramids sitting amidst sand dunes.

290 Ptolemy founds library at Alexandria, Egypt.
264–241 First Punic War between Rome and Carthage; Rome wins.
250 Roman nobles begin collecting works of art.
• Arsaces founds kingdom of Parthia in eastern Persia.
247–183 Life of Hannibal of Carthage.
221 Antiochus III becomes ruler of the Syrian empire.
221–210 Shih Huangdi is first emperor of Qin dynasty in China; builds the Great Wall.
218–201 Second Punic War; Rome wins.

206 Liu Bang founds Han dynasty in China.
c. 200–50 Rock-cut Buddhist cave temples made in India along the Western Ghat hills.
189 Romans defeat Antiochus III.
• Pushyamitra Shunga founds new dynasty in north India.
171 Mithridates I becomes Parthian king.
c. 166 Roman dramatist Terence writes his first comic play, *Andria*; the plots of his comedies influenced later European writers.

Across the ancient world, multiple gods were worshipped. But at the same time, this period saw the rise of advanced philosophies, especially in Greece, India, and China.

Greek philosophy

The foundation for all later Western philosophy was laid by the Greek thinkers who worked between c. 600–200 BCE. Socrates (470–399 BCE), his disciple Plato, and Plato's student Aristotle, were the most influential Greek philosophers. Socrates sought truth through dialectical questions. He put forward the idea that *arete* (goodness or virtue) is an innate aspect of life, and is linked to self-knowledge. Socrates did not write anything himself, but his dialogues were recorded by others. Plato systematized Socratic philosophy, and defined the goal of the philosopher as that of knowing and understanding eternal forms, and instructing others in this truth. Plato's book, *The Republic*, presents a description of the perfect state. Aristotle wrote many works on logic, on the natural world, metaphysics, and ethics. His ideas were pervasive until modern times.

Other great philosophers included Thales, Anaximander, and Heraclitus, who all provided explanations of matter; Pythagoras (582–500 BCE), who used mathematics to understand the natural world; and Anaxagoras, who introduced the concept of Nous, the mind or intellect that permeated all living beings, and believed matter was made up of tiny particles or atoms. In the fifth century BCE Sophists such as Protagoras focused on material success, as they believed understanding the ultimate truth was not possible. Cynics, Epicureans, Sceptics, and Stoics were other groups of ancient Greek philosophers, and overall, Greek ideas also influenced later politics and aesthetics.

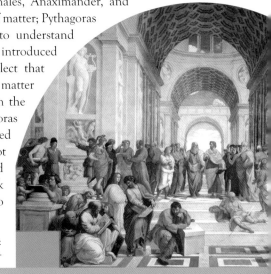

Right: Michelangelo's rendering of Aristotle's Lyceum at Athens, on the Sistine Chapel ceiling in the Vatican.

165 BCE–1 CE

165 Judas Maccabeus defeats Seleucids in Jerusalem, and rededicates the Jewish Temple.

c. 160 Bactrian Greeks begin rule in northwest India.

c. 150 Famous statue, Venus de Milo, sculpted in Greece.

• Xitle volcano erupts in Mexico.

149–146 Third Punic War; Rome extends control over North Africa.

146 Romans invade Greece.

141 Chinese emperor Wu-ti expands control of Han dynasty across East Asia.

138–78 Civil wars in Rome; ends with a dictatorship.

c. 112 Silk Road from China to the Mediterranean opens.

106–43 Life of Cicero, Roman scholar and orator.

c. 99–55 Life of Roman philosopher and poet Lucretius; wrote *De Rerum Natura* (On the Nature of Things) in six volumes.

Indian philosophy

Six classical systems of philosophy developed: Nyaya, Vaisheshika, Mimamsa, Samkhya, Yoga, and Vedanta. These laid the foundation for all future developments in Hindu philosophy, but at the same time, the new religions of Buddhism and Jainism were spreading. Jains follow the teachings of Mahavira and believe in strict non-violence and harming no living being, including insects.

BUDDHISM

Gautama Siddhartha, known as the Buddha or "Enlightened One," founded the religion known as Buddhism. He was born a nobleman in Nepal, but in his 29th year, moved by sights of suffering, he became an ascetic, wandering and meditating until he reached Enlightenment. His basic teachings are the Four Noble Truths that ascribe suffering to desire, and the Eightfold Path, which lays down the way of life that can lead one beyond material suffering.

The preaching Buddha, Sarnath, India, fifth century.

Chinese philosophy

Confucius (551–479 BCE) lived in China at the time of the declining Zhou dynasty, when corruption was rampant. In order to recreate an ideal state, he believed the principles of the ancient sages of China should be revived, and that society should be a heirarchy with both ruler and subjects behaving ethically, giving loyalty to superiors and justice for those below them. Confucius' philosophy became widely adopted and his teachings, collected in the *Analects*, are still popular.

At roughly the same time, the philosophy of Daoism developed. Dao (the Way) implied understanding the free-flowing, changeable nature of the world and of oneself, and being free of dogma.

Confucius.

The Sasanians

In Iran, Ardashir I defeated the Parthians in c. 224 CE, and established the Sasanian dynasty. The Sasanian empire soon extended from the Euphrates river up to northwest India. Iran's position as a gateway of trade and commerce between the Western and Eastern worlds was reflected in its wealth and abundance of luxury items such as silver plates, stucco panels, glass ware, silk, and fine wool textiles. Elaborate gem and stone seals were carved and impressed on clay to seal documents. Huge reliefs, of scenes of royalty, hunting, and battle, were hewn on rocky mountain cliffs. Zoroastrianism was made the state religion.

Bas relief showing the investiture of Ardashir I by Ahuramazda, Naqsh-e-Rustam, Iran.

The Sasanid empire came to an end with its defeat at the hands of the Arabs in the seventh century.

Kushans and Guptas

Gold coin of Samudragupta.

The Central Asian Kushans gradually acquired a large territory, extending to the Tarim Basin in northwest China, and through Afghanistan to north India. In the third century, the Kushans in Afghanistan were subjugated to the Iranian Sasanids. In north India, they were succeeded by the Gupta dynasty. The greatest Gupta king, Samudragupta (c. 335–80 CE), established a vast empire. Art and culture flourished under the Guptas. Beautiful and refined sculptures were produced, particularly at Sarnath and Mathura. Gold coins were used, and great literature composed. Kalidasa, one of the greatest writers in Sanskrit, lived at this time.

1–135 CE

1–300 Cholas rule in part of south India; Sangam literature composed in Tamil language.

8 Julian calendar introduced in the Western world; used till 1582.

23 Greek historian Strabo completes 17-volume work on geography.

23–79 Life of Roman Pliny the Elder, author of *Historia Naturalis*, an encyclopedia.

30 John the Baptist imprisoned by King Herod of Judea.

c. 33 Jesus Christ crucified.

c. 40 Trung Trac and Trung Nhi, two sisters in Vietnam, lead revolt against Chinese.

43 Claudius, Roman emperor, invades Britain.

46 Plutarch, Greek scholar, born in Chaeronia.

54–68 Nero is emperor of Rome.

c. 56–c. 120 Life of Tacitus, Roman official; wrote historical works in Latin: *Germania*, on Germanic tribes; *Historiae* and *Annals*, on different phases of Roman empire.

The Maya

Possibly the greatest of the elaborate civilizations of South America, dating back to at least 1500 BCE, was the Maya. The Maya covered a very large area, including parts of Mexico, the Yucatan peninsula, and northern Central America. The civilization reached its height between *c.* 250–900 CE, with about 80 city-states, each with a distinct line of kings. The states practiced large-scale agriculture, and had urban and religious centers, with palace complexes, pyramids, and temples. Tikal, Caracol, Dos Pilas, and Calakmul were among these centers.

The Maya are known for their architecture, art, pottery and ceramics, system of writing, calendar, and complex mathematical and astronomical systems. They also practiced human sacrifice, and most cities contained a court for a ritual ball game. The Maya calendar, beginning with a date equivalent to 3114 BCE, predicts a great change in 2012.

An illustrated version of the Mayan calendar.

Han dynasty

In China, the Han dynasty overcame a usurper and reestablished themselves in 25 CE as the Eastern Han, ruling from a new capital at Luoyang. Trade flourished and new inventions of the period included paper, water clocks, astronomical instruments, and a seismograph. The Han declined by *c.* 220 CE, giving way to the Period of the Three Kingdoms.

An Eastern Han pottery soldier, *c.* first century CE.

TEOTIHUACÁN

Teotihuacán, the most important pre-Aztec city in central Mexico, was occupied from around 400 BCE. It reached its zenith in *c.* 500 CE, covering an area of 7.7 sq miles, with an estimated population of 100,000–200,000. The origin of its people is so far unknown. The city contained 2000 house compounds, great plazas, temples, palaces, and pyramids, but the central area burnt down around 750 CE and the city declined.

64 Large areas of Rome destroyed by fire.
79 Roman cities Pompeii and Herculaneum, in Italy, destroyed by eruption of Mt Vesuvius.
79–81 Titus is Roman emperor.
• **100** Soap begins to be used as a cleaning agent.
c. 100 Emperor Trajan constructs city of Thamugadi, in North Africa, on a Roman plan.
c. 100–170 Life of Ptolemy, astronomer, mathematician and geographer; lived in Egypt.
c. 105 Paper invented in China.

118 Pantheon rebuilt in Rome.
c. 120 Kanishka I, Kushan king, begins rule in Central Asia, Afghanistan, north India.
122–138 Hadrian's wall built to defend Roman province of Britain.
129–c. 216 Life of Galen of Pergamum (now in Turkey); synthesized Greek and Roman medicine.
132–135 Jews of Judea, led by Simon bar Kokhba, revolt against Romans, but are defeated.

GREAT EMPIRES & CIVILIZATIONS

The Roman empire

THE ROMAN EMPIRE
c. 150 CE

The greatest empire in the world at this time was that of Rome. The empire reached its height between the first and second centuries CE, with provinces in Europe, Asia, and Africa enjoying a period of peace and prosperity that ended about 180 CE. Rome was known for art, architecture, and literature, and for its vibrant social life. In 285 CE, Emperor Diocletian divided the empire into the Western and Eastern empires for easier governance. The empire was twice reunited for brief periods, but after 395 remained permanently divided, with the Eastern capital at Constantinople (Byzantium). In the fifth century, Rome's continental provinces were invaded by the Visigoths, Huns, and Vandals, but while the Western Roman empire declined, the Eastern Roman empire, also known as the Byzantine empire, continued to exist.

ROMAN RELIGION

The Romans worshipped several deities, some, such as Jupiter and Mars, originating in early Etruscan and Latin traditions, and others, such as Diana, Minerva, Hercules, and Venus, derived from Greece and Iran. Mithra or Mithras, originally an Indo-Iranian deity, became the center of a mystical cult.

The emperor was also the Pontifex Maximus (chief priest), the head of the Roman state religion and guardian of the old Roman cults. In the first century, Paul of Tarsus (c. 10–67 CE) began to propagate Christianity, but the Roman state responded with fear and persecution until Emperor Constantine converted and enforced Christianity in parts of his empire. Earlier deities and the Mithra cult declined.

Emperor Constantine.

150–350 CE

- **c. 150** Kingdom of Champa established in Vietnam.
- **198–217** Roman Emperor Caracalla rules; Roman citizenship extends to all free-born citizens.
- **c. 200** Bantu people move into central and southern Africa; cultivate cereal; from **c. 300** herd cattle.
- **c. 200–650** Paintings made at Ajanta caves, India.
- **206** Construction of Roman baths of Caracalla begins; has hot and cold rooms.
- **c. 240** Mani establishes religion of Manichaeism in Iran; later spreads to other areas.

- **248** Trieu Au, Vietnamese woman patriot, leads revolt against China; wins several battles, but finally defeated.
- **251–66** Plague epidemic in Roman world.
- **271–76** Aurelian walls constructed around Rome.
- **284–305** Diocletian is Roman emperor; brings in reforms, peace, and order; **294** divides empire.
- **c. 300** Tiridates III of Armenia makes Christianity the official religion; Armenia is first Christian state.
- • Yamato clan extends control in Japan.

Roman cities

Ruins of the Roman Forum, Rome, Italy.

Amongst the empire's many cities, the greatest was Rome itself. Rome was dominated by the Forum, originally an open space for public functions, later the site of huge buildings, temples, and archways. Begun in 600 BCE, and added to by many emperors, the Forum was the centre of public life. Political discussions, victory processions, sacrifices, worship in temples, games, amusements, and theatrical performances took place here. Wheeled vehicles were prohibited within till four p.m., and it was surrounded by huge market centers. Later, there were separate forums for legal and administrative matters, and for markets.

A typical Roman home.

Each city in the empire had public buildings, forums, theaters, amphitheaters, bridges, aqueducts, arches, and statues, modeled on Rome, though the architecture varied in different regions. Public baths, where men met to discuss various issues, were another common feature.

AKSUM

Many different societies at varying levels of development existed in Africa at this time. The coastal regions of the north were under the Roman empire. The Kush kingdom, with its capital at Meroe, was declining, and in c. 300 CE it was taken over by the state of Aksum. In the fourth century, Aksum became a Christian state, and finally declined in the seventh century with the spread of Islam in Africa.

- Early eastern Polynesian culture begins.
- **305** Palace of Roman Emperor Diocletian is built at Split (Spalato), Croatia, for his retirement.
- **312** Constantine becomes emperor of the Western Roman empire; **324** sole emperor of both Western and Eastern empires.
- **319** Arius of Alexandria puts forward doctrine of Arianism; distinguishes between God and Christ.
- **320–550** Gupta empire in north India.

- **325** First Council of Nicaea; founds Nicene Creed, on the divine nature of Jesus Christ.
- **c. 326–56** First Basilica of St Peter constructed in Rome.
- **c. 329–79** Life of St Basil; founds order of monks.
- **c. 330** New city of Constantinople founded on the site of Byzantium.
- **c. 345–405** Life of artist Gu Kaizhi of China.
- **c. 350** *Panchatantra*, a book of fables, composed in India, in Sanskrit.

Mosaic of Jesus Christ at the Hagia Sophia museum, Turkey, 13th century.

Jesus, a Jew born in Bethlehem in Judea, was the founder of the religion later known as Christianity. Around the age of 30, he gathered 12 disciples (also known as the Apostles) who would be his main companions, and began to teach people about love, forgiveness, and compassion. He is also said to have performed miracles. He came to be known as "Christ," a term meaning "messiah," and his followers came to be called Christians. Threatened by his growing stature, the Jewish clergy pressed the Roman administration to sentence him to be crucified. The office of the pope, first at the head of the entire Christian Church, and later exclusively of the Catholic Church, is traced to St Peter, the leader of the Apostles.

Christianity's basic text is the Bible, consisting of the Old Testament and the New Testament. The four Gospels of the New Testament, the Gospels of Matthew, Mark, Luke, and John, record the life and teachings of Jesus, and were composed sometime in the first century. They chronicle the Sermon on the Mount, a message of love and forgiveness, which is the essence of Jesus's teachings. In c. 380 CE, Christianity became the religion of the Roman empire, and by this time it had also reached North Africa, Armenia, Persia, India, and some other areas.

Developments in Judaism

Judah, to the south of Israel, was occupied by the Romans in 63 BCE. In 70 CE the Jewish Temple was destroyed by the Romans and many Jews left their homeland and settled in different parts of the world.

In the first century CE Jewish scribes divided into two camps following the ideas of scholars Shammai or Hillel. Towards the end of the century the patriarch Gameliel II unified the community, and allowed a lenient interpretation of Jewish law. The Jewish calendar was standardized. By 136 CE, Jewish resistance to the Romans had collapsed and instead, led by the rabbis, they began to develop their scripture. This included the Mishnah, on various Jewish laws, and the Talmud, with commentaries and elaborations on the Mishnah. After Christianity became the official religion of the Roman empire, the Jews retained freedom of worship, but suffered some limitations, for instance in collecting taxes from other Jews or building synagogues. The office of the Jewish patriarch was abolished in c. 425.

360 CE–500

360s Huns of Central Asia invade Europe.
372 Huns drive Ostrogoths and Visigoths out of Ukraine.
378 Visigoths defeat Romans at Adrianople.
c. 378 Maya city Tikal captures rival Uaxactin.
c. 387 St Augustine of Hippo begins composition of *De Musica*, on musical aesthetics.
391 Library at Alexandria in Egypt destroyed by fire.
399–414 Chinese Buddhist pilgrim Faxian travels through India and records what he sees.

c. 400 Use of iron spreads in East Africa.
406 Vandals, Alans, and Sciri (Germanic tribes) cross the Rhine; Roman power collapses.
410 Visigoths loot Rome; Huns force Rome to pay tribute.
428 Gaiseric becomes king of Vandals.
429 Vandals conquer Carthage; later annex Corsica, Sardinia, and Sicily.
c. 430 St Patrick arrives in Ireland; spreads Christianity.

Mahayana Buddhism

In India, Mahayana, a new form of Buddhism, emerged. It embraced the worship of images and Buddhist deities, along with the concept of the Bodhisattva, a being who vows to help all, and take on the suffering of others. Each person who embarks on the Mahayana path is recognized as a Bodhisattva.

Second-century sculpture of a Bodhisattva, Mathura, India.

Hinduism

The Hindu religion, mostly prevalent in India, developed over time, and consists of both high philosophy and popular practices. It has no single founder or canon. Among its features is the belief in deities, who represent aspects of a supreme being. It also embodies the concepts of *dharma*, or right action; *karma*, or action and its results; reincarnation; and the division of society into castes related to birth and occupation.

The form of Hinduism that developed during 1–500 CE was similar to that practiced today: Images, temples, and the worship of major deities such as Vishnu and his incarnations, as well as Lakshmi, Shiva, Parvati, Ganesha and Kartikeya. Their myths and stories were consolidated in the *Puranas*, a series of religious texts in Sanskrit. Other texts, including the *Dharma Shastras*, or "great law books," were written, which described and explained customary laws and practices. At the same time, philosophy continued to develop.

Vishnu, one of the prominent deities of the Hindu religion.

CULTURAL DEVELOPMENTS

Indian dynasties

Kingdoms rose and fell. The Gupta empire declined after attacks by the Huns, while Harsha (r. 606–47) of the Pushyabhuti dynasty established control over much of northern India. In the south, the Chalukyas, Pandyas, and the Pallavas were among the most powerful dynasties. The great Buddhist monastery of Nalanda thrived at this time, with 10,000 monks affiliated to it.

The ruins of Nalanda.

The Suis and Tangs

Although the Sui dynasty ruled for a short period (581–618), it is remembered for starting the Grand Canal, the longest in the world, and for reconstructing the Great Wall. The succeeding Tang dynasty (618–907) saw an increase in urban centers and trade, along with cultural developments in literature and art. Woodblock printing was developed, and medical texts were compiled.

XUANZANG, THE CHINESE PILGRIM

Unable to get a travel permit, this intrepid Buddhist scholar left China secretly in 629, and walked for a year across high mountains to reach India. There he spent more than 13 years traveling and recording everything he saw, particularly anything on Buddhism. He returned to China in 643–44, carrying hundreds of sacred Buddhist texts on mules.

Buddhism grows in Japan

Empress Suiko (r. 593–628) made the Asuka valley in Yamato province her capital. Her nephew and regent, prince Shotuku, reformed the administration and drafted the first Japanese constitution, consisting of 17 principles of good government. He also promoted Buddhism throughout Japan, building a Buddhist temple complex with 41 buildings at Horyu-ji, southwest of Nara, which became the capital in 710.

500–595

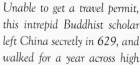

c. 500 Thale people occupy Alaska.

• Polynesians settle on Hawaiian islands and Easter Island.

508 Clovis I of Merovingian dynasty occupies most of France and Belgium; Paris becomes the capital.

510 Huns invade India.

c. 520 Indian monk Bodhidharma reaches China; considered founder of Chan (Zen) Buddhism.

c. 523 Boethius (c. 484–524), Roman philosopher and statesman, writes *De Consolatione*

Philosophiae (The Consolation of Philosophy).

525 Kaleb of Aksum conquers Yemen; builds churches.

529 St Benedict establishes monastery of Monte Cassino at Nurse, Italy.

531–79 Hussar I of the Sasanian dynasty extends Persian empire.

534 Byzantine military commander Balearics defeats Vandals in North Africa.

541 Plague sweeps through Europe.

c. 550 David brings Christianity to Wales.

Americas: Hohokam and Huari cultures

Among the several Native American cultures of North America, the Hohokam flourished between 300 BCE and 1400 CE in central and southern Arizona. During 500–900 CE, they lived in villages with pit houses, and cut deep irrigation channels to grow corn and cotton. They had several varieties of pottery, mainly buff ware, decorated in iron red.

South America had a number of civilizations, among which were the Moche and Nazca cultures, and the Huari and Tiahuanaco civilizations. The Huari, in the highlands of modern Peru, reached its height between 600–1000, with an urban site that was probably the center of an empire. Large stone structures, temples with naturalistic sculptures, and metal artifacts, including gold masks, have been found there. The "Doorway God," a figure with a rectangular face and headdress with rays, is often depicted on their pottery. Huari artistic styles were closely linked with Tiahuanaco, near lake Titicaca in Bolivia, and also influenced the Late Nazca culture.

Nazca Lines, Peruvian desert.

NAZCA LINES

The Nazca civilization of Peru (200–700) drew mysterious lines in the Nazca desert, creating giant drawings of birds, plants, lizards, and geometric figures, some of them 400 feet long. Formed by removing surface stones to reveal a lighter layer beneath, the lines' purpose remains unknown. While some see them as extra-terrestrial landing spots, anthropologists believe that they are connected with ancient water rituals and that the lines may mark underground aquifers.

The Tegai gate at Todai-ji Buddhist temple, Nara, Japan.

- Kalabhras, a group of unknown origin, defeat kings of south India.
- Tendai Buddhism established in Japan by Zhiyi.
- **550–600** Nubians in Sudan become Christian.
- **c. 550–1190** Rule of various Chalukya dynasties in west and central India.
- **553** Justinian I holds Second Christian Council of Constantinople (Fifth Ecumenical Council).
- **560–636** Life of St Isadore, Archbishop of Seville, Spain; composes *Etymologiae*, an encyclopedia.

563 St Columba begins conversion of Picts in Scotland to Christianity.
c. 570–632 Life of the Prophet Muhammad who receives the message of Islam and inspires the creation of the Arab Empire.
581–617 Yang Jian of Sui dynasty rules China; reunites country, known as Emperor Wen-di.
584 Kingdom of Mercia founded in England.
590 St Gregory the Great elected Pope.
595 Indian mathematicians use decimal system.

The Merovingians and the Carolingians

After the decline of the Western Roman empire, new rulers and kingdoms emerged in the region. The Frankish King Clovis I of the Merovingian dynasty ruled in Gaul up to 511. However, on his death, the empire was partitioned among his four sons, and later among their sons, causing frequent wars. Monks and missionaries brought Christianity to the Franks at the time of the Merovingians.

The Merovingians were followed by the Carolingians, who officially took power under Pepin in 751. Their greatest king was Charlemagne, who ruled from 768–814. He united much of western Europe, and was made Holy Roman Emperor by Pope Leo III in 800. (The Holy Roman Empire's actual foundation is considered to be under king Otto II, in 962.) The title was based on the concept of a Christian empire, which would revive the glory of the Western Roman empire, as well as establish papal sovereignty in Italy. Charlemagne's empire included France, northern Italy, and parts of Spain and Denmark. The blossoming of literature, education, art, and architecture during his reign and the succeeding period has been called the Carolingian Renaissance.

Charlemagne.

THE MIDDLE AGES

Beginning in the fifth century and lasting up to the Renaissance, the Middle Ages in Europe saw the decline of the advanced culture of the Western Roman empire. Political and economic developments were largely local, although some areas then saw a limited and static feudal society develop, which gradually changed into the dynamism of the Renaissance.

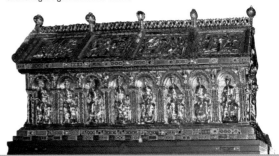

Charlemagne's gold and silver casket.

600–700

597 St Augustine of Rome reaches England to convert Anglo-Saxons to Christianity; becomes first Archbishop of Canterbury.

c. 600–700 Welsh bard Aneirin composes *Book of Aneirin*.

c. 602 Slavic tribes begin to settle in the Balkans.

c. 605–10 Canal built in China, linking Yangtze river with the capital, Changan.

608–42 Reign of Pulakeshin II, king of Chalukya dynasty, in India.

617–86 Life of Wonhyo Daisa, an influential Korean Buddhist.

618 Tang dynasty begins in China under Li Yuan; unites China; **628** adopts Buddhism.

629 Dagobert I of Merovingian dynasty unites Frankish lands.

c. 632 Queen Sondok begins rule in Silla kingdom of Korea.

632 King Penda of Mercia takes control of northern Britain after killing King Edwin of Northumbria.

Anglo-Saxons in England

A folio from the *Lindisfarne Gospels*.

Numerous invasions and internal wars were a feature of this period. By around 600, the Angles and Saxons from Germany had occupied most of England. According to a 12th-century source, there were seven separate kingdoms of Kent, Sussex, Wessex, Mercia, East Anglia, Essex, and Northumbria, though research shows these emerged at different times and were not equal in power, and that, in addition, other kingdoms existed. Anglo-Saxon kings and chiefs were sometimes buried in ships, which were pulled onto land. These ship-graves such as at Sutton Hoo were filled with elaborate ornaments and other goods. Religious art flourished, a fine example being the illustrated Lindisfarne Gospels of the eighth century that was bound in leather and encrusted in jewels and metals.

Justinian I and the Byzantine empire

Meanwhile, the Eastern Roman, or Byzantine, empire flourished from Constantinople, with a widespread trade network. Under Justinian I (r. 527–65), it expanded to include parts of Spain and Italy, the Balkan peninsula, Asia Minor and Palestine, as well as Egypt and other areas in North Africa. Justinian is remembered for his codes of law, and the grand church of Hagia Sophia (Church of the Holy Wisdom) was constructed during his reign.

THE GHANA EMPIRE

One of Africa's numerous kingdoms was the Ghana empire, south of the Sahara (nowhere near modern Ghana). Well established by the eighth century, around 700 it was ruled by the Soninke or Serahule people, with their capital at Kumbi Saleh, a leading trading center. The empire was first called Wagadou or Aoukar, but came to be known as Ghana as this was one of the titles of the king. Gold was the most valuable product of this rich and powerful state.

636–713 Life of Huineng, Sixth Patriarch; most important figure of Chinese Zen Buddhism.
640–41 Arabic Caliph Omar conquers Egypt.
641 Last Sasanid king Yazdgird III defeated by Arabs.
646–700 Political and social reforms in Japan.
c. 650–888 Later Pallava dynasty in south India erects temples at Mamallapuram.
650–1150 Sri Vijaya kingdom of Sumatra dominates the Malay region.
c. 651 Arab traders bring Islam to China.

661–750 Umayyads rule Arab Caliphate; continue rule in Spain up to 1031.
c. 675 Bulgars from Russian steppes settle south of Danube river.
c. 690–91 Dome of the Rock, earliest surviving Islamic monumental building, built in Jerusalem at a site sacred to Muslims and Jews.
697–98 Arabs build city of Tunis.
699–759 Life of Chinese poet and painter Wang Wei; starts the "pure landscape" style of painting.

Advance of Christianity

In the sixth century, Christianity reached Wales and Scotland, and spread through England over the next two centuries. Pope Gregory the Great (590–604) reformed the structure and administration of the Church. Between 500 and 800, three Christian Councils were held during which bishops decided on matters of Christian doctrine and practice.

PADMASAMBHAVA

Buddhist ideas are believed to have spread to Tibet by the second century, but gained prominence from the seventh and eighth centuries, especially through the Buddhist monk Padmasambhava's efforts. By way of his teachings, debates, and magical demonstrations, Padmasambhava convinced the adherents of the prevailing animistic Bon religion of the "superiority" of Buddhism. Various schools of Tibetan Buddhism developed later, some incorporating deities.

Padmasambhava, a typical Tibetan Buddhist image.

Buddhism evolves

Buddhism became the state religion of Japan in 594. New schools emerged in both China and Japan. In India, Mahayana Buddhism, which had emerged around the first century BCE, declined around the seventh and eighth centuries, and Vajrayana, a new form, gained prominence. Vajrayana incorporated several aspects of Mahayana, such as the worship of Buddhist deities, and elements of Tantra, a Hindu religious philosophy. Buddhism grew in Tibet, and with the efforts of the monk Padmasambhava (c. eighth century), the Vajrayana form was firmly established in the region.

700–800

- **c. 700** Polynesians settle on Cook Islands.
- Tang capital of Changan is the largest and richest city in world.
- **c. 700–92** Life of Wu Daozi of China, painter of Buddhist frescoes.
- **c. 700–900** Pueblo people in Arizona, North America, build houses above the ground.
- **710–70** Life of Du Fu, Chinese poet.
- **712** Arab Muhammad bin Kasim conquers Sind (now in Pakistan).

- **715** Islamic forces conquer most of Spain.
- **c. 716** Traditional date for arrival in India of a group of Zoroastrians from Iran; came to be known as Parsis.
- **c. 718–1492** Period of Reconquista: attempt of Spain and Portugal to regain control of territories in Iberian peninsula from Arabs.
- **721–c. 815** Life of Jabir, Arab alchemist.
- **729** Kingdom of Nanzhao founded in western Yunan, China; declines after **836**.

Emergence of Islam

Muhammad, the founder of Islam, was born in Mecca (in today's Saudi Arabia) in 570. In 610 he began to receive messages from god through the angel Jibril (Gabriel). Muhammad began to spread these messages, but facing hostility in Mecca, left for Medina in 622. This departure, known as the Hegira, is the beginning of the Islamic era.

Muhammad's influence spread, and he re-entered Mecca in 630, setting up the Kaaba as the center of Islamic pilgrimage. This cube-like shrine originally contained several pagan idols, which Muhammad destroyed in order to promote the worship of one god, Allah. By the time of his death in 632, most of Arabia was unified under Islam.

The caliphs

Spiritual successors of Muhammad, the caliphs (Arabic *khalif*) also held political power in the Arab empire. The early caliphs were:

632–34 Abu Bakr.
634–44 Umar al-Khattab.
644–56 Usman.
656–61 Ali.
661–750 The Umayyads.
750–1258 The Abbasids.

The Quran

The word of god, as conveyed to Muhammad, forms the Quran, Islam's sacred text. Consisting of 114 suras or chapters, the Quran defines the nature of god, and explains beliefs, religious duties, and right actions.

SUNNIS AND SHIAS

After his death, some of Muhammad's followers elected Abu Bakr–a faithful disciple and father of Aisha, one of Muhammad's favorite wives–as the caliph. This group later became known as Sunnis ("people of custom and community"). Others felt Muhammad had wanted Ali, his cousin and son-in-law, to be his successor. They became known as Shias ("partisans") of Ali.

BATTLE OF KARBALA

In 661, Ali's son Hasan was chosen as his successor, but was opposed by Muawiya, governor of Syria, who founded the Umayyad dynasty. The succession of Muawiya's son Yazid was opposed by Husain, brother of Hasan, leading to the battle of Karbala in Iraq in 680. There Husain was killed and his followers were defeated by Yazid's forces.

---

731 Benedictine monk, the Venerable Bede, completes *Historia Ecclesiastica Gentis Anglorum* (Ecclesiastical History of the English People).

c. 740–1000 Rashtrakuta dynasty rules in central India.

746 Greeks reoccupy Cyprus, drive out Arabs.

c. 750 *Beowulf*, epic poem in Old English, composed.

765 Ismaili sect founded in Islam.

773 Charlemagne annexes Lombard kingdom.

779 Offa, king of Mercia, becomes king of England.

787 Second Council of Nicaea held; allows veneration of images in Christianity.

• Vikings raid Britain.

c. 787–886 Life of Abu Mashar (Albumazar), Arab astrologer; synthesizes Indian and Iranian astrology with Greek philosophy.

788 Idris rules Morocco.

• Charlemagne annexes Bavaria.

794 Emperor Kammu unites Japanese islands.

794–1185 Heian period in Japan.

CONTINUITY AND CHANGE

Rule of the caliphs

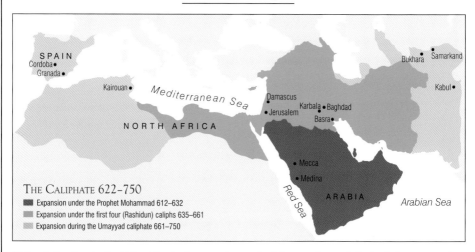

SPAIN
Cordoba•
Granada•

Kairouan•

Mediterranean Sea

NORTH AFRICA

Damascus
•Jerusalem Karbala •Baghdad
Basra•

Bukhara• •Samarkand

Kabul•

•Mecca

•Medina

Red Sea

ARABIA

Arabian Sea

THE CALIPHATE 622–750
▨ Expansion under the Prophet Mohammad 612–632
▨ Expansion under the first four (Rashidun) caliphs 635–661
▨ Expansion during the Umayyad caliphate 661–750

In Asia, the Arab Abbasid caliphs overthrew the Umayyads, and shifted their capital to Baghdad, but the political and religious authority of the caliphs began to decline after about 850. The 800–1000 period was known for developments in science, technology, medicine, philosophy, education, and culture. Among the caliphs, Haroun al-Rashid (r. 786–809) encouraged arts, culture, and scholarship. An embellished account of life at his court is given in *The Thousand and One Nights*. Another notable caliph was Haroun's son Al-Mamun (r. 813–33) who set up the Baitul Hikmah or the House of Wisdom. Here, literature from various parts of the world was translated into Arabic.

The Arab world was known as a melting pot of different cultures and ideas. Philosophers like Al-Kindi, Al-Farabi, and Ibn Sina imbued Islamic thought with ideas from Greek philosophy. In addition, the Arabs disseminated algebra, Arabic numerals, and knowledge from other parts of the world, such as paper-making and gunpowder (both from China).

Politically, however, other dynasties began to assert themselves. A branch of the earlier Umayyads ruled independently from Spain. Cordoba, in Spain, was a great center of learning and culture, and, during the 10th century, it was the largest city in Europe. Iran, Afghanistan, and North Africa were among other areas over which the Abbasids gradually lost control.

800–870

c. 800 Compositions of woman poet, Ono-no Kamachi of Japan.

• First castles built in western Europe.

800–909 Aghlabid dynasty rules in Tunis, North Africa.

c. 800–950 Aksum empire declines, but Christianity continues in Ethiopia.

c. 801–73 Life of Al-Kindi, Islamic philosopher.

809–17 Wars between Byzantine empire and Bulgars.

c. 815–77 Life of philosopher John Scotus Erigena; introduces Neoplatonism in Christianity.

827–69 Life of St Cyril, a Byzantine monk; created Glagolitic, a Slavonic alphabet; along with his brother St Methodius, converted Danubian Slavs to Christianity.

830–70 Life of Al-Bukhari, compiler of *Al-Sahih*, a collection of hadiths, or sayings of Muhammad.

843 Treaty of Verdun; sons of Louis I agree on division of Carolingian empire.

c. 845–925 Life of Al-Razi, Islamic physician from Rey, Iran; wrote *Al-Hawi*, a medical encyclopedia.

Tangs to Sungs

In China, the Tangs saw their authority reduced by the rise of regional military governors. In 907 the dynasty was overthrown, and a period of unrest followed until the founding of the Sung dynasty in 960.

The Fujiwara regents

The Japanese capital shifted to Heian-kyo (Kyoto) in 794, the start of the Heian period. Members of the Fujiwara clan began to dominate the government, ruling as regents on behalf of the emperor. There was a great flowering of art and culture. Distinctively Japanese paintings, different from the earlier Chinese-influenced styles, depicted court life and stories of gods. Japanese Buddhist art was heavily influenced by Shingon beliefs, depicting mandalas or cosmic diagrams. Two types of Japanese script developed.

Despite clashing with other powerful clans such as the Taira and the Minamoto, the Fujiwara continued to control the throne until the mid 11th century.

THE SUFIS

Tracing their origin to an inner circle around the Prophet Muhammad, the Sufis are esoteric Islamic sects. Over time, many different Sufi schools developed. Meditation, asceticism, devotion, repetition of the word of god, music, and specific breathing techniques are used by Sufis to unite with the "god within."

Rabia al-Adawiyya, the first female Sufi saint.

Indian dynasties, Shankara's philosophy

Chola temple at Pudukkottai, Tamil Nadu, India.

From around 700, a number of dynasties rose in north India who called themselves Rajputs (from "*raja putra,*" "sons of kings"). In the south, the Chola dynasty became the most prominent. Both in the south and the north, great temples were built. Perhaps the greatest and most influential philosophy of India, known as Advaita Vedanta, was propagated at this time by the saint Shankara (c. 788–820). In essence, it states that there is only one true reality known as Brahman, the Absolute: Uncreated, unchanging, and eternal.

- **c. 850** Borubodur, large Buddhist temple, constructed near Magelang, in Java, Indonesia.
- Louis II becomes Holy Roman Emperor.
- **c. 850–900** Early Cyrillic alphabet, related to Glagolitic, devised by a follower of St Cyril.
- **850–1846** Kanem-Bornu empire flourishes in Africa.
- **c. 858–929** Life of Al-Battani, Arab astronomer and mathematician.

- **858** Fujiwara clan begins to control Japanese emperors.
- **862** Vikings rule north Russia.
- **c. 865** Vikings conquer parts of England.
- **868** Tulunid dynasty founded in Egypt.
- Buddhist text *Diamond Sutra* printed in China with wood blocks; oldest extant printed book.
- **c. 868–1000** Vikings colonize Iceland, Greenland, and parts of North America.

CONTINUITY AND CHANGE

After the death of Charlemagne's son Louis the Pious in 840, the Carolingian empire in western Europe began to decline and disintegrate. The Byzantine empire was still flourishing, and reached its height under Basil II (963–1025).

A Viking longboat.

The Vikings

Much of Europe at this time was dominated by Viking raids. Also known as Norsemen or Northmen, the Vikings were warriors from Scandinavia who crossed the seas in their longships, invading and setting up trading centers. In England, the Vikings began to plunder coastal towns and settle in some areas in the late eighth century. They settled in Iceland from around 900, and then colonized Greenland. They also settled in Ireland and in Normandy, and even reached Russia. Viking raids died out by the end of the 11th century.

NORSE GODS AND LITERATURE

Thor and Hymir in an 18th-century Icelandic manuscript.

Thor, the god of thunder, and Odin, a wizard and warrior god, were among the main Viking deities. Dating back to an earlier period, the gods attained their full form at the time of the Vikings, though most accounts of them were written down later. Viking myths and legends were composed in Iceland and Scandinavia, in works known as "sagas." Two main works of this type are known as Eddas. Snorri Sturluson (1172–1241) of Iceland compiled the Prose or Younger Edda, consisting of a prologue and three parts. The first two parts provide instruction on earlier meters used in poetry, so that the poems of the oral tradition could be understood. The third part includes a number of Norse myths. The Poetic, or Elder Edda, is contained in a manuscript of the 13th century, but has a collection of poems on heroes and gods composed between 800–1100.

Magyar invasions

Other European invaders during this period were the Magyars from Romania and Hungary. They penetrated Germany, northern Italy, and France, but were defeated by Otto, king of Germany, in the Battle of Lechfield, in 955. In 962, Otto was crowned Holy Roman Emperor, and later became king of Italy.

870–935

873–950 Life of Al-Farabi, Islamic philosopher; proposes universal approach to religion.

875 Charles the Bald is Holy Roman Emperor.

878 Alfred the Great allows Danes to occupy parts of England.

881 Pope John III becomes Charles III, Holy Roman Emperor.

886–1267 Chola dynasty rules in south India.

891 *Anglo-Saxon Chronicle*, a history of England, written by monks.

895 Magyars settle in present-day Hungary and part of Romania.

c. 900 Liturgical polyphony known as organum has developed; important step in growth of western music.

• Post-classic period of Maya civilization begins.

• Kingdom of Chimor established in Peru.

900 Settlers from Cook Island reach New Zealand.

906 Annam (Vietnam) frees itself from Chinese rule.

Kievan Rus

The name Russia derives from Rus, a people whom some scholars believe were Vikings, although others think they were Slavic. Slavic tribes had occupied western Russia from around the seventh century, but Vikings came to the region evidently as traders. According to the *Primary Chronicle*, a 12th-century account, a Viking named Rurik became the elected ruler of Novgorod in *c.* 860. His successors extended their territory to Kiev, and Kievan Rus became a large and prosperous state in the 10th and 11th centuries. A differing opinion says that Kievan Rus was a Slavic state, only briefly occupied by Vikings, who were later absorbed by the Slavs. Vladimir the Great (980–1015) adopted Byzantine Christianity, and Byzantine art styles influenced Russia.

A painting showing the baptism of Vladimir I, c. 1890s.

Alfred the Great.

England, Scotland, and Wales

England began to unite under Athelstan, king of Wessex (r. 925-39), who was the first to rule the whole of England after he gained control of Northumbria in 927. In Scotland, the Picts, Scots, Britons, and Angles were the four main groups, and in 843 the Scot Kenneth MacAlpin conquered the Pictish lands, creating a kingdom known as Alba. In 940 Malcolm I of Alba expanded the territory, and during the next two centuries the whole of Scotland was united. Meanwhile Rhodri Mawr (d. 878), prince of Gwynned, defeated the Vikings and the English, and became king over most of Wales.

907–26 Khitan Mongols conquer Inner Mongolia and part of north China.

909–1171 Fatimid dynasty rules North Africa and Sicily.

910 Benedictine Abbey of Cluny founded in France.

911 Rollo, Viking chief, settles in France.

912–61 Abd Al-Rahman III, Umayyad caliph, rules in Cordoba, Spain.

915–65 Life of Arab poet Al-Mutanabbi; also wrote political satires.

925 Athelstan becomes king of Wessex; unites all the English kingdoms into one.

933 Jewish scholar Saadia Ben Joseph writes *Book of Opinions and Beliefs* on Jewish religion, law, and traditions.

c. 935–c.1002 Life of German woman poet and chronicler Hrosvitha; best known for her moral comedies.

935 Koryo dynasty founds a united kingdom in Korea.

The caliphate loses its hold

Al-Azhar mosque, Cairo, Egypt.

Parts of North Africa remained under the Abbasid caliphs, while some areas asserted their independence. Sicily was conquered during the time of emir Ziayadat Allah I (817–38). Kairouan (Al-Qayrawan), the Aghlabid capital, flourished in the ninth century. Its great mosque, first constructed in the seventh century, was rebuilt at this time, and still stands today.

In northern Algeria, the Rustamid state, known for its learning and religious tolerance, was independent from 761–909. Other independent states were the principality of Banu Midrar, and the Idrisid state, in southern and northern Morocco, respectively. A new Shia Muslim dynasty, the Fatimids, emerged under Abaidullah, in CE 909, and annexed Ifriqiyah and the other states in the region. The Fatimid dynasty reached its height under Al-Muizz (r. 953–75), who conquered Egypt, Palestine, and part of Syria, and founded the town of Al-Qahirah (Cairo). The great Al-Azhar mosque, as well as Al-Azhar University, was constructed in Cairo. Fatimid power began to decline after 1100. In West Africa, Ghana remained prosperous. There were several other states in the rest of the continent.

The Anasazi

Various groups lived in settlements across North America, including those later known as Pueblos. The early Pueblos, sometimes referred to as the Anasazi, date back to about 100, but their society began to increase from around 700. Their houses had circular underground rooms, probably used for ceremonial purposes.

Anasazi pottery had black painted designs on a white or grey background, while petroglyphs and pictographs were other artistic forms. After about 1050 the Anasazi built extraordinary stone and molded-brick houses along cliff walls.

An Anasazi pot.

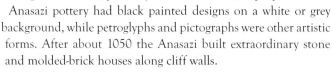

935–1000

937 Battle of Brunanburh in northern England; Athelstan of England defeats Scots, Irish, and Danes.

939 Ngo dynasty founded in Vietnam; marks end of Chinese supremacy.

942–50 Welsh law codified and written down.

950 *Njal's Saga* composed in Iceland.

950–1050 Igbo-Ukwu culture in eastern Nigeria.

• Temples with erotic sculptures built at Khajuraho, India.

959 Edgar, king of Wessex, becomes king of England.

960 Sung dynasty reunifies China.

962 Otto the Great of Germany crowned Holy Roman Emperor.

• Alptigin founds Ghaznavid dynasty in Afghanistan.

963 Mieszco I founds kingdom of Poland.

c. 964 Great Mosque (Mezquita) constructed in Cordoba.

The Toltecs

The Maya civilization began to decline around the 10th century, and most of their temple complexes were abandoned. However, in the Yucatan peninsula, cities like Chichen Itza, Uxmal, Ednza, and Coba still flourished. A new people, the Nahuatl-speaking Toltecs, appeared. Probably an agglomeration of several different ethnic groups, they migrated from northern Mexico, and reached central Mexico around 900 or even earlier. With their capital at modern Tula, they probably occupied some Maya centers.

According to traditional accounts, the Toltecs under the leadership of Mixcoatl sacked and burned Teotihuacan. His son, Toplitzin, united a number of states into an empire, and established the cult of Quetzalcoatl. Skilled in medicine, astronomy, and craft, the Toltecs constructed huge statues, monumental porticoes, serpent columns, and reclining Chac-Mool figures.

The Mixtecs

The Zapotecs, who had been in southern Mexico from the first century BCE or earlier, were replaced by the Mixtecs. The latter flourished from the ninth to 16th centuries. The Mixtecs specialized in stone and metal work, polychrome pottery, feather mosaics, and fine embroidered textiles. They used a calendar similar to the Aztecs. Monte Alban, in the Oaxaca valley, has both Zapotec and Mixtec remains, including plazas and pyramids, a ball-game court, and a number of tombs.

The ruins of Monte Alban in Oaxaca, Mexico.

QUETZALCOATL
A god of the Toltecs and Aztecs, his name is usually translated as "feathered serpent." The god was earlier worshipped at Teotihuacan and by the Maya under the name Kukulcan. Under the Toltecs, he was god of the morning and evening star, and the central deity in ceremonial worship.

Two seemingly contradictory trends were a feature of this period. On one hand, there was the growth in long-distance trade and new ideas, while on the other hand, some groups were stagnant and tied to the land. New routes were discovered, and roads were built across borders, facilitating economic activity. Towns increased in number, and with universities opening in Europe, there was a new impetus to learning.

Feudalism

Manuscript illustration of emperor Charlemagne accepting the fealty of his vassal, Roland.

Wars and unrest gave rise to a static organization of society with a hierarchical framework of land ownership that came to be called feudalism. This structure existed in western Europe between c. 800 and 1400, and in other areas of the world at different times. Feudalism involved the grant of large tracts of land by the king—who was at the apex of the structure—to people of high standing, such as noblemen, important officials, rich merchants, and influential lawyers. Monasteries were also beneficiaries.

In return, the landowner paid rent or taxes to the king, and provided certain services, including an army in times of war. The landlord maintained peace and dispensed justice within the area under his control. His manor or estate was the economic and social unit of life, and included the manor house, tracts of cultivated and forest land, and one or more villages. Castles were built by kings and lords for the defense and protection of their lands.

The two types of land in the estate were those which the landowner cultivated himself, and those he sublet to vassals, who could cultivate or further sublet them. In return for the land (a fief), the vassal had to pledge allegiance (fealty) to the lord.

The 12th-century Bamburgh castle on the coast of Northumbria is a typical example of a medieval castle.

1000–1060

c. 1000 Chinese invent gunpowder.
• Maoris settle in New Zealand.
1000 People speaking Bantu languages form kingdoms in South Africa.
1000–38 Under Stephen I, Christianity becomes state religion of Hungary.
c. 1000–1200 Italian towns Rome, Venice, Florence, and others become city-states.
c. 1008–20 Court lady of Japan, Murasaki Shikibu, writes Tale of Genji, a novel.

1010–1225 Ly dynasty rules territory of present-day Vietnam.
1016–35 Canute (Knut) II of Denmark is king of England; 1018 becomes king of Denmark; 1028 of Norway.
1019–30 Airlangga becomes king of Java; frees country from rule of Malay Sri Vijaya kingdom.
c. 1021–58 Life of Spanish Jewish philosopher and poet Solomon ibn Gabirol; writes Neoplatonic treatise Mekor Chayim (The Fountain of Life).

KNIGHTS

Symbol of the
Knights Templar.

Initially, "knight" was just a term for a horseman, but gradually it came to indicate warrior nobles. In the early feudal period, the vassals of a manor were usually knights. In battle knights wore heavy armor and helmets, and were identified through painted designs on their armor and shields. There were also military knights who had no individual land holdings, but were organized into orders to which land grants were made. Among these orders were the Teutonic Knights, Knights Templar and Knights Hospitaller. Stories of knights, such as the legends of King Arthur and his Knights of the Round Table, were popular in medieval days.

The Knights of Christ, an offshoot of the Knights Templar.

Peasants and serfs

In England, two types of peasants lived in the manor villages: Those who were free and those who were serfs. Free peasants had a hard life but were better off than serfs, who were peasants tied to the land and under the rule of the lord. In the highest category of serfs were villeins, who voluntarily entered into an arrangement with the landlord to gain land and his protection. The institution of serfdom was probably the successor of the Roman slave system, though some serfs were granted the use of land by the lord, and in return had to provide a certain amount of free labor, and some produce. The system was not uniform, and functioned in varying degrees in different parts of the world. In much of Europe, serfdom died out between the 14th and 16th centuries although it continued in Austria-Hungary, Russia, and some parts of eastern Europe till the 19th century. In Asia, some elements of feudalism existed in several countries.

A 14th-century painting showing serfs tilling the land around a French lord's castle.

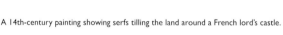

1023–91 Muslim Abbadid dynasty rules from Seville, Spain; known for opulence and patronage of arts.

c. 1025 Italian Benedictine monk Guido d'Arezzo develops musical notation.

1027–1137 Traditional dates of life of Indian philosopher Ramanuja; put forward philosophy of qualified non-dualism.

1037 Spanish kingdoms of Castile and Leon unite.

1044 King Anawrahta establishes kingdom of Pagan (Burma), uniting northern Burmese and Southern Mon peoples of present-day Myanmar.

1046 Clement II appointed Pope by German king Henry III; crowns Henry Holy Roman Emperor.

c. 1050 Port of Mombasa established in East Africa.

1051–1107 Life of Mi Fei, Chinese landscape painter; introduces ink-splash technique.

1058–1111 Life of Islamic philosopher and theologian Al-Ghazali.

The Kharaghan twin towers (1067): Seljuk tombs in Qazvin, Iran.

In Asia, the Arab empire was breaking up, though the Abbasids continued to be the caliphs of Baghdad. The Buyids or Buwayids (945–1055) from Iran captured Baghdad and seized political power, but allowed the caliph to retain his title.

Seljuk Turks

Among the rising powers were the Seljuks, a group of Turks originally from Central Asia. Tughril (Togrul) Beg, their leader, conquered most of Iran and Iraq, including Baghdad, in 1055, and became protector of the caliph. His successors, Alp Arslan and Malik Shah, extended control into Syria, Palestine, and Anatolia (Rum). Alp won a great victory in the Battle of Manzikert in 1071 against the Byzantine empire. The Seljuks, with their capital at Isfahan, Iran, were great patrons of Persian art and literature. After the death of Malik Shah, the empire was divided among his sons, and different lines of Seljuk sultans ruled from Hamadan, Kerman, Syria, and Anatolia.

Muslims and Cholas in India

The Rajput dynasties were prominent in north India. Like the European knights, Rajputs had a tradition of chivalry and protection of the weak. From the region of Afghanistan, Mahmud of Ghazni (997–1030) made several raids into India, followed in the next century by Muizuddin Muhammad of Ghur (1173–1206), who defeated the combined Rajput kings in the Battle of Tarain (1192), and paved the way for the rule of Muslim sultans in north India.

South India was dominated by the Chola dynasty which had a strong army and navy, and an efficient administration with self-government in the villages. Devotees of the god Shiva, they built a number of temples, the greatest being the Brihadeshvara at Thanjavur.

SELJUKS OF ANATOLIA

By the end of the 12th century, only the Anatolian line of Seljuks remained. They lasted till 1308, and are known for their art and architecture. More than 100 caravanserais, trading posts and shelters for traveling caravans, were established on roads across their territories. The largest of these, the Sultan Han, built in 1229 between Konya and Aksaray, covers an area of 42,000 sq ft. Persian literature flourished. Among the best Persian poets was Omar Khayyam (1048–1123) known for his *Rubaiyat*, a series of verses.

1060–1100

1066 Norman conquest of England.

c. 1070 Somadeva of India composes *Katha Sarit Sagara* in Sanskrit, a collection of stories and fables.

1070 Tilantongo kingdom, a Mixtec state in Oaxaca, expands.

1073 Gregory VII becomes pope; introduces Church reforms.

c. 1075–1141 Life of Judah Ha Levi, Jewish physician and philosopher of Judaeo-Arabic school; composes religious and secular verse.

1078 Philosopher St Anselm composes *Proslogium* (Discourses), containing ontological proof of the existence of god.

1079–1142 Life of Peter Abelard, French philosopher; Paris becomes center of religious learning.

1080 Toledo in Spain captured by Christians as part of Reconquista; 1118 Saragossa.

1084 Kyanzittha becomes king of Pagan dynasty in Burma; strong and tolerant rule.

Advances under the Sung

Chinese movable type.

In China, the Sung dynasty came to power in 960. Kaifeng was the capital under the Northern Sung (960–1126). The Southern Sung (1127–1279), with their capital at Hangzhou, controlled southern China. The Sung period saw a growth in the economy, and new techniques in agriculture and craft production. Double-cropping began in rice cultivation, and iron and textile production increased. Varieties of pottery were made. A highpoint was reached in art, particularly in landscape painting. Poetry and music flourished, and in printing, movable type was invented, leading to the production of books.

Shoguns and samurai

The power of the Fujiwaras declined in Japan, and the Minamoto family gained supremacy. In 1192, Yorimoto declared himself shogun, or military ruler, at Kamakura. The samurai, the hereditary warrior class, became powerful. At the end of the 12th century, Zen Buddhism was introduced in Japan, and soon became the religion of the samurai. The modern Japanese language began to develop at this time.

A samurai warrior.

SHAH NAMAH

Firdausi, a Persian Muslim, resented the Arab and Turk occupation of Iran. He wrote the Shah Namah (Book of Kings) in 1010. The epic story, in 60,000 couplets, has semi-mythical and historical accounts of pre-Islamic Persia.

An illustrated folio from the Shah Namah.

1086 *Domesday Book* provides detailed land survey of England.

1088 Chinese Su Sung constructs a water-powered mechanical clock.

1095 Pope Urban II asks Christians to fight a crusade against Muslims; **1096** First Crusade starts.

1095–1139 Life of Avempace, philosopher in Islamic Spain; combines ideas from Neoplatonism and logic.

1099 Jerusalem captured by Christians in the First Crusade.

c. 1100–1200 Jayadeva in India composes *Gita Govinda*, devotional poem on the god Krishna, in Sanskrit.

1100–1200 Hohokam people in Arizona, North America, make platform mounds.

1100s Polynesians settle on Pitcairn Island in the south Pacific.

c. 1100–1300 *Mabinogion*, a collection of Welsh stories, including those on Arthurian legend, are composed.

The Holy Roman empire, in the west, and the Byzantine empire, in the east, dominated Europe and parts of Asia and Africa. Their borders were not static, and were constantly changing. Whereas the court language of the western empire was Latin, the eastern empire used Greek, and their views on Christianity also varied. A formal split between the Western and Eastern branches of the Church took place in 1054. There were also conflicts between the pope and secular authorities of both empires.

Robert Curthose (c. 1051-1134), Duke of Normandy, at the seige of Antioch in the First Crusade.

The Crusades

After the Turkish victory at the Battle of Manzikert in 1071, the Byzantine emperor Alexius I (1081–1118) appealed to Pope Urban II (1042-99), who authorized a holy war to recapture Jerusalem. A series of wars then began, known as the Crusades. Though ostensibly motivated by religious factors, the Crusades were also fought for economic reasons and the control of valuable lands. The First Crusade succeeded in capturing Antioch and Jerusalem, however the Second Crusade (1147–49) ended in disaster. The Seljuks re-established their hold on Anatolia in 1176. Saladin (Salah ad-din), the Kurdish prime minister of Egypt, overthrew the Fatimid dynasty in 1171, and formed a kingdom from the Nile to the Tigris rivers. In 1187, he invaded the Latin kingdom of Jerusalem and the Frankish states. The Third Crusade (1189-92) did not succeed in recapturing Jerusalem. More Crusades took place in succeeding centuries.

TOWNS

Despite the wars and battles, trade increased, and numerous urban centers emerged by the 11th century. Some of the great cities were London, Paris, Cordoba, and Venice. Town dwellers, who were artisans, merchants, and craftsmen (often organized into guilds), paid a tax to the lord who owned the land, but otherwise did not owe him service or obedience. Some towns in Europe were autonomous.

1100–1154

1114–c. 1186 Bhaskara of India composes works on mathematics; uses decimal system.

c. 1115–80 Life of John of Salisbury, English prelate and scholar; composes biographies of St Anselm and Thomas Becket, as well as works on logic, religion, philosophy, and history.

1115–1234 Rule of Jin dynasty in China.

1118–90 Life of Saigyo, Japanese Buddhist poet.

1119 Bologna University founded in Italy.

1120 Order of the Poor Knights of Christ and the Temple of Solomon (Knights Templar) founded.

• English ship *White Ship* sinks; William Aethling, son and heir of Henry I of England, is among those drowned.

1122–79 First three Lateran Councils held in Rome.

c. 1126–90 Life of Persian poet Anvari; composes elegy *Tears of Khorasan*.

1126–98 Life of Ibn Rushd (Averroes), Islamic philosopher.

William, and Brian Boru

The Normans, under William the Conqueror, won the Battle of Hastings against Harold II of England in 1066, thus beginning a new era in English history. A land survey was carried out during William's reign to assess the amount of taxes he could raise. The *Domesday Book*, as the compilation is called, is an invaluable source for English history of that period.

In Ireland, Brian Boru, king of Munster, began to unite the different kingdoms, making himself high king. He was killed in 1040 fighting Vikings.

Romanesque and Gothic architecture

Art, architecture, literature, and philosophy flourished. Universities were established at Bologna, Paris, and Oxford. Romanesque architecture, typified by strong pillars and rounded arches, emerged around 1000. Another new style, Gothic, developed from around 1135. It was expressed particularly in religious themes: Cathedrals were built with tall spires, flying buttresses, and vaulted ceilings, and were decorated with stained glass windows. Arches were pointed and pillars were tall and slender. In art, strong and bright colors were used.

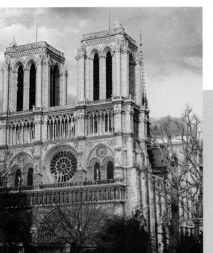

MONASTERIES, CENTERS OF CHRISTIANITY
Christianity and the Church formed an important part of life in Europe, and also provided an impetus to learning, art, and music. New monastic orders were formed, building monasteries where monks or nuns could devote themselves to the service of Christ, and where monks studied, preserved, copied, and illustrated manuscripts. Music was composed for church services, leading to the development of polyphony.

The Gothic-style Notre Dame cathedral, Paris, France.

c. 1128–1203 Life of theologian and philosopher Alain de Lille, a Flemish Cisterian monk; writes allegorical poem *Anticlaudianus*.

1133–41 French theologian and philosopher Hugh heads monastery school at St Victor, Paris.

1136 Church of St Denis, France, constructed in new style; marks beginning of Gothic architecture.

c. 1150 Angkor Wat temple constructed in Cambodia.

• Kamban writes Tamil *Ramayana* in south India.

c. 1150–1200 Life of French poet Chretian de Troyes; composes *Percival* and other works on Arthurian legend.

1150 Paris University founded in France.

• Hopewell culture in North America ends.

1152 Frederick I becomes king of Germany; crowned Holy Roman Emperor; dies during Third Crusade.

• Henry II is king of England.

c. 1154 Arab geographer Al-Idrissi draws world map and writes commentary on it.

CULTURES AND KINGDOMS

The Viking Leif Ericson sailed from Greenland and established a settlement in Newfoundland. Elsewhere in North America, there were numerous cultures, including the early Pueblos (Anasazi), the Mississippi, and the Mogollon. In Mesoamerica, Maya and Toltec cities continued to be occupied.

Several changes were taking place in Africa, as dynasties and kingdoms rose and fell. The Shia Fatimid dynasty was overthrown by Saladin in 1171. Shewa, on the central Ethiopian plateau, was an independent kingdom from c. 950–1400. In South Africa, Bantu peoples set up kingdoms. In West Africa, the kingdoms of Tukrur and Gao flourished on the back of the gold trade.

Mississippi culture

A painting by Herbert Roe (2004) of the Kincaid site in Illinois, an important center of the Mississippi culture.

Large towns and intensive maize cultivation were features of this widespread culture, which had emerged along the Mississippi river around 750. It existed in the Midwestern, eastern, and southeastern United States up to 1500. The central point of each town was a ceremonial plaza. Around this there were earthen oval or pyramidal mounds, on which temples or important houses were built.

CAHOKIA

The most important city of the Mississippi culture, Cahokia possibly had a population of 50,000 by around 1200. The grand plaza of Cahokia measured 16 hectares (40 acres). One of the Cahokia mounds contained the remains of a man in his 40s, who could have been a ruler. He was buried on more than 20,000 marine-shell disc beads, arranged in the shape of a falcon. There are several other burials at the site some of which seem to be of sacrificial victims.

1154–1200

1154 Nicholas Breakspear becomes the only English pope, Adrian IV.

1154–91 Life of Al-Suhrawardi, Islamic Sufi philosopher.

c. 1159 Spanish rabbi Benjamin of Tudela begins travels through Europe and Asia to contact dispersed Jews.

1159 Alexander III becomes pope.

1164 Henry II of England issues Constitutions of Clarendon, laws to restrict power of the Church.

c. 1170–1240 Life of Leonardo Fibonacci, Italian mathematician; contributes to algebra and number theory.

1170 Thomas Becket, Archbishop of Canterbury, murdered.

1171 Saladin seizes Egyptian throne.

1173–74 Construction of Leaning Tower of Pisa, in Italy, begins.

1177 Chinese Xhu Xi writes commentaries on Confucian texts, founding Neo-Confucianism.

Mogollon culture

Located mainly in western Texas, Arizona, and New Mexico, in high altitude desert regions, the Mogollon culture had several branches, the most distinctive being the Mimbres Mogollon. It began around 200 BCE, along the Mimbres river in New Mexico, and reached its height during 1000–1200. From around 1000, the earlier pit houses were followed by two- to three-story-high structures made of adobe and masonry, built on the surface. The Mimbres Mogollon are known for their distinctive pottery, black with geometric lines on a white background. Pottery bowls are often found along with burials.

The Almoravids

The Almoravids, a Berber Muslim dynasty, rose to power in 1040 in the Sahara region of Africa, and soon spread to include a large area of northwest Africa, as well as Spain and Portugal. In 1076, Ghana was conquered. Marrakesh, in Morocco, was founded in 1062 as the Almoravid capital. It became one of the largest and richest cities of North Africa, with markets selling goods from all parts of the empire. The Almoravids declined by 1147, when Marrakesh was conquered by the Almohads (1121–1267), another Berber dynasty.

St Giorgis church, Lalibela, Ethiopia.

The Zagwes

According to traditional accounts, a non-Christian queen named Gudit took over the Aksum state (approximately the same area as Ethiopia) around 960, and her descendants continued to rule until 1137. The Agew, one of the subject people of the Aksum, founded a new dynasty, the Zagwe, and ruled Ethiopia between 1137–1270. The Zagwe were staunch Christians. One of their greatest kings was Lalibela (r. c. 1185–1225), who created 11 churches carved out of rock, below ground level.

- *c.* 1180 Chartres cathedral constructed in France, in Gothic style.
- Philip II becomes king of France.
- 1183 Peace of Constance leads to agreement between Lombard League and Holy Roman Emperor Frederick I.
- 1184 New Canterbury cathedral constructed.
- 1187 Saladin wins Battle of Hattin against Christians; takes Jerusalem; unites Egypt, Syria, Palestine, northern Mesopotamia.

- Richard the Lionheart becomes king of England.
- *c.* 1190 Jewish philosopher Maimonides writes *Guide for the Perplexed*; attempts to reconcile Greek and Jewish philosophy.
- 1190 Teutonic Order of Knights set up in Germany.
- 1191 Henry VI becomes Holy Roman Emperor.
- Chinese Buddhist Ensai spreads Zen Buddhism in Japan.
- 1197 Civil war in Germany after the death of Henry VI.

51

THE MONGOL EMPIRE, C. 13TH CENTURY

GOLDEN HORDE

CHAGHATAI
KHANATE

EMPIRE OF
THE
GREAT KHAN

IL KHANATE

The Mongols

In 1206 the nomadic tribes of Mongols chose Temuchin (c. 1155-67) as their leader or Khan. Temuchin, the son of Yesugei, a member of a royal clan, took the title Gengis ("lord"). With his capacity to gain the loyalty of different groups, Gengis unified the tribes of Mongolia. Karakoram was established as his capital. He then embarked on a series of conquests, and by the time he died in 1227, his empire occupied a vast territory from the Caspian Sea to the Sea of Japan. Apart from being a great conqueror, Gengis was an efficient organizer. After Gengis's death, the empire was divided among his sons, from whom separate Mongol dynasties arose. However, all owed allegiance to one leader known as the great khan, chosen through election by an assembly of Gengis' descendants.

Gengis Khan.   Kublai Khan.

In 1260, Kublai became the great khan. He extended control over China, defeating the Southern Sung dynasty in 1279, and founding the Mongol Yuan dynasty. Other Mongol dynasties were those of Greater Iran, Central Asia or Turkestan, and Russia. Kublai reorganized China and built roads throughout the country. He made Buddhism the state religion, and introduced paper money. Porcelain, metalwork, and textiles were produced. His capital was at Dadu (Beijing); the wealth of his summer capital at Shangdu was described by the traveler Marco Polo. After the death of Kublai, in 1294, the power of the Mongols in China began to wane. In 1368, they were replaced by the Ming dynasty.

THE TRAVELS OF MARCO POLO

Marco Polo (1254–1324), a Venetian, along with his merchant father and uncle, reached Kublai Khan's court at Shangdu in 1275. Marco was employed by the emperor as his agent. All three Italians came back to Venice in 1295. In the war between Venice and Genoa, Marco served as commander of a Venetian fleet. He was captured and imprisoned, during which time he dictated an astounding account of his travels.

1200–1260

c. 1200 Ceremonial coral platform built in Tonga.
c. 1200–50 Dwelling complexes built at Cliff canyon and Fawkes canyon, Colorado.
c. 1201 Venice is an important commercial centre under the doge, an elected ruler.
1203 Hojo family rules Japan.
1209 St Francis of Assisi founds Franciscan order.
• German prince Otto IV invades Italy; is crowned Holy Roman Emperor.

1216 Llewellyn the Great is recognized as ruler of Wales.
c. 1220 German epic poem Nibelungenlied composed, on mythical hero Siegfried.
1220–44 French scholar Vincent of Beauvais compiles encyclopedia, Speculum Majus.
1220–92 Life of Roger Bacon, British scientist and philosopher.
1225 Cathedral of Notre Dame constructed in Paris, in Gothic style.

The Il khanate

There was a great flowering of culture under the Il khanate (Persian for "subordinate khan") of Greater Iran. Mongol influence led to the development of new art, combining East Asian, Persian, and Islamic styles. Illuminated and illustrated manuscripts were produced with new motifs and the influence of Chinese styles. Mosques and Sufi shrines were constructed. A network of roads, with post-houses as halting places, connected the different Mongol states. Messages were swiftly passed through a relay system using horses. Caravans were protected along the routes.

Religion under the Mongols

At the time of Gengis, Tangri, a sky god, was the major deity of peoples of the Asian steppes. Like the Mongol rulers that followed him, Gengis was tolerant of all religions. His followers included Buddhists, Nestorian Christians, and a few Turkish Muslims. Later, Kublai Khan became a Buddhist, though he was also influenced by Christianity. Ghazan of the Il khanate accepted Islam.

The Delhi sultanate

From 1206, northern India was ruled by various sultan dynasties. The first sultan, Qutbuddin Aibak (r. up to 1210), was initially a Turkish slave-general of Muhammad of Ghur. Succeeding dynasties were the Khaljis (1290–1316) and the Tughlaqs (1320–1412). Under Alauddin Khalji, the sultanate reached its greatest extent. Mosques and tombs were built, introducing new styles in architecture, particularly the true arch and dome. The Qutb Minar, a tower at Delhi, is a signature structure of this period.

The Qutb Minar, Delhi.

1231 Pope Gregory IX initiates the Inquisition.
c. 1233 Coal mining begins in Newcastle, England.
1236 Ferdinand III conquers Cordoba; 1248 Seville, as part of Reconquista.
1237 Mongol khanate of Golden Horde formed in Russia by Batu Khan, grandson of Gengis.
1238 Nasrid dynasty established in Granada, Spain.
1240 Alexander Nevsky of Novgorod, Russia, defeats Swedes; 1242 defeats Teutonic knights in the Battle of Lake Peipus.

1241 German cities Lubeck and Hamburg unite; beginning of Hanseatic League.
• Holy Roman Emperor Frederick II invades papal states.
1245 Westminster Abbey, London rebuilt.
c. 1258 Persian poet Sadi composes his masterpiece, *The Rose Garden*.
1258 English House of Commons formed.
c. 1260 Nicola Pisano, Italian architect and sculptor, integrates classical art into Gothic style.

A 14th-century manuscript of the Magna Carta.

The Magna Carta

England faced unrest in the 12th century, and the king increasingly came to depend on the support of the barons, the owners of landed estates. They requested king John (r. 1199–1216) to sign the Magna Carta, a charter or list of demands, and he finally did so in 1215. It regulated the relationships between the king and his barons, and the latter and their tenants. It also stated that even the king was subject to the law of the land.

This document is considered significant as it marked the beginning of constitutional government in England, placing limits on the right of the king.

The Hanseatic League

The rise of towns and trade led to the Hanseatic League in Europe, a group of towns to protect trade. The League began with Hamburg and Lubeck, who created a hansa (association) for self-protection, as the government was weak. By the mid-14th century, the League had around 70 towns across Northern Europe.

GREAT LITERATURE

Dante Alighieri (c. 1265–1321), Francesco Petrarca (1304–74), also known as Petrarch, and Giovanni Boccaccio (1313–75) are the three great Italian writers of this time.

Dante's most famous poetic work is *Divina Commedia* (The Divine Comedy), which describes a journey through hell, purgatory, and paradise. Petrarch wrote sonnets which provided a model for later literature. Boccaccio's masterpiece is the prose *Decameron*, consisting of stories narrated by 10 characters.

Fresco of Dante Alighieri at the Uffizi gallery, Florence, Italy.

1260–1309

1260 Sufi poet Rumi, founder of Mevlevi sect, composes *Masnavi*, spiritual couplets.

1265–73 St Thomas Aquinas composes *Summa Theologica*, influential work on theology.

1270 Navigational charts used in Europe.

1271 Edward I becomes king of England; introduces administrative and legal reforms.

1273 Rudolf I crowned Holy Roman Emperor; is first Habsburg king of Germany.

1274 Second Council of Lyons brings short reunion of Eastern and Western Churches.

1275 Ramkhamhaeng is king of Sukothai (Thailand); expands kingdom.

c. 1280 Kabbalah, Jewish mystical philosophy, emerges in Spain and Portugal.

1282 Pedro III of Aragon becomes king of Sicily.

1284 Edward I of England annexes Wales.

c. 1285 Florentine painter Cimabue (Bencivieni di Pepo) creates naturalistic paintings.

The Reconquista

The Alhambra palace in Granada, Spain.

The Umayyad Muslims had conquered much of Spain in the eighth century. The few remaining Christian states were keen to reconquer the region, and by the 13th century had achieved some success. The Reconquista (reconquest) continued, and the great cities of Cordoba and Seville were captured by the Christians in 1236 and 1248 respectively. Granada, ruled by the Nasrid dynasty, remained the only Muslim state. In 1238 it became a tributary of Castile, and continued to exist till 1492. The grand Alhambra palace complex was built during the Nasrid period.

BLACK DEATH

Possibly originating in Central Asia, the virulent bubonic plague known as the "Black Death" struck China and India and reached Constantinople in 1347. From here it was transmitted to Sicily, France, England, and then to the rest of Europe. In Europe, the first and worst phase of the Black Death ended in 1351, although there were later epidemics. Some saw the plague as the wrath of god, some blamed it on beggars and the poor who lived in unhygenic conditions, and others on the Jews. The latter belief led to the massacre of Jews in some cities. The population of Europe was much reduced after the epidemics. As a result, there were temporary benefits for the survivors: Wages rose for the remaining available workforce, the rents for tenants on the landed estates fell, and food prices were lower.

Plague victims being blessed by a priest, manuscript detail c. 14th century.

CONFLICT AND CHANGE

European rulers continued to organize Crusades, and fought other wars in Europe, such as the Hundred Years' War. At the same time new trade routes opened and commercial towns emerged.

The Crusades continue

Five Crusades took place during this period.

1. The Fourth Crusade (1202–04) aimed to reconquer Jerusalem, but ended in a conflict among Crusaders and an attack on Constantinople.

2. The Fifth Crusade (1218–21) called for by Pope Honorius II, ended in failure.

3. The Sixth Crusade (1228–09) was led by Frederick II (1194–1250), Holy Roman Emperor. He negotiated a 10-year truce, which allowed Christians to return to Jerusalem. Frederick made himself king of Jerusalem in 1229. However, the Templar and Hospitaller knights fought over territory, and mercenary Turks seized Jerusalem in 1244.

4. The Seventh Crusade (1248–54) was begun by Louis IX of France (1215–70). He attacked Cairo, but was taken prisoner. A ransom was paid to free him, and he rebuilt Jaffa and Acre, making peace with Muslim leaders.

5. The Eighth Crusade was initiated by Louis IX in 1270, but he died at Tunis. Prince Edward of England then went to Acre and negotiated an 11-year truce. However, in 1289 the Mamluks took Tripoli, and in 1291 captured Acre.

EASTER ISLAND STATUES

This southeastern Pacific island was first settled by the Polynesians in the sixth century. Around 700–850, they built rectangular platforms, known as ahus, along the coasts. Medium-sized stone  *statues, probably depicting important people, were erected on them. These were destroyed later, and the platforms reconstructed to make them stronger. Between 1200 and 1680 more statues, this time much bigger, were dragged on to the platforms with the help of ramps. More than 600 such sculptures have been found. Between 10 and 40 feet high, some weigh over 80 tons.*

1310–1370

1314 Scots under Robert the Bruce defeat Edward II in Battle of Bannockburn; Scotland becomes independent for the next 300 years.

c. 1320–80 Life of Welsh bard Dafydd ap Gwilym.

c. 1325 Kachina cult established in Colorado river valley by Native Americans.

1326–27 Queen Isabella kills her husband Edward II; makes her son king of England, as Edward III.

1328 Philip VI begins Valois dynasty in France.

1329 French rabbi Gersonides writes *The Wars of the Lord*, a study of philosophical theology.

c. 1330–36 Italian sculptor Andrea Pisano founds Florentine school of sculpture.

1331 First Swabian League formed by 22 cities in southwest Germany to unite against local rulers.

c. 1333 In Japan, Emperor Go Daigo removes shoguns (hereditary warlords) and restores power to imperial line.

1338 Muromachi period begins in Japan.

Hundred Years' War: the first two phases

Born in 1312, Edward III of England was the son of Edward II of England and Isabella, daughter of Philip IV of France. When he laid claim to the throne of France in 1337, a series of wars started between England and France, generally known as the Hundred Years' War. This war had three main periods of conflict. In the first phase, known as the Edwardian War (1337-60), England gained control over Calais in the northeast, and part of southwest France. A new weapon, the longbow, helped England to win the first phase of the war. During the second phase, termed the Caroline War (1369-89), Charles V of France regained most French territories. A truce was signed in 1389.

The English longbow.

Edward III of England.

An interrogation under the Inquisition: a priest exhorts the condemned to confess as he is being tortured.

THE INQUISITION

Christian Councils were held from the fourth century onwards to define the essentials of Christian belief. Anyone who differed was considered a heretic and was excommunicated. Then, in 1231, Pope Gregory IX set up the office of Inquisitor to pressurize Christians into accepting Church doctrines. Often torture was used, and those who refused were executed. In some regions, the Inquisition lasted up to the early 19th century.

---

c. 1338–9 Sienese painters Ambrogio and Pietro Lorenzetti create naturalistic art.

1340 Kimono, Chinese robe, introduced in Japan.

1343 Hanseatic League, N. European trading cities, set up in 13th century, gains power.

1348–50 Black Death kills millions in Europe.

c. 1350 African kingdom of Kongo founded in region of Angola.

• Thai kingdom of Ayutthaya established; continues till **1767**.

1356 Golden Bull, edict on electoral procedures, issued by Charles IV, Holy Roman Emperor.

1361 Murad I becomes Ottoman sultan; expands empire.

1366–67 Statutes of Kilkenny restrict use of Irish language and customs among English settlers.

1368–70 King Waldemar IV of Denmark defeated by Hanseatic League.

1369 Timur, of Mongol descent, occupies Samarkand in Central Asia.

The empire of Mali

In 1240, Ghana was absorbed into the growing empire of Mali, which had developed from the earlier state of Kangaba on the upper Niger river. Under Mansa Musa (c. 1307–32), Mali reached its greatest extent, incorporating the great trading centers of Timbuktu and Gao. Mali traders dominated West Africa, ambassadors were sent to Egypt and Morocco, and Egyptian scholars were brought to the kingdom. The empire broke up by 1550.

Mansa Musa of Mali holding a gold nugget, Catalan Atlas c. late 14th century.

The Mamluks

In 1250 the Mamluks, originally Turks or Circassian slave-soldiers, overthrew the Ayyubid sultanate founded by Saladin in Egypt. In 1260, though Baghdad was taken by the Mongols and the caliphate ended, it was restored by the Mamluk sultans in Cairo. The Mamluk state continued till 1517. During its height under the Turkish sultans who ruled till 1382, Mamluk control extended to Syria and Palestine. Egypt and Syria became great commercial and trading centers, rich in art and craft. The Mamluk period was known for its woven carpets, metal and glass work. Its architectural achievements were vast; more than 3000 buildings, including mosques, tombs, and seminaries were constructed.

Mamluk enameled lamp, c. 13th century.

CHIMU CULTURE

The Chimu state came into being along the coast of Peru around Chan Chan (c. 1200–1400), the capital. This was divided into separate areas, one for the ruling lords and priests and another for the common people. The Chimu built roads, wove textiles, and made fine pottery. In 1465–70, they were conquered by the Incas.

A Chimu mantle, c. 14th century.

1370–1400

c. 1370 Construction completed of palace of Comares at Alhambra, residence of Islamic rulers of Granada (entire complex dates between 11th and 14th centuries).

1370–1430 Life of Andrei Lubyov, Russian monk and icon painter.

1372 Tezozomoc is ruler of Azcapotzalco, most powerful city-state in Mexico.

1375 Scottish poet John Barbour writes epic poem, *The Bruce,* on king Robert the Bruce.

1376 Second Swabian League formed.

1378 Byzantine icon painter Theophanes the Greek creates frescos.

1378–1417 Great Schism of Christian Church; two rival popes claim authority.

1379 John Wycliffe, English theologian, attacks accepted Church doctrines.

c. 1380 Japanese actor and playwright Zeami develops Noh theatre, writes 50 plays.

1380 Tarot cards begin to appear in Italy and France.

Mayas, Incas, and Aztecs

Manco Capac, founder of the Inca dynasty.

Maya power in the Yucatan had shifted to the new capital city of Mayapan. In other areas there were independent Maya city states. The *Popul Vuh*, a famous Maya work of myth and history, was composed by the Kiche Maya.

Of uncertain origin, the Incas settled in Peru, South America, with their chief center at Cuzco, around 1200. They had a dynasty of kings with the title Sapa Inca, or "unique Inca," who was considered a descendant of Inti, the Sun God. According to tradition, the Incas began to expand in the 14th century. In c. 1390, King Hatun Tapac called himself Viracocha, after the supreme creator deity.

Inca rulers wore gold-threaded garments, decorated with brightly-colored feathers. Quipus, knotted strings in bundles, were used to record information and for accounting purposes. Roads were constructed throughout their territories. Textiles with intricate motifs were woven; painted ceramics, and gold and silver objects, were crafted. The Incas cultivated potatoes, maize, squash, tomatoes, peanuts, and cotton, among other crops, in their mountainous kingdom.

The Aztecs, also known as the Mexica, probably arrived in the valley of Mexico in the 12th century when Toltec power was declining. A Nahautl-speaking community, they settled at various places in the northwest of the valley. In 1325, the city of Tenochtitlan was founded on a swampy island at the edge of Tezcoco lake. Tlatelulco was a sister settlement to the north. The Aztecs did not at first control the region. There were other city-states—Azcapotzalco was one—and, for some time, the Aztecs were subject to them. In the 15th century, Aztec power rose to dominate the rest. Their calendar of 365 days was divided into 18 months of 20 days each, and five extra days.

The pyramids at the Aztec capital at Tenochtitlan.

1381 Peasant revolt in England.
1382 Poland's Baltic provinces conquered by Teutonic Knights.
1386 University of Heidelberg (Ruprecht-Karls Universitat) founded; oldest in Germany.
• Jagellion dynasty of Poland and Lithuania established.
• Construction of Milan cathedral begins; is completed in the 20th century.

1389 Turks invade Serbia and win Battle of Kosovo Polje; execute King Lazarus of Serbia.
c. 1390 English writer Geoffrey Chaucer completes *Canterbury Tales*.
1391 Huitilihuitl is Aztec ruler; frees them from rule of Azcapotzalco.
1392 Yi dynasty established in Korea; lasts till 1910.
1394 Timur conquers Iran; 1398 destroys Delhi.
1397 Union of Kalmar unites Norway, Denmark, Sweden; lasts till 1523.

THE AGE OF DISCOVERY

An illustration from the *Akbarnama* (the biography of Akbar), showing the author Abul Fazl presenting a copy of his work to the emperor.

Explorers set out to discover and settle in new areas. Empires declined and new dynasties emerged. New crops were grown, and different parts of the world were linked through trade, commerce, and adventure.

Among the great dynasties of Asia were the Mughals in India, the Safavids in Iran, and the Mings in China. The power of the Ottoman Turks crossed beyond Asia to Europe and Africa.

The Mughals

The Delhi sultanate was declining. Meanwhile, in 1494, Babar, a 12-year-old boy, became king of Farghana, in Central Asia. Babar extended his sway over Kabul, and invaded north India, founding the Mughal dynasty. Babar's grandson, Akbar (r. 1556-1605), was the greatest Mughal ruler. Through his conquests, he united much of north India, dividing his territory into provinces. Stone and ivory carved into fine objects, brocades, and embroidered textiles, were among the goods produced. Trade and commerce prospered, and large cities emerged.

The Safavids

Ismail I established the Safavid dynasty in Iran in 1502. Under Abbas I (1587-1628), a period of peace and prosperity began. The capital was moved to Isfahan, the administration was reorganized, and literature, art, and architecture flourished. Isfahan was said to have 500,000 residents, and beautiful gardens. The Safavid period is particularly known for miniature painting, textiles, and intricately-woven carpets.

Ismail I.

1400–1440

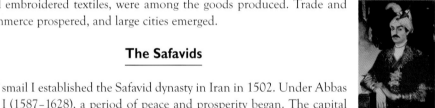

1400–1511 Kingdom of Malacca established in Malaya; becomes important trading center.

1402 The Yongle emperor is Chinese Ming emperor; constructs palace complex of Forbidden City in Beijing; dynasty reaches its pinnacle.

1405 Timur dies; his empire disintegrates.

c. 1410 Andrei Rublev (c. 1360–1430), Russian icon painter, paints *Old Testament Trinity*.

1410 Kiche Mayas of Central America expand kingdom.

• Battle of Tannenberg; Polish and Lithuanian armies defeat Teutonic Knights.

1414–92 Life of Nuruddin Jami, Iranian Sufi poet; wrote *Haft Aurang* (The Seven Thrones).

1416 Ottoman Turks defeated by Venice at Dardanelles.

1419 Philip III (Philip the Good) becomes duke of Burgundy; creates a powerful state in Europe.

c. 1420–1506 Life of Japanese Zen Buddhist artist Sesshu, master of ink painting.

The Mings

The first Ming emperor had to reestablish control over the country. As stability was restored, China's prosperity increased and trade expanded. The tributary position of several other East Asian states was restored. Admiral Zheng He (1371–1433) made seven expeditions to far flung ports for trade, including those in Thailand, India and Iran, Jeddah in Saudi Arabia, and along the coast of East Africa. Silk, textiles, and ceramics were among the products exported from China. Around 1400, their capital Yintiang (Nanjing), with a population of around one million, was the largest city in the world. In 1421, the capital was moved to a reconstructed Beijing.

Chinese culture flourished under the Mings. Books, including novels, were written. New styles in painting developed. Wars against the Mongols and Japan, weak emperors, and rival factions in the government contributed to the Mings' decline. The dynasty finally came to an end in 1644.

Ottoman Turks

Osman, who died in 1326, founded the Osmanli or Ottoman state, northeast of Turkey. His dynasty lasted for 600 years as his successors extended their realm into Byzantine lands through war and diplomacy. By 1398, the Ottomans controlled Anatolia, Thrace, Macedonia, and parts of Bulgaria and Serbia. Bayazid was defeated by Timur in 1402, but later the Ottomans regained their lands and continued to expand their territories. Their greatest victory was the capture of Constantinople in 1453, thus bringing to an end the declining Byzantine empire. Under the Ottomans, great literature was composed in Persian and Turkish, while Arabic was used for scientific and religious works.

OTTOMAN ART AND ARCHITECTURE

Glazed pottery and silver and gold metalwork reached a high degree of excellence. Intricate designs were woven on textiles and carpets. The great Topkapi palace in Constantinople (formally renamed Istanbul in 1930), as well as mosques and tombs, were constructed. Heavy domes were raised on square bases and brilliantly colored tiles decorated the buildings.

The Suleimaniye mosque, built in the 1550s in Istanbul by the Ottomans.

c. 1425 Pueblo people in New Mexico build multi-storied buildings with stone and sun-dried bricks.

1428–29 Orleans in France rescued from the English by Joan of Arc.

1429 Cosimo de Medici is head of Medici banking house in Florence; richest man of his time.

1430 Order of Golden Fleece, an order of knights, founded by Philip the Good of Burgundy.

c. 1430–1435 Italian sculptor Donatello (c. 1386–1466) creates bronze image of David; first sculpture in Western Europe cast in the round, and first nude, since ancient times.

1431 Angkor, capital of Khmer kingdom in Cambodia, invaded and destroyed by people from Thailand; new capital at Phnom Penh.

1438 Emperor Pachacuti in Peru expands Inca empire: Machu Picchu probably built for him.

There were wars between England and France in Europe, and civil war within England. The Byzantine empire fought its last battle against the Turks. In Russia, the state of Muscovy began to expand; in 1480, Ivan III declared himself grand prince of all Russia. Among the Scandinavian countries, Sweden asserted her independence in 1523.

At the same time Europe saw a flowering of culture. Protestantism developed within Christianity; urban centers flourished along with trade and commerce; and Europeans went on voyages of exploration, establishing colonies and settlements around the world.

Hundred Years' War: the final phases

There was political confusion in France and England before the third phase of the Hundred Years' War (1415–35). Eventually the French regained lost territory. In 1435, peace negotiations began with Charles VII of France. However, due to this, Philip the Good of Burgundy, who had supported the English, withdrew support, and France regained Paris in 1436. Using the mobile cannon to its best advantage, France wrested back more territories. A five-year truce was signed in 1444, but hostilities were resumed. Eventually, the Hundred Years' War ended after the Battle of Castillon, in 1453. In France, only Calais remained under the control of the English.

The Battle of Castillon, by the French painter Charles-Phillippe Larivière, 19th century.

JOAN OF ARC

In 1428, during the Hundred Years' War, a 17-year-old girl convinced Charles VII, king of France, that she had received visions directing her to save Orleans from the Engish siege. Charles gave Joan of Arc an army that relieved Orleans and won battles at Ptay and Reims. But she was captured by the English in 1430 and the following year she was burned to death as a heretic.

1440–1485

- **c. 1441** Maya city of Mayapan destroyed; region divided into separate city-states.
- Portuguese bring first African slaves to Lisbon.
- **1448** Portuguese navigator Dinis Dias discovers and names Cape Verde, the western-most part of Africa.
- **c. 1450** French painter Jean Fouquet (c. 1416–80) paints the Melun Diptych.
- Vatican Library, originating from earlier papal collections of books and documents, established.

- **1452–1519** Life of Italian polymath Leonardo da Vinci.
- **1453** Hundred Years' War between France and England ends.
- **1455** Civil war, Wars of the Roses, in England.
- Johannes Gutenberg of Germany prints first book in Europe using fully moveable type.
- **1458** Matthias Corvinus becomes king of Hungary; recognized by Holy Roman Emperor in **1462**.
- **1461** Louis IX becomes king of France.
- **1461–83** Reign of Edward IV of England.

The Wars of the Roses

The Hundred Years' War had hardly ended when a civil war, known as the Wars of the Roses, was fought between the Houses of York (white rose emblem) and Lancaster (red rose emblem) in England. The main battles took place between 1455 and 1485. Henry VI of Lancaster, backed by his powerful queen, Margaret of Anjou, was challenged by Richard, Duke of York. Both sides were descended from King Edward III, and were aided by feudal lords, their vassals, and mercenaries. The worst battle was that of Towton, in 1461, when 28,000 men were killed in one day. Edward, son of Richard, was crowned king as Edward IV after this battle, but the Wars were not over. Richard, duke of Gloucester, seized the throne from Edward V (son of Edward IV) and became King Richard III. The Lancastrian Henry Tudor then defeated Richard III at the Battle of Bosworth and was crowned Henry VII. He united the factions through marriage and established the Tudor dynasty in England.

Top: The red rose of the House of Lancaster. Middle: The white rose of the House of York. Bottom: The Tudor rose symbolizing the union.

ELIZABETH I

The queen of England and Ireland (1558–1603), Elizabeth was the last ruler of the Tudor dynasty founded by Henry VII. She faced numerous problems during her reign, including a conflict with Mary, Queen of Scots, war with Spain and the French Catholic League, and rebellion in Ireland. At the same time, her reign is known as the Golden Age of the English Renaissance. Writers of this time included William Shakespeare, Edmund Spenser, and Philip Sidney. Elizabeth herself was a scholar and linguist. She had a love for theater and plays were performed in her honor.

1462 Ivan III is grand duke of Muscovy.
1466–77 Onin War between two rival clans in Japan.
c. 1469–70 Thomas Malory (d.1471), English writer, composes prose epic *Le Morte d'Arthur* (The Death of Arthur).
1470 Portuguese explorers reach Gold Coast in Africa.
1471–1528 Life of German painter Albrecht Durer.
1475–1564 Life of Italian artist and sculptor Michelangelo.

1476 First English printing press set up by William Caxton, at Westminster.
1478 Tarascan and Aztec empires clash in Central America.
• Start of the Spanish Inquisition.
1483 Richard III becomes king of England; he is the last of the House of York.
• Dominican monk Tomas de Torquemada appointed to conduct Spanish Inquisition.
1483–1520 Life of Italian painter Raphael.

Martin Luther (1483–1546).

THE AGE OF DISCOVERY

The Reformation

From the 14th century onwards, some people openly challenged practices that had crept into Christianity. In 1517, a German monk, Martin Luther, published his *Ninety-Five Theses*, protesting against various aspects of Church functioning. He believed that people should be freed from the authority of the pope, and should be able to gain direct experience of god themselves through the Bible. His views had a huge impact, and other reformers began to preach similar ideas. Among them were Huldreich Zwingli in Zurich, and John Calvin, a French theologian settled in Geneva. Gradually, entire groups, and even countries, broke away from the Roman Catholic Church. They came to be known as Protestants, and set up their own churches. Despite attempts to reform the Catholic Church, known as the Counter Reformation, Protestantism flourished and expanded.

Explorers and traders

Vasco da Gama (1460–1524).

Flourishing cities and the expansion of trade led to a search for new lands. The occupation of Constantinople by the Turks forced Europeans to find different routes to the East. The early explorers and colonizers were largely Portuguese and Spanish, though the English and French also ventured into Africa, the Americas, and the East.

The Portuguese were the first Europeans to tap into Africa's lucrative trade in gold, copper, and slaves. Henry the Navigator, prince of Portugal, organized numerous voyages of exploration from 1434 onwards. In the late 15th century, the Portuguese discovered the sea route around Africa. In 1497–98, Vasco da Gama followed the route around the Cape of Good Hope and reached India.

THE KREMLIN

The citadel of a Russian city is known as a kremlin. Under Ivan III (r. 1462–1505), the Moscow kremlin was rebuilt with a new wall and towers, a new palace, and three new cathedrals. The great bell tower was built by Ivan's son Vasily III between 1505 and 1508. Construction at the Kremlin under Ivan III.

1485–1522

1485 Jewish philosopher Joseph Albo writes *Sefer ha-Ikkarim* (Book of Principles), explaining aspects of Judaism.

1485–1603 Tudor dynasty rules England.

1486 Aztecs defeat Guarrero and Oaxaca people.

1488–1576 Life of Italian painter Titian.

1490 Portuguese explorers reach Congo.

1492 Christopher Columbus sets sail for the East Indies; **1494** instead reaches the Caribbean Islands.

1497–98 Spanish explorer Amerigo Vespucci explores North America; Americas are named after him.

1499 Plague epidemic kills thousands in London.

1500 Pedro Alvares Cabral reaches Brazil; makes it a Portuguese dominion.

1502 Safavid dynasty of Persia assumes power in Azerbaijan.

1505 Portuguese conquer African kingdoms of Quiloa and Mombasa; reach India.

The Renaissance

Italy in the 14th century saw the beginning of a period called the Renaissance ("rebirth"), characterized by a revival of interest in the arts of classical Greece and Rome. It is a period of history seen as a glorious age, whereas the Middle Ages were condemned for cultural stagnation. The renewed interest in the classical was combined with new concepts and ideas. The background for the Renaissance lay in economic change. Trade and commerce had led to the rise of wealthy cities in Italy, among which were Florence, Venice and Milan. Rich families such as the Medici of Florence, the Gonzaga of Mantua, the dukes of Urbino, and the doges of Venice, patronized Renaissance art and education. Though Christianity and the Church continued to be important, there was a growth of secular ideas. "Humanism" is a term used to describe these ideas, emphasizing the importance of the human being, rather than god. Secular histories, which did not incorporate Christian theories of creation and the Last Judgment, were written. Theological questions addressed by Humanists came to have an impact on Christianity.

In art, classical forms were revisited. A technique, called the linear perspective, that gave depth to a drawing or painting, was understood. Among the greatest artists of the Renaissance were Raphael, Leonardo da Vinci, and Michelangelo. In sculpture, the human body once again became important. There were fresh trends in architecture. Literature began to be composed in regional languages. Ancient Greek treatises were translated. Nicolaus Copernicus, Tycho Brahe, Johannes Kepler, and Galileo were among the pioneers who opened new dimensions in science.

Left: Raphael's *Marriage of the Virgin*, now housed in a Milan art gallery.
Right: Johannes Kepler (1571–1630).
Far right: Nicolaus Copernicus (1473–1543).

1507 Shaibanid dynasty established in Transoxiana area of Central Asia.

1508 Pope Julius II founds League of Cambrai; fights against Venice.

1509 Henry VIII becomes king of England.

1510 Portuguese conquer Goa, in India.

1513 Italian Niccolo Machiavelli writes *The Prince*.

• Portuguese reach China via sea-route.

1514 Ottomans defeat Safavids of Persia; capture Persian capital Tabriz.

1516–17 Ottomans conquer Syria and Egypt; end Mamluk sultanate; control Mecca.

1517 Martin Luther begins Christian Protestant movement.

1519–21 Ferdinand Magellan, Portuguese-born Spaniard, explores Asia.

1522 Revolt by African slaves in Hispaniola; probably first such slave revolt.

• Defeat of Christian Knights Hospitaller by Ottomans at Rhodes.

THE AGE OF DISCOVERY

Christopher Columbus (right) lands on an island in Central America (1492).

By 1400 the population of North America, (north of Mexico) is estimated to have been between one and 10 million, with most people living in the area of today's USA and only about 250,000 living in the Canada region. There were about 240 tribal groups of Native Americans such as the Apache, Navajo, Iroquois, and others, most speaking different languages.

In South and Central America, where the empires of the Incas, Aztecs, and others thrived, the population would have been much higher.

Europeans reach the Americas

A population explosion in Europe as well as a desire to find new sources of wealth and gold prompted its inhabitants to seek new lands. In the late 15th century, Christopher Columbus, sponsored by the government of Spain, reached parts of the American continent. He was followed by other Spanish explorers. The Venetian John Cabot (1450–99), sailing for England, arrived on Newfoundland, in present-day Canada, in 1497. Jacques Cartier (1491–1557) of France reached the Strait of Belle Isle, off Canada's east coast, in 1534.

In the region of North America which later became the USA, the first permanent European settlement was founded in 1565 by the Spaniard Pedro Menendez de Aviles, at St Augustine in Florida. This was an area populated mainly by Seminole tribes. Sir Walter Raleigh of England attempted to set up settlements in the late 16th century, but these did not last. The first permanent English outpost was established in the 17th century.

THE IROQUOIS

By the 16th century, five Native American tribes of the Iroquoian language family, the Mohawk, Onondaga, Cayuga, Oneida, and Seneca, founded a confederacy. They dominated the region of present-day New York, and later expanded to neighboring areas. Their staple diet was corn, though they also grew pumpkin, beans, and tobacco.

1523–1564

1523 Sweden independent from Denmark.
1528–72 Christian missionaries convert native populations in Mexico.
1530 Spaniard Alvarado defeats the Mayas.
• Knights Hospitaller settle on island of Malta; become known as Knights of Malta.
1530–84 Life of Ivan IV (the Terrible) of Russia.
1531 Protestant Schmalkaldic League formed against Holy Roman Emperor.

1534 Protestant Christianity established in England; king is supreme head of Church.
1535 Wales incorporated into the English legal and government system by Act of Union.
1536 Spanish conquest of Aztec and Inca empires complete.
1538 Ottoman Turks led by Khair ad-Din (Barbarossa) defeat combined forces of Venice, Holy Roman Emperor Charles V, and Pope Paul III in naval battle; control Mediterranean.

Course of the Maya, Aztec, and Inca empires

South and Central America saw conquests by Spain and Portugal. Civilizations that had existed for hundreds, even thousands, of years were destroyed, and new ways of life imposed. Spain occupied Maya, Inca, and Aztec lands. In the early 16th century, the Portuguese settled in Brazil.

The great Maya civilization had declined, but several distinct groups still existed until the arrival of the Spanish in 1517. As the Maya had many different centers, it took the Spanish a long time to establish control over them. The last states were conquered in 1697. Though the Maya produced a large number of books, only a few survive, as most were destroyed by the Spanish.

In 1427 the Aztec ruler Itzacoatl, with his capital at Tenochtitlan, joined with the cities of Tlacopan and Texcoco to defeat the Tapanec city of Azcapotzalco. The Aztecs now expanded into a large empire. By this time, Tenochtitlan, and its neighboring city Tlatelolco, were inhabited by more than 200,000 people. In 1502, Montezuma became Aztec emperor. The empire finally ended when Hernando Cortes (1485–1547), a Spanish soldier, reached Mexico and defeated the Aztecs in 1521.

In the first half of this period, the Inca empire continued to expand, and extended along the coast from northern Ecuador to Chile, a distance of 2983 miles. The Incas had a state religion and a centralized administration. Priests conducted sacrificial rituals and prophesied the future. The Incas had developed an advanced system of medicine, even conducting successful surgeries. The beautiful city of Machu Picchu, with stone buildings

and terraced fields, was built between two mountain peaks in the Andes in c. 1450.

In 1532, the Spaniard Francisco Pizarro's attack brought the main empire to an end. However, a new Inca empire was created in the northwest mountainous region of Vilcabamba. It survived till 1572, before being subjugated by the Spanish.

Machu Picchu.

1541–1614 Life of Spanish painter El Greco.

1545–96 Life of British explorer Francis Drake.

1546 Catholic forces defeat Schmalkaldic League in Battle of Muhlberg.

1553 Mary, Queen of England, suppresses revolt of supporters of Lady Jane Grey.

1555 Peace of Augsberg allows German states to follow their chosen Catholic or Protestant religion.

• French astrologer and physician Nostradamus writes his prophecies.

1556 Philip II becomes king of Spain.

• Tobacco introduced in Europe (Spain) from Central America; reaches England by 1585.

1559 Peace treaty of Cateau-Cambresias ends wars between France and Spain over territory in Italy.

1560 Religious reformer John Knox establishes Presbyterian Church in Scotland.

1561–1636 Life of Italian physician Sanctorius Sanctorius; initiates studies in human metabolism.

TRADING EMPIRES

Africa saw continuous changes in boundaries and dynasties, often due to conflict over natural resources or trade. Islam, initially a religion of the ruling classes and urban centers, began to be accepted by ordinary people, especially in Sudan.

The Songhe empire

Artist's impression of Askia Muhammad of Songhe.

In West Africa the Songhe state, with its capital at Gao near the Niger river, annexed some of the Mali empire's territories. The cities of Timbuktu, Jenne, and Gao were great trading centers as well as places of Islamic learning. During the reign of Askia Muhammad (1493–1528), the area of Songhe sway increased, but in 1591 Morocco conquered Gao.

The Bornu kingdom

Idris Alooma (r. c. 1580–1617) of the Saifawa dynasty was the best known ruler of the Bornu kingdom which existed in the Sudan region from the eighth to the 17th centuries. Idris reformed the administration and introduced Sharia or Islamic law.

His army included a camel corps, and Bornu was the only state in the region with firearms, bought from the Ottomans.

TIMBUKTU

Founded probably in the 11th century, Timbuktu, north of the great bend in the Niger river, was incorporated into the kingdom of Mali by the 14th century. It developed into a renowned center of Islamic culture and learning. The city reached its height under the Songhe empire, and in the 16th century, held a population of around 40,000. It was an important center on the trans-Sahara trade network.

Timbuktu's Sankore mosque had evolved into a great university by the time the Songhe empire was established.

1564–1600

1564–87 Life of Tintoretto, Italian artist.
1564–1616 Life of English poet and playwright William Shakespeare.
1568 Oda Nobunaga ends control of Ashikaga shoguns in Japan.
1569 Gerardus Mercator, Flemish geographer and cartographer, creates a map projection named after him.
1570 Panama, in Central America, becomes important trading post.

• Jewish rabbi and mystic Isaac ben Luria develops influential school of Kabbalah.
1571 Ottoman fleet defeated in Battle of Lepanto; Turkish control over Mediterranean ends.
• Ridolfi plot to assassinate Queen Elizabeth I and place Mary, Queen of Scots, on the throne of England fails.
1572 Danish astronomer Tycho Brahe discovers supernova in Cassiopia constellation.

The Ottomans in Egypt

The Mamluks were conquered in 1517 by the Ottoman Turks, who extended their control over North African coastal areas. The Mamluks however were retained in the administration, and by the 17th century assumed real power, while acknowledging the supremacy of the Ottomans.

East African city-states

Malindi, Mogadishu, and Mombasa were some of the city-states of the inland inter-lake region. The rulers were Arab-Africans, while the ordinary people were Bantu speakers. Swahili, a new language, emerged from the mixing of Arabic and Bantu.

Great Zimbabwe

The ruins of Great Zimbabwe.

A great civilization emerged in south-central Africa, located on the Zimbabwe plateau between the Zambezi and Limpopo rivers. Its founders were the ancestors of the modern Shona people of Zimbabwe. Around 1100, settlements within thick stone walls were built. Trade in gold and copper crossed the Indian Ocean to China. Luxury goods were imported in return. By c. 1450, the settlement at Great Zimbabwe was at its pinnacle. Massive stone walls surrounded the complex, though the houses were simple thatched structures. Other centers have been found in modern Zimbabwe and in neighboring states.

THE HAUSA

In northern Nigeria the Hausa people founded a number of city-states from around 1000. Textiles, glass, leather, and metal work were among their crafts, and they had an extensive trade. By the 16th century the state of Kano was the largest and most prosperous, with trade in ivory, gold, leather, and slaves. Arab and Berber traders, as well as local merchants lived there, and it was a center of Islamic culture. The Hausa states survived till the early 19th century.

1576 English explorer Martin Frobisher discovers Baffin Island off Canada.
- Spanish Carmelite monk St John of the Cross describes mystical experiences in his poems.

1577–1640 Life of Flemish painter Peter Paul Reubens.

1578 Mongolian ruler Altan Khan bestows title of Dalai Lama (spiritual leader) on leader of Tibet's Gelugpa Buddhist sect.

1578–1606 Manila becomes important trading town in the Philippines.

1582 Pope Gregory XIII introduces Gregorian calendar.

1584 El Escorial, palace of the kings of Spain, completed near Madrid.

1587 Mary, Queen of Scots, executed by Elizabeth I of England.

1588 English defeat Spanish Armada, near Calais.

1591 French mathematician Francois Viete introduces new system of algebraic notation.

1597 Jacopo Peri writes *Dafne*, the first opera.

WARS, COLONIES, AND NEW STATES

The Manchu

I n China, the Ming were replaced by the Qing dynasty, also known as Manchu, in 1644. Though the Chinese resented the new rulers, who were from Manchuria, they gradually came to accept them. The Manchu were familiar with Chinese ways, and did not make drastic changes in the system of government, though they retained the top posts. The Manchu also introduced the practice of wearing the hair in a pigtail. In 1661, emperor Shunzi was succeeded by his seven-year-old son Kangxi, who reigned for 61 years. He respected Chinese traditions, maintained the Chinese as high officials in the civil service, and rebuilt Beijing. Old books and manuscripts were collected, and a 5000-volume encyclopedia was produced. Confucian ideals were emphasized.

Emperor Kangxi.

Emperor Qianlong (r. 1736–96) destroyed Mongol power in Central Asia, and brought the Xinjiang Ughyur region under Chinese control. During his reign China had a period of peace and prosperity. Qianlong was a great patron of arts, and himself studied painting and calligraphy. China became famous for its glazed pottery, textiles, art, and learning. Trade increased and new towns emerged. Tea and porcelain were exported to the Western world.

The Tokugawa

T here was a civil war between rival claimants for power in Japan. Ieyasu, of the powerful Tokugawa feudal family, won the Battle of Sekigahara against Ishida Mitsunari, and became the shogun in 1603. The Tokugawas ruled from Edo (modern Tokyo), while the emperors lived in luxury at Kyoto. Samurai warriors kept peace in the empire; another type of warrior were the ninja, trained in martial arts and employed as spies or assassins. Distrusting foreigners, Japan isolated itself from the rest of the world, becoming insular and dated. The period of Tokugawa shoguns lasted till 1868.

1600–1631

1600 English East India Company formed.
• William Gilbert (1544–1603), English physicist, writes De Magnete (Of Magnets) on magnetism.
1602 Dutch East India Company formed.
1608 English East India Company ship reaches Surat, India.
1609 Johannes Kepler formulates laws of planetary motion.
• Japan and Korea inaugurate period of friendship.

1609–10 Galileo Galilei confirms Copernicus' theory that the earth and planets revolve around the sun.
c. 1610 Christianity spreads through South America.
1611 King James Bible published in England.
1611–32 Gustavus Adolphus is king of Sweden.
1612 Spanish writer Cervantes composes Don Quixote.
1613 English playwright John Webster writes The Duchess of Malfi.

SIKHISM

In India, Guru Nanak (1469–1539) founded the Sikh religion. His basic tenets—belief in one god, who has no shape or form; an emphasis on ethical behavior; meditation on the divine name—were expanded by nine gurus (spiritual teachers) following him. The fifth guru, Arjan Dev, compiled the sacred teachings in what was later known as the Guru Granth Sahib, the holy book of the Sikhs.

Guru Nanak.

Mughals: peak and decline

In north India, Mughal rule continued under Jahangir (r. 1605–27), Shah Jahan (1628–58), and Aurangzeb (1659–1707). Wars and conquest were pursued by all three, but Aurangzeb became entrapped in attempts to conquer the independent kingdoms of central India. He spent 25 years away from the capital, Delhi.

Art and culture were vibrant under the Mughals. Jahangir's reign is known for its fine miniature

The Taj Mahal, Agra, built by Shah Jahan in memory of his wife.

paintings, and Shah Jahan's for grand buildings, including the white-marble Taj Mahal. Aurangzeb did not promote the arts, but, in his absence, Delhi became a center of learning and culture. With the devastation caused by the invasion of Nadir Shah (1739), and later by the Afghan Ahmad Shah Abdali, the center of culture moved for some time to Lucknow.

Meanwhile, the Sikhs and Marathas were also struggling for control in India. Europeans, including the Portuguese, French, Dutch, and English, were establishing trading centers, while battling with each other and with indigenous rulers. By 1800, the British were the dominant power on the subcontinent.

1613–29 Gabor Bethlen is prince of Transylvania; also king of Hungary **1620–21**.

1616 Manchurian forces invade China.

1619–24 Dutch dominate Indoneseian spice trade.

c. 1620 Cornelis Drebbel, Dutch inventor, designs first submersible craft; tested on Thames river.

1620 Ottoman Turks invade Poland; are driven out.

1623 Tommaso Campanella, Italian philosopher, writes utopian treatise *La Citta del Sole* (City of the Sun) when imprisoned in Naples, Italy.

1624 Dutch settlers acquire Manhattan from local tribes and name it New Amsterdam.

1625 Plague in London kills at least 40,000 people.

1626 French colonizers settle in Madagascar.

1627 Korea invaded by Manchus; **1636** Seoul captured.

1631 Mughal emperor Shah Jahan begins construction of Taj Mahal in India.

• French mathematician Pierre Vernier devises scales for measuring lines and angles.

WARS, COLONIES, AND NEW STATES

While various European powers had begun colonizing the world, within Europe wars continued. Some, such as the Seven Years' War (1756–63), fought both within and outside Europe, were over territory and trading rights, whereas the Thirty Years' War was based on religious differences. Other conflicts arose from challenges to the "divine right" of kings to rule.

Civil war in Britain

Oliver Cromwell.

In 1640 King Charles I (1625–49) asked parliament for funds to suppress a long-lasting Scottish revolt. In return, parliament demanded more powers, and in 1642 civil war began between the king and representatives of the people, who raised their own armies. Charles was executed in 1649, and a republic, the English Commonwealth, was established, with the anti-royalist general Oliver Cromwell appointed as its leader or Protector in 1653. He provided stable government until his death in 1658, but in 1660 the royalty was revived under Charles II.

Politically unsuccessful, Charles I was a patron of the arts, commissioning portrait-painter Anthony van Dyck (1599–1641) and the architect Inigo Jones (1573–1652).

THE DUTCH STATE

After a long fight for independence from Spain, the Dutch Republic of the United Provinces was established in 1648. The new state became rich through trade. Dutch blue and white pottery from Delft gained worldwide fame. There was significant scientific advancement: Christian Huyghens (1629–95) discovered that light travels in waves. Antonie van Leeuwenhoek (1632–1723) described the composition of blood, and observed bacteria and protozoa with a simple microscope. In painting, Rembrandt van Rijn (1606–69) and Johannes Vermeer (1632–75) are the great names from this time.

A Delft blue and white vase.

1632–1680

1632–54 Queen Christina rules in Sweden.

1633 Italian scientist Galileo faces charges of heresy from the Inquisition for defending Copernicus' theory of heliocentrism.

1635 Zaidi imams reestablish themselves as rulers of Yemen.

1637–1709 Safavid dynasty declines; Ghalzai Afghans occupy Kandahar.

1640 French mathematician Blaise Pascal invents early form of calculator.

1640 Portugal asserts independence from Spain.

1641 Tibet becomes a religious state under fifth Dalai Lama.

1648 Treaty of Westphalia ends Thirty Years' War in Holy Roman Empire and Eighty Years' War between Spain and Netherlands.

1650 Sultan bin Saif al Yarubi drives Portugese out of Muscat and founds Yarubid dynasty that rules Oman up to 1749.

1652–54 First Anglo-Dutch War.

The Thirty Years' War

Beginning in Bohemia as a Protestant struggle against the Catholic Habsburg king Ferdinand II, who was also the Holy Roman Emperor, the war (1618–48) gradually involved Denmark, Norway, Sweden, France, and numerous German states, many of them worried about Habsburg power. At that time the family ruled Austria, Bohemia, Hungary, Spain, and other areas. The struggle ended with the Peace of Westphalia. France emerged as the major power in Europe, while the Habsburgs and the Holy Roman Emperor were weakened. The German states were devastated, losing at least 20 per cent of their population and going into economic decline.

Ferdinand II.

Wars of Succession

The War of the Spanish Succession (1701–14) was fought by the Habsburg Holy Roman empire, England, Portugal, and other European powers against Philip, Duke of Anjou, the successor to Spanish Habsburg territories. Philip was supported by France, Bavaria, and Hungary. The war ended with Spain under the Bourbons of France.

Another major conflict was the War of the Austrian Succession (1740–48), when rival claimants challenged the accession of a female, Maria Theresa, to the Habsburg Austrian lands. Most European countries were drawn in before her claim was recognized.

PETER I

Tsar Peter I (r. 1682–1725) who traveled outside the country, brought in reforms, and built the city of St Petersburg, which became Russia's capital in 1714. Under him, Russia became a major European power.

1655 British capture Jamaica from the Spanish.
1657 Great fire kills thousands in Edo, Japan.
1660 Royal Society founded in London, England.
1662 Robert Boyle, English scientist, formulates law on the pressure-volume relationship of gas.
1663 and '65 Plague epidemics in Amsterdam and London.
1665–67 Second Anglo-Dutch War.
1666 Great fire destroys London.

1668 John Dryden becomes England's first poet laureate.
1669 Hanseatic League comes to an end.
• Famine kills three million in Bengal, India.
1676 Observatory established at Greenwich, England.
1679 Habeas Corpus Act passed in England, no imprisonment allowed without court appearance.
1680–92 Pueblos of New Mexico revolt against Spanish colonists.

REVOLUTION AND LEARNING

The French Revolution

A series of events, collectively called the French Revolution, took place in France between 1787 and 1799, stimulating the development of new ideas in other parts of the world.

When Louis XVI was crowned in 1774 France was undergoing a financial crisis, which continued despite his economic reforms. So he authorized elections for the first Estates-General assembly since 1614. This body consisted of representatives from three groups: The clergy, the nobility, and the common people. Meeting at Versailles on May 5, 1789, the assembly could not reconcile the conflicting demands of the elite and the common people, and the latter formed a new National Assembly. Louis's plans to cancel this led to protests in Paris, and the storming of the Bastille, the fortress-prison, on July 14.

LOUIS XIV
The reign of Louis XIV (1643–1715) of France, known as the "sun king," is remembered for his patronage of art and culture, and for the glorious palace he built at Versailles. Louis founded academies of painting and sculpture, science, and architecture. A national theater, the Comédie Française, was established in 1680. Playwrights Molière (1622–73) and Jean-Baptiste Racine (1639–99) thrived.

The National Assembly then assumed power and drew up a constitution that proclaimed

The storming of the Bastille.

the basic rights of man: Liberty, equality, and respect for life and property. A new assembly, the National Convention, declared France a republic on September 21, 1792. Louis and his wife Marie Antoinette were executed and the Jacobins, a radical group in the Convention, started a "reign of terror" under Maximilien Robespierre, during which thousands accused of opposing the Revolution were executed. In 1794, Robespierre was himself executed by an rival group, and, in 1795, another government was formed.

1681–1711

1681 Pennsylvania founded in North America.
• Languedoc canal constructed in France; connects Atlantic Ocean and Mediterranean Sea.
1683 Formosa (Taiwan) taken over by China.
1684 English East India Company establishes first trading post in Canton, China.
1685–1750 Life of Johann Sebastian Bach, German musician.
1685–1759 Life of Georg Friedrich Handel, German musician.

1687 Venice gains Athens from Ottoman Turks.
1689 Russia and China sign Treaty of Nerchinsk whereby Russia cedes some territory to China, but retains other important areas.
1694 Bank of England established in London.
1697 After 11 years' fighting, France loses War of the League of Augsburg to European coalition.
1697–1718 Charles XII rules in Sweden.
1698 London Stock Exchange established.

Cultural and scientific flowering

Wolfgang Amadeus Mozart.

Despite the turmoil, this was an age when new ideas came to the fore, and great strides were made in the arts and sciences. The baroque style in painting, sculpture, architecture, and music emerged in the first half of the 17th century. In art and architecture, it was characterized by dramatic effects and contrasts of light and shadow. Baroque evolved into the lighter, more decorative rococo in the early 18th century. In music, the opera took shape. Classical styles developed between about 1750 to 1820, with great composers Joseph Haydn (1732–1809) and Wolfgang Amadeus Mozart (1756–91) of Austria, and the German Ludwig van Beethoven (1770–1827).

Jean-Jacques Rousseau.

Great philosophers included the Englishman John Locke (1632–1778), the Frenchmen Voltaire (1694–1778) and Jean-Jacques Rousseau (1712–78), and the British-American Thomas Paine (1735–1805). Isaac Newton (1642–1727), another Englishman, discovered the laws of gravity and motion; French chemist and physicist Antoine Lavoisier (1743–94) put forward a new combustion theory; and plants and animals were classified for the first time by Swedish botanist Carl Linnaeus (1707–78).

Isaac Newton.

FREDERICK THE GREAT

Prussia, one of the main states of Germany, began to expand from the time of Frederick I (r. 1701–13). Frederick II (the Great), king from 1740 to 1786, made Prussia a major power in Europe. He was a patron of culture, and was himself a prolific writer and a musician.

OCEANIA DISCOVERED

The Spanish, Portuguese, and Dutch explored the islands of Asia and Oceania. Portuguese explorer Luis Vaez de Torres reached New Guinea in 1606, while Dutch seafarers reached Tasmania, New Zealand, Tonga, and Fiji, and the northern coasts of Australia.

Jacob Roggeveen, a Dutch navigator, landed on Easter Island in 1722. Though Europeans had reached Australia, the aboriginals continued their peaceful lifestyle there.

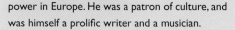

- First steam engine made by English engineer Thomas Savery; used to pump water from coal mines.
- **1699** Sikh leader Guru Gobind Singh founds the Khalsa, order of baptized Sikhs, in India.
- Habsburgs acquire most of Hungary by Treaty of Karlowitz.
- **1702–14** Anne is queen of England and Scotland.
- **1703** Peter the Great founds city of St Petersburg in Russia.

- **1704** First newspaper of North America, *The Boston News-Letter*, published.
- **1705–11** Joseph I is Holy Roman Emperor.
- **1707** By Act of Union, England and Scotland join to create Great Britain.
- **1708–09** King Charles XII of Sweden invades Russia; is defeated in Battle of Poltava.
- **1711** North American tribes fight against North Carolina planters in the Tuscarora Indian War.

COLONIES AND TRADE

There were numerous kingdoms all over Africa, each with their own myths and stories, indigenous religion, arts and crafts, and forms of music and dance. European colonization began and the slave trade grew. The Portuguese, Dutch, and British established bases and settlements.

The Ottoman empire was so large by this time that local pashas or governors assumed various degrees of control. Tripoli, Tunis, and Algiers in north Africa asserted their autonomy. The latter became virtually independent in 1710. In the 18th century, there was a revival of Islamic dynasties among the Fulani, Mandingo, Soso, and Tukolor people.

African kingdoms and the slave trade

African kingdoms that carried out a slave trade included Asante, Dahomey, and Benin (different from today's state of Benin). Slaves were sent to America, the Caribbean islands, Asia, and Europe, and by 1730, about 50,000 slaves were being transported every year to the Americas alone. By the 1780s, the number had risen to about 90,000.

The Asante were united in 1701 by Osei Tutu, chief of the small Asante state of Kumasia. They controlled gold mines and supplied slaves to European nations, receiving firearms in return. Kings of Yoruba origin founded three kingdoms—Allada, Abomey, and Whydah—in the early 17th century. By 1727 they were united by king Agaja of Abomey as the kingdom of Dahomey and began supplying slaves to the Europeans. He is also known for creating a corps of women soldiers.

In the 16th and 17th centuries, Benin, in what is now Nigeria, traded in palm oil, spices, ivory, and textiles. In the 18th century, it was also a slave-trading kingdom. Benin city's wide streets had large palaces and houses with wooden pillars. It was known for ivory and bronze carvings.

THE YORUBA

The first remains at the ancient sacred city of Ife, to which the Yoruba people trace their origin, date between the 12th and 15th centuries. In the 17th century Oyo was the most important Yoruba state, controlling a large area between the Volta and Niger rivers.

Wooden sculpture of the head of a Yoruba king.

1712–1757

1712 British inventor Thomas Newcomen (1663–1729) makes steam engine using atmospheric pressure.

1713–14 Treaties of Utrecht end War of the Spanish Succession and Queen Anne's War.

1714 Gabriel Fahrenheit, German physicist, makes first mercury-filled thermometer and develops scale for measurement of temperature.

1714–27 George I is first Hanoverian king of Great Britain.

1717 Tibet comes under Chinese rule.

• In India, Mughal emperor Farrukhsiyar allows East India Company to trade in Bengal.

1723–90 Life of Scottish economist Adam Smith.

1727 Coffee first planted in Brazil.

1727–88 Life of English landscape artist Thomas Gainsborough.

1739 John Wesley founds Methodist Society.

c. 1740 Hasidism, Jewish movement, founded by Baal Shem Tov.

Developments in Ethiopia

Though Islam was followed by some, the kingdom's main religion was Monophysite Christianity of the Orthodox Church. Jesuits tried to convert Ethiopian Christians to the Western Church, though with little success. Emperor Fasilides (r. 1632–67) established a new capital at Gondar, which became a great center of trade, art, and culture. Castles, palaces, and churches, including the Debre Berhan Selassie Church, were constructed here. Ethiopia continued to resist colonial inroads. A period of feudal anarchy persisted during 1700–1850, with several local rulers holding sway.

QUEEN NZINGA

From 1624 Ndongo, a kingdom in modern Angola, was ruled by Queen Nzinga, who was opposed to the slave trade. She fought the Portuguese, who had occupied part of Angola, and provided shelter to fugitive slaves. Defeated in 1626, Nzinga conquered the neighboring kingdom of Matamba (1630) and continued to harass the Portuguese from there. Resistance to the slave trade also came from King Maremba of the Congo.

Fasilides's palace in Gondar.

1740 Maria Theresa becomes archduchess of Austria.

1741–62 Elizabeth Petrovna, daughter of Peter the Great, is empress of Russia.

1742 Swedish astronomer Anders Celsius creates centigrade thermometer.

1744 Islamic Wahhabi creed established in Dariya, Arabian Peninsula.

1748 War of the Austrian Succession ends with Treaty of Aix-la-Chapelle.

1749–1832 Life of German writer Johann Wolfgang von Goethe.

c. 1750–1850 Classical period of Western music.

1755 Earthquake in Lisbon kills 30,000.

• Samuel Johnson compiles English dictionary.

• Smallpox spreads through Cape Town, South Africa.

1757 Battle of Plassey in India marks beginning of British rule.

1757–1827 Life of English poet and painter William Blake.

The Boston Tea Party.

COLONIES AND TRADE

Colonization of North America

Europeans began to extend their settlements in America. The French, English, Swedish, and Dutch were in North America, while the Spanish and Portuguese were prominent in South and Central America.

The first permanent English settlement was founded in 1607 at Jamestown, and, in 1624 the British crown took control of the area. As the economy expanded through the cultivation of tobacco, the importation of African slaves to serve as cheap labor began. In 1620, a dissident religious group of English Protestants, later known as the Pilgrim Fathers, landed in Massachusetts. They composed a self-governing agreement known as the Mayflower Compact (named after their ship, the *Mayflower*). It is considered the first constitution of America. More colonies emerged in this region, which came to be known as New England. A small college founded here in 1636 developed into Harvard University by 1780.

The French gained control over the fur trade in Canada, and in 1604 established their first settlements. In 1627 the colony of New France was founded along the St Lawrence river. Expansion continued into the Mississippi valley area and the territory known as Louisiana. By the Treaty of Paris in 1763 after the Seven Years' War, New France came under the British. Deeply in debt after the series of wars, the British tried to gain revenue in its American colonies by taxes and duties. These were resisted by the colonists, and finally, only a tax on tea was retained.

After a monopoly on the tea trade was granted to the English East India Company in 1773, the colonists destroyed boxes of tea landing at Boston—an event later known as the Boston Tea Party. The British reacted with repression.

Spanish and Portuguese in South America

In 1717 Spain founded the viceroyalty of New Granada, made up of the present-day states of Panama, Ecuador, Colombia, and Venezuela. Spain later expanded its empire into Mexico and Peru, while the Portuguese controlled Brazil. Native Americans and African slaves worked under poor conditions in Peruvian and Mexican silver mines, and in gold and diamond mines in Brazil.

1758–1800

1758 British forces defeated by French at Fort Ticonderoga in Canada.

1761 Afghans defeat Marathas in Third Battle of Panipat, India.

1762–96 Catherine the Great is empress of Russia.

1764 Scottish inventor James Watt designs first steam engine; improved model in **1782**.

1767 English inventor James Hargreaves develops spinning jenny, a hand-operated spinning machine: Important development in early Industrial Revolution.

1767–1847 Life of Indian musician Tyagaraja.

1768 Royal Academy of Arts founded in Britain.

1768–74 Russo-Turkish War; Russia gains navigation rights on Black Sea.

1769 Richard Arkwright invents "water frame" for spinning cotton yarn.

- Nicholas-Joseph Cugnot, French engineer, invents steam-powered tricycle, which can draw carriages.

American Independence

Representatives from the American colonies formed the First Continental Congress in 1774, and sent a petition containing their grievances to king George III of Britain. As this had no effect, a second Continental Congress was held in 1775, when the Americans declared independence. The Revolutionary War began the same year, with colonists fighting against British troops. On July 4, 1776, the colonies adopted the Declaration of Independence,

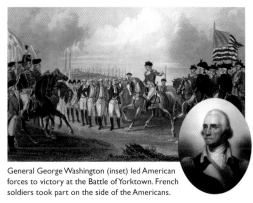

General George Washington (inset) led American forces to victory at the Battle of Yorktown. French soldiers took part on the side of the Americans.

and the United States of America, comprising 13 states, came into existence. Fighting continued for five years until the British surrendered at Yorktown, Virginia. In 1783, by the Treaty of Paris, the USA was recognized as a separate nation.

State delegates drew up a constitution for the new nation in 1787, and in 1789 George Washington became the first president of the United States.

AMERICAN COLONIAL ART AND ARCHITECTURE

In the 17th and 18th centuries, Europeans in North America developed art styles based on those in Europe. There were Spanish influences in the west, and British, Dutch, and French styles in the east. Native American styles also contributed. Early buildings in New Mexico were made of adobe (sundried mud), whereas the English used wood, first of all for log cabins, then as boards for larger

houses. Cities laid out on grid plans were built from the 18th century. Portrait painting was predominant, while religious art was also common.

Palladian-style home of Thomas Jefferson, third president of the U.S., in Virginia, built between 1768 and 1826.

- Major famine in Bengal, India.
- 1770–1850 Life of William Wordsworth, English poet.
- 1774 Warren Hastings becomes first British governor-general in India.
- 1775 French philospher and scholar Denis Diderot completes his *Encyclopedia*.
- 1775–83 American Revolution.
- 1780–84 Fourth Anglo-Dutch War, over secret Dutch trade to American colonies.

1781 William Herschel, German-born British astronomer, discovers the planet Uranus.
1782–1840 Life of Italian composer and violin player Nicolo Paganini.
1789 French Revolution.
1792–1822 Life of English poet, Percy Bysshe Shelley.
1794 English writer Ann Radcliffe writes *The Mysteries of Udolpho*; develops genre of Gothic novel.
1796–1869 Life of Mirza Ghalib, Indian Urdu poet.

A NEW WORLD ORDER

Napoleon Bonaparte

Born in Corsica in 1769, Napoleon made his mark as a general in the French army. Returning to France in 1799 after the Egyptian campaign, he began to take control of the government then, in 1804, declared himself emperor and began a series of wars against other nations to further French power. The Napoleonic Code of civil law instituted by him laid emphasis on written law, and influenced the legal codes of many other countries.

In Europe, the first 15 years of the 19th century were dominated by the Napoleonic wars between French forces and various other countries. Finally, Napoleon was decisively defeated in 1815 at the Battle of Waterloo, and exiled to St Helena.

He died in exile in 1821 but his legend lived on. His life caught the imagination of writers, artists, and musicians. Historians believe his reforms were more important than his conquests, and had long-lasting effects. At the Congress of Vienna (1814–15), French territories acquired by Napoleon were distributed among other European nations. The Congress also condemned the slave trade, and provided for free navigation of rivers across different European nations.

The Battle of Austerlitz (1805), at which Napoleo (above) defeated the combined forces of Russia and Austria (right), was one of his greatest victories.

1799–1817

1799 Socialist Robert Owen establishes model factory in Scotland.
- Swiss educationist Johann Pestalozzi develops new educational system; founds school.

1799–1837 Life of Alexander Pushkin, Russian writer.
1799–1852 Civil War and disorder in Tonga.
1800 U.S. Library of Congress founded.
1801 Act of Union; Great Britain and Ireland join to form the United Kingdom (UK).
- Thomas Jefferson becomes president of USA.

1801–25 Tsar Alexander I rules Russia.
1802 Madame Tussaud of France establishes museum of wax figurines in Britain.
1802–20 Emperor Gia-long unifies Vietnam.
1803 USA buys Louisiana, a large territory in North America, from France.
1804–30 Black War fought in Tasmania; Europeans kill aborigines.
1805 Japanese doctor Hanaoka Seishu uses anesthetics in surgery.

Revolutions of 1848 and nationalism

The inequalities and economic hardships created by the Industrial Revolution, demand for social reform, and nationalist movements, all led to a series of revolutions across Europe. Prince Klemens Wenzel von Metternich (1773-1859), the powerful chancellor of Austria, was forced to abdicate, and in France, the Second Republic was established, though it did not last long.

Prussian Chancellor Otto von Bismarck.

Nationalist ideals continued to gather momentum. The movement for the unification of Italian states, driven by the endeavors of Giuseppe Mazzini (1805-72), Giuseppe Garibaldi (1807-82), and Count Cavour (1810-61), achieved its objective in 1870. Similar efforts by Otto von Bismarck (1815-98), prime minister of Prussia, brought about the unification of the various states of Germany in 1871.

TRENDS IN ART, LITERATURE, AND MUSIC

A painting by Claude Monet in the Impressionist style.

In Europe and America the 1800–1850 period is considered the era of Romanticism, typified by an imaginative and emotional intensity, and freedom of thought and approach. In music, Beethoven's and Franz Schubert's (1797–1828) compositions helped build a bridge between classical and Romantic styles. Other great Romantic musicians were Robert Schumann (1810–56), Hector Berlioz (1803–69) and Frederic Chopin (1810–49). William Blake (1757–1827), Eugene Delacroix (1798–1863), and John Constable (1776–1837) were some of the Romantic artists.

Impressionist art developed in the latter half of the 19th century, inspired by French artist Edouard Manet (1832–83). Impressionist paintings rejected classical formalism and Romanticism, while placing importance on capturing the effects of light. Realism was another artistic trend. In post-Impressionistic styles, the use of color was similar to that of the impressionists, but the paintings were freer and not accurate representations of reality. Major artists of this late 19th-century genre were Vincent van Gogh (1853–90), Paul Gauguin (1848–1903), and Henri de Toulouse-Lautrec (1864–1901).

A poster by Henri de Toulouse-Lautrec.

1809 Finland brought under Russian rule.

1809–82 Life of Charles Darwin, British naturalist; wrote *On the Origin of Species*, seminal book on evolutionary biology

1810 Mexico revolts against Spanish rule.

• Hawaiian islands united by king Kamehameha I.

1811–18 Muhammad Ali of Egypt overruns much of Arabia; first Saudi empire ends.

1811–32 Evariste Galois, French mathematician, develops group theory.

1812–15 War between the U.S. and Britain.

• Jacob and Wilhelm Grimm publish their collection of folk tales, *Grimm's Fairy Tales*, in German.

1812–70 Life of British author Charles Dickens.

1813 English novelist Jane Austen writes *Pride and Prejudice*.

1815 British restore Java to the Dutch.

1817 James Monroe is fifth U.S. president.

• German philosopher GWF Hegel composes his *Encyclopedia of the Philosophical Sciences*.

Spurred on by the Industrial Revolution, European powers raced to carve out spheres of influence and control in Asia. Towards the end of this period nationalist movements for independence began.

British ascendancy in India

In north India, Mughal emperors retained their hegemony only in name, as British control over the subcontinent strengthened. In 1857–58, a widespread revolt, beginning as a mutiny in the army, broke out, proclaiming Bahadur Shah Zafar, the titular Mughal emperor, as the ruler of India. The British emerged victorious. Delhi was destroyed. Bahadur Shah's sons were killed, and he was exiled to Rangoon (Yangon), where, in 1862, he died a lonely death.

Memorial to the Revolt of 1857–58, in Delhi.

As a result of the revolt, the English East India Company, which had so far managed affairs in India, was abolished, and India came directly under the British crown.

The Great Game

Central Asia was the battleground for the "Great Game" a shadowy war between Britain and Russia for control of the area that took place from about 1839 to the early 20th century. The British fought wars in Afghanistan, and gained control of its foreign relations, while the Russians advanced into Khiva and Turkistan. In Iran, Russian influence pervaded in the north, whereas the British dominated in the south.

Dost Mohammad, emir of Afghanistan (1826–1863) during the Great Game.

THE BAHÁ'Í RELIGION

Babism emerged in Iran as a religious offshoot of Islam in 1843, and, in 1863 developed into a separate religion founded by Mirza Husain Ali, known as Bahá'u'lláh (Glory of God). The Bahá'ís believe in one god, whose divine messengers or prophets, including Abraham, Moses, Jesus, and Muhammad, proclaimed the truth through the ages. God's final message, to unite everyone through universal love, was revealed through Bahá'u'lláh.

1817–1840

1817–18 First Seminole War between the Seminole tribe of Florida and U.S. troops.

1818 Florida transferred to the U.S from France.

1819 Pomare II establishes first legal code on Society Islands, in the South Pacific.

1820 Missouri Compromise in the U.S. establishes balance between free and slave states.

• George IV rebuilds Windsor Castle, U.K.

1821 Scottish philosopher and economist James Mill writes *Elements of Political Economy*.

1821–48 Prince Klemens von Metternich, chancellor of the Austrian Habsburg empire, creates a German confederation under Austrian leadership.

1823 Monroe Doctrine promulgated; U.S. requests European powers not to interfere in its affairs; in return, guarantees non interference in Europe.

1830 Revolution in France; king Charles X replaced by Louis Philippe.

1830–34 Great Trek of Boers in southern Africa to lands across Orange river.

Opium Wars

China admitted foreign traders but confined them to the ports of Canton (Guangzhou) and Macao, mainly to stop the opium trade carried out by the British. After the Chinese burned a consignment of the drug at Canton, two "Opium Wars" (1839–42 and 1856–60) were fought with Britain, who had the support of other foreign nations. China was forced to provide more trade concessions and to grant Hong Kong to the British.

Chinese junks destroyed by British warships in the Battle of Anson's Bay (1841), during the First Opium War.

Taiping rebellion

From 1850 Hong Xiuquan, a schoolteacher and religious visionary, organized an uprising against the Manchu rulers of China. The Taiping rebellion, as it was known, extended to 15 provinces and led to the deaths of twenty million people. In return for helping the Manchu rulers crush the rebellion, European powers were given trade facilities. Despite the unrest, Chinese arts thrived, and a type of Chinese opera, known as Beijing opera, developed in the late 18th century.

Hong Xiuquan.

KATSUSHIKA HOKUSAI

Japanese arts flourished in the 19th century. Hokusai (1760–1849) was a painter and a master of woodcut

print-making, whose series, Thirty-six Views of Mount Fuji *(1826–33) is considered the highest development of landscape printing.*

The print *Red Fuji,* from Hokusai's series on the mountain.

The Meiji restoration

In Japan, opposition to the shoguns led to the restoration of the rule of the emperor in 1868. Japan developed a nationalist ideology, with a revival of the traditional Shinto religion, and new industry and railways were promoted.

1835 Arc de Triomphe constructed in Paris.
1836 Texas gains independence from Mexico.
1837 German educationist Friedrich Froebel establishes first kindergarten, an educational system of activity and play.
• Victoria becomes queen of England.
1837–39 Working class Chartist movement in Britain.
1839 Ottomans start modernization program in Turkey.

1839–42 *Amistad* revolt, a shipboard uprising on the coast of Cuba, leads to debates on slavery.
• First Anglo-Afghan War; British troops massacred.
1839–1906 Life of French painter Paul Cézanne.
1840 Treaty of Waitangi signed in New Zealand.
• Kamehameha III introduces a constitutional monarchy in Hawaii.
• Postage stamp introduced in Britain; soon becomes widespread.

A NEW WORLD ORDER

This was a period of great change. There were far-reaching developments in industry and technology, accompanied by political change. Colonialism expanded.

Age of machinery begins

The Crystal Palace in Hyde Park, London, built for the Great Exhibition of 1851.

The term Industrial Revolution describes the major changes brought about by a host of inventions and discoveries enabling the development of new technology, machinery, and modes of production. Machinery was used to complement or substitute human labor. For example, wind, water, human, and animal power were replaced to some extent by the use of steam power. Steam generation needed coal, leading to a massive increase in demand. The harnessing of electricity was another important stride. Machine tools and parts were standardized, and factories became the centers of production. The railways ushered in a transport transformation, linking cities and distant areas. New methods of making iron, glass, and steel were developed. Pride in technology was displayed as in the Great Exhibition held in London in 1851.

The Industrial Revolution, which began in Great Britain in the 18th century, spread by the end of the 19th century to other countries in Europe, the United States of America, and Japan. The enormous potential of the new modes of production induced a shift from the focus on agriculture towards the accumulation of capital. Skills such as marketing and management emerged, along with new practices in banking and insurance.

With an unprecedented capacity for mass production, industries now needed large quantities of raw materials as well as markets to sell the finished goods. These two factors helped drive the acquisition of colonies by European powers. In the 19th century, capitalist economics were best analyzed by Karl Marx, in his voluminous work, *Das Kapital*.

Left: Karl Marx.
Right: Smoke billows from the chimneystacks of dozens of cotton mills in Manchester, England, 19th century.

1840–1858

1840–89 Pedro II rules Brazil; introduces reforms.

1840–1917 Life of French sculptor Auguste Rodin.

1843–72 Maoris and British battle in New Zealand.

1844–1926 Life of Italian physician Camillo Golgi; identifies two types of nerve cells.

1845–49 British annex Punjab in India.

• Catastrophic famine in Ireland after failure of potato crop.

1845–1918 Life of German mathematician Georg Cantor; develops set theory.

1846 Planet Neptune discovered by German astronomer Johann Galle.

1846–48 U.S.–Mexican War; U.S. gains territory.

1847 Briton Charlotte Bronte writes *Jane Eyre*.

• William Makepeace Thackeray writes *Vanity Fair*, a novel depicting English society.

1848 Karl Marx and Friederich Engels publish the *Communist Manifesto*.

1848–1916 Rule of Francis Joseph I, last Habsburg emperor of Austria, king of Hungary (from 1867).

The working class

A new class emerged: Industrial workers, including children, who toiled for long hours, often in terrible conditions, for low pay. In protest against this and against the machines themselves, groups such as the British Luddite movement (1811-12) smashed machinery. Gradually workers united into unions, which bargained for fewer working hours and better pay.

As people flocked to cities for work, new ideas emerged along with new social relationships. Robert Owen (1771-1858) envisaged a cooperative society, while Karl Marx (1818-83) and Friedrich Engels (1820-95) analyzed class struggle in *The Communist Manifesto*.

Davy's safety lamp.

SOME 19TH-CENTURY INVENTIONS AND INNOVATIONS

1800 Alessandro Volta (1745–1827), Italian. Early form of electric battery or cell.
1804 Joseph Marie Jacquard (1752–1834), French. Jacquard loom, to weave textiles with elaborate patterns.
1810 First tin cans.
1814 George Stephenson (1781–1841), British. Railway locomotive.
1815 Humphry Davy (1778–1829), British. Miner's safety lamp.
1829–30 Barthelemy Thimonnier (1793–1857), French. Sewing machine.
1832 William Sturgeon (1783–1850), British. Electric motor.
1836–37 Samuel Morse (1791–1872), American; Charles Wheatstone (1802–75), British. Telegraph/Morse code.
1849 Walter Hunt (1796–1859), American. Safety pin.
1855 Robert Bunsen (1811–99), German. Spectroscope, spectrum analysis, gas burner.
1876 Alexander Graham Bell (1847–1922), American. Telephone.

Thomas Alva Edison.

1879 Karl Benz (1844–1929), German. Car engine (two-cylinder).
1883 Thomas Alva Edison (1847–1931), American. Light bulb.
1893 Rudolf Diesel (1858-1913), German. Diesel engine.
1895 Guglielmo Marchese Marconi (1874–1937), Italian. Wireless telegraph.

Alexander Graham Bell.

1850 Four Australian colonies gain some powers from the British.
• English poet Alfred, Lord Tennyson composes *In Memoriam*.
c. 1850s Black African journalism and secular literature emerge.
1851 Mongkut becomes king of Thailand; brings in reforms.
1852 Louis Napoleon of France becomes Emperor Napoleon III.

1853–78 King Mindon reigns in Burma.
1854 British mathematician George Boole develops Boolean algebra.
• Florence Nightingale organizes nursing during Crimean War.
1855 English novelist Elizabeth Gaskell writes *North and South* showing conditions in factories.
1858 Fenian movement for Irish independence founded.

A NEW WORLD ORDER

The Sokoto caliphate

The Fulani, originally pastoral nomads, started expanding from north Nigeria in 1804, and established a number of kingdoms between Senegal and Cameroon. Osman bin Fodio led the Fulani jihad (1804–8), which integrated the Hausa states of this area into a political and religious entity: The Sokoto caliphate (sometimes called the Fulani empire). The Sokoto were defeated by the British by 1903.

Events in various states

Seku Ahmadu, a Muslim, founded a state in 1818 in Macina (the region of modern Mali). In 1862, al-Haji Umar, an Islamic scholar and mystic, conquered Macina and created the Tukolor empire, which was annexed by the French at the end of the century.

Algeria was wrested by the French from the indirect rule of the Turks in 1834. The Sufi Abd al-Qadir (1808–83) organized a revolt against the French. Though he did not succeed, he remains a heroic figure in Algerian history.

Ethiopia saw a revival in stature under three powerful emperors: Tewodros II (r. 1855–68), Yohannes IV (r. 1872–89), and Menelik II (r. 1889–1913).

The Mahdi war

Egypt under Muhammad Ali, viceroy of Oman, asserted its independence, and extended his sway over Sudan (1819) and parts of the Middle East. However, Sudan rejected Egyptian dominance, and in the 1870s, Muhammad Ahmad proclaimed himself the mahdi (the "guided one," an Islamic messiah), and instigated a revolt against Egypt and Britain. The Mahdists managed to gain control after a long struggle, but were ousted by the British in 1898.

SLAVE TRADE: EXTENT

Though the figures are controversial, some historians estimate that between 1650 and 1900 at least 28 million Africans from the western and central part of the continent were transported across the Atlantic as slaves by European traders. This has been called the Black Holocaust, although the slave trade organized by Arabs had commenced much earlier, in the seventh century. Estimates place the number of African slaves exported by them, up to 1911, as anywhere between 14 to 20 million.

1861–1882

1861 Serfdom abolished in Russia.
1861–65 American Civil War leads to end of slavery in the U.S.
1862 French encroach on Indochina.
1864–70 Paraguay fights war against Argentina, Brazil, and Uruguay.
1865 Wellington becomes capital of New Zealand.
• Lewis Carroll writes *Alice's Adventures in Wonderland*.
• British surgeon Joseph Lister discovers antiseptics.

• U.S. president Abraham Lincoln assassinated.
1866 Seven-Weeks' War between Prussia and Austria.
1867 Alaska purchased by U.S. from Russia.
• Swedish chemist Alfred Nobel invents dynamite.
1868–1910 Rama V modernizes Thailand.
1869 Suez Canal opened.
1870 Frenchman Jules Verne writes *Twenty Thousand Leagues Under the Sea*; considered originator of modern science fiction.

The Scramble for Africa

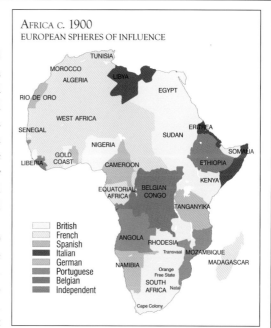

AFRICA C. 1900
EUROPEAN SPHERES OF INFLUENCE

TUNISIA
MOROCCO
ALGERIA
LIBYA
EGYPT
RIO DE ORO
WEST AFRICA
SENEGAL
ERITREA
SUDAN
NIGERIA
GOLD
LIBERIA COAST
CAMEROON
ETHIOPIA
SOMALIA
KENYA
EQUATORIAL BELGIAN
AFRICA CONGO
TANGANYIKA

British
French
Spanish
Italian
German
Portuguese
Belgian
Independent

ANGOLA
RHODESIA
Transvaal MOZAMBIQUE
NAMIBIA
MADAGASCAR
Orange
Free State
SOUTH
AFRICA Natal
Cape Colony

As their explorers ventured deeper into Africa, European nations struggled for control of the continent. Britain acquired Cape Colony in 1814. The Dutch Boers in the Cape moved away from British control, and clashed with the Zulus and other Bantu people. They first settled in Natal, and established the Republic of Transvaal (1852), and Orange Free State (1854).

Cecil Rhodes (1853–1902) expanded British power beyond Cape Colony, while King Leopold II (1835–1909) of Belgium acquired Congo (Zaire). Around 1880, what is known as the "Scramble for Africa" began. At the Conference of Berlin (1884–85), European powers decided their spheres of influence on the continent. Following the Anglo–Boer War of 1899–1902, the British appropriated Boer territories, but gave them certain concessions. By the end of the 19th century most of Africa was parceled between various European nations. Only Ethiopia and Liberia were independent.

SLAVE TRADE: ABOLITION

In 1822 the American Colonization Society established the African colony of Liberia for freed slaves. Gradually, through the 19th century, Western nations banned the practice.
1794 *Abolished by France's National Convention;* **1848** *final abolition.*
1807 *British ships prohibited from engaging in the trade; Slavery after* **1833** *abolished in Britain.*
1808 *USA prohibits importation of slaves;* **1865** *slavery abolished.*
1814 *William I of Netherlands forbids his subjects to engage in slavery.*

1870–71 Franco-Prussian War.
1870s Zulu Wars against Britain.
1870–88 Antonio Guzman rules Venezuela; introduces reforms.
1871–1940 Third Republic in France.
1872 Yellowstone, America's first National Park, founded.
1874 Benjamin Disraeli is prime minister of England for the second time.
1874–91 Prince David Kalakaua rules Hawaii.

1876 German musician Johann Brahms composes *Symphony No I*, first of his great orchestral works.
• Alexander Graham Bell invents the telephone.
1877–78 Russo-Turkish War; some Balkan states gain freedom.
1879–84 Chile, Peru, and Bolivia involved in War of the Pacific.
1880 France annexes Tahiti.
1882 Tsar Alexander II of Russia assassinated.
• Triple Alliance between Germany, Austria, Italy.

A NEW WORLD ORDER

The USA expands

In 1800, the U.S. consisted of 13 colonies. Three years later, the new nation bought from France the vast territory known as Louisiana, extending west from the Mississippi river to the Rocky mountains. Gradually, the USA gained more territories, and new settlers moved westward. The southern states, who wished to continue with slave labor, seceded from the U.S., causing a civil war (1861–65) in which the southern Confederacy was defeated. By 1900, the country consisted of 45 states.

Uprooting of Native Americans

The herds of buffalo that had been the mainstay of the Native American way of life on the Great Plains were wiped out. Many people died of diseases brought in by European settlers, and the Indian Removal Act

The Sioux Ghost Dance.

of 1830 forced the tribes to move to the west onto reservations; thousands died along the way. The Sioux formed the main Native American opposition, defeating American forces under George Custer at the battle of the Little Bighorn in 1876. Native American resistance ended after the massacre at Wounded Knee (South Dakota) in 1890, where 200 unarmed men, women, and children were killed by U.S. troops.

Art and literature

Winslow Homer (1836–1910) and Thomas Eakins (1844–1916) were some of the great American painters, and literary figures included Mark Twain (1835–1910), Herman Melville (1819–91), Harriet Beecher Stowe (1811–96), Nathanievl Hawthorne (1804–64), and the poets Walt Whitman (1819–92) and Henry Wadsworth Longfellow (1807–82).

JOHN JAMES AUDUBON

In 1838 the artist and natural historian John James Audubon (1785–1851) produced Birds of America, *with 435 hand-colored plates. Between 1831 and 1839 he wrote* The Ornithological Biography, *on the characteristics of birds, with the Scottish naturalist William MacGillivray.*

Right: White gerfalcons drawn by Audobon.

1883–1898

1883 Peter Carl Fabergé, Russian jeweler and goldsmith, creates elaborate art objects.
• *The Story of an African Farm,* a novel by Olive Sriner, a white South African, explores race and gender relations.
• Eruption of Krakatoa volcano; thousands die in Java and Sumatra.
1884–85 The Berlin Conference; European powers and USA define spheres of influence in Africa; no African state is invited.

1885 Indian National Congress founded; spearheads movement for independence.
• Canadian Pacific Railway completed.
1886 American Federation of Labor formed.
• German philosopher Friedrich Nietzsche writes *Beyond Good and Evil,* rejecting traditional Christian morality.
1886–1900 Neo-Impressionist movement in French art.
1887 Ferdinand of Coburg becomes king of Bulgaria.

Canadian consolidation

Meanwhile, Canada resisted U.S. incursions, and became a self-governing dominion of the British empire in 1867. At this time, it was a federation of Nova Scotia, New Brunswick, Québec (Lower Canada), and Ontario (Upper Canada). The opening of the transcontinental Canadian Pacific Railway helped to expand settlement and unite the vast area.

The Canadian Pacific Railway.

Liberation of South American states

Simon Bolivar.

By 1830, the Spanish and Portuguese yoke had been thrown off, and most states had gained independence. Prominent revolutionary leaders included José de San Martin (1778–1850) in Chile, Argentina, and Peru; and Simon Bolivar (1783–1830), founder of Bolivia, in Venezuela. Revolutions, conflicts, and border disputes continued.

Europeans colonize Australia, New Zealand

Convicts were transported to Australia from Britain until 1868, and wealthy settlers also emigrated there. Sheep breeding began, and between 1809 and 1821 governor Lachlan Macquarie improved the economy. By the end of the century Australia consisted of six colonies, which agreed to join together in a federation.

In New Zealand, British colonists established settlements in 1840, and founded the town of Wellington. A treaty made with the native Maori leaders, offering them land rights and British citizenship, was not honored, and war resulted.

1888 August Strindberg (1849–1912), prominent Swedish literary figure, writes realist plays, including *Froken Julie* (Miss Julie).
1888–1918 William II rules Germany.
1890 First election in Japan.
1893 New Zealand is first country to grant voting rights to women.
• Czech musician Antonin Dvorak composes *Symphony From the New World (No 9)*, using Native American themes.

1894 Tower Bridge completed in London.
1894–95 Japan-China War; Japan occupies Korea.
1895 Bulgarian prime minister Stefan Nikolov Stambolov assassinated.
1896 Ethiopians defeat Italians at Battle of Aduwa.
• First modern Olympics, in Greece.
1898 U.S. wins Spanish-American War; gains territories in the Caribbean and Pacific.
• Cuban independence.
• U.S. annexes Hawaii.

WAR AND THE WORLD

Contemporary cartoon expressing the nervousness of the great European powers with the volatile state of affairs in the Balkans in 1912-13.

The early 20th century saw increasing development, with the USA becoming highly industrialized, more so than any country in Europe. Within Europe, Germany had become a leading industrial nation, overtaking Britain in the production of pig-iron and steel. In Asia, Japan had become a major power, defeating Russia in a 1904-05 war. Despite the rapid changes that were taking place, Europe continued to dominate world affairs, and World War I, beginning in Europe, involved practically the whole world.

Prior to World War I there were several other wars in Europe. The huge Ottoman empire faced internal problems, with the rise of the Young Turks and the growth of nationalism in its subject countries. The Italo-Turkish War of 1911–12 ended in victory for Italy, who occupied three Ottoman provinces that later became Libya. The Ottoman defeat inspired two Balkan Wars that took place in 1912 and 1913. In the first, Bulgaria, Greece, Montenegro, and Serbia (The Balkan League) attacked the Ottoman empire gaining some victories, while in the second, Bulgaria attacked Serbia and Greece. Montenegro, Romania, and the Ottoman empire later joined in against Bulgaria. Albania gained independence from the Ottomans, and Serbia emerged as a stronger state.

The Balkan Wars did not directly lead to World War I, but created a volatile situation within Europe.

SCIENCE AND TECHNOLOGY

During this period science and technology continued to develop. Max Planck's quantum theory (1900), Albert Einstein's special theory of relativity (1905), and Niels Bohr's theory of atomic structure (1913–15), were among the most notable scientific advances. The first airplane flight took place, and mass production of cars began. Sigmund Freud introduced theories of the subconscious and of psychoanalysis, publishing The Interpretation of Dreams *in 1899–1900.*

Albert Einstein.

Sigmund Freud.

Niels Bohr.

1900–1906

1900 Boxer rebellion in China.
• Manchuria occupied by Russia (up to **1904**).
• New Zealand appropriates Cook Islands (formal annexation in 1901).
1901 Commonwealth of Australia established.
• Nobel Prizes awarded for the first time.
• Asante in west Africa annexed by Britain.
• USA takes over Philippines.
EARLY 1900s British mathematician Karl Pearson (1857–1936) contributes to theories of statistics.

1901–71 Life of American jazz musician Louis Armstrong.
1902 Irish Nationalist Party Sinn Fein founded.
• Influential French novelist André Gide writes *L'Immoraliste* (The Immoralist), exploring individual freedom.
1903 Britain takes over Sokoto caliphate in Africa.
• First airplane flight, by Orville and Wilbur Wright.
• First crayons created from charcoal and oil.
• Alexander, king of Serbia, assassinated.

World War I begins

Austrian archduke Franz Ferdinand and his wife Sophie.

The main underlying cause of World War I (1914–18) was competition for land and resources, both in Europe and elsewhere. Europe was already divided into two groups of protective alliances. The Triple Entente comprised the UK, France, and Russia, with Japan, the U.S., and Spain becoming affiliated to this group. On the other side was the Triple Alliance of Germany, Austria–Hungary, and Italy, although Italy later switched sides. The trigger for war was a conflict between Austria and Serbia, originating in the rise of Serbian nationalism. Serbia wanted to unite the Serbs and Croats and create a separate nation of Yugoslavia, encompassing Bosnia, which was part of Austria. On a visit to Sarajevo in Bosnia, the Austrian archduke Franz Ferdinand was shot dead by a Serbian terrorist group on June 28, 1914. Austria declared war on Serbia on July 28.

THEODORE ROOSEVELT

Theodore Roosevelt became president of the USA in 1901. His policies favored small businesses rather than large monopolies, and he referred to his actions as aiming for a "square deal" between labor and business. He made this a slogan for his 1904 election campaign, and after his reelection he extended the term Square Deal to refer to other programs that would help ordinary citizens. He also expanded forest reserves and national parks. In 1906 he won the Nobel Peace Prize for helping end the Russo–Japanese war of 1904–05. Roosevelt remained president until March 1909.

1904–09 Ismael Montes is president of Bolivia; brings in reforms.

1904–1990 Life of BF Skinner, exponent of behavioral school of psychology.

1905 Alberta and Saskatchewan provinces formed in Canada.

- In Russia, revolt against tsar Nicholas II leads to grant of constitutional reforms.

1905–06 British New Guinea comes under Australia; renamed Territory of Papua.

1905–07 Maji Maji revolt against German colonial rule in East Africa.

c. **1906** Bakelite, the first synthetic resin, invented.

1906 Protestant Pentecostal movement begins in USA.

- Cuba occupied by USA.

- Simplon railway tunnel built through Alps linking Switzerland to Italy; 12 miles long, it was longest railway tunnel till the English Channel tunnel was opened in 1993.

WAR AND THE WORLD

World War I

Affter Austria's declaration of war on Serbia, Russia ordered a troop mobilization to support the latter, and Germany declared war on Russia (August 1, 1914) and France (August 3). Germany invaded Belgium and besieged Liège, on the way to France. This caused Britain to enter the war, and other powers soon joined the fray. European countries also pulled in native troops from their colonies. Machine guns, tanks, aerial bombing, and poison gas were used in the war. Casualties were higher than in any war before: Around 10 million soldiers died, 21 million were wounded, and about eight million were taken prisoner or went missing. Civilian deaths amounted to about 10 million.

The four-year war ended in a crushing defeat of the Central Powers (Germany, Austria–Hungary, Turkey, Bulgaria). An armistice was agreed on November 11, 1918, and a series of peace treaties were signed. Though the objective was to bring about a lasting peace, the humiliation suffered by Germany led to the growth of militarism and nationalism in that country. Another result of the war was the transfer of European colonies in Africa from German or Italian control to France or Britain. Some of the Asian colonies such as India expected to be given more self-government, as had been promised during the course of the war.

One positive aspect of World War I was the creation of the League of Nations, the first organization created in an attempt to maintain peace in the world.

ART, LITERATURE, AND MUSIC

At this time, the modern period of individualistic styles, based on the artist's own vision, began. Expressionism, futurism, Fauvism, and Cubism were some of the new trends. Dadaism emerged out of a rejection of the War and sought new themes and methods that aimed to shock and scandalize. Constructivism developed in the USSR, with three dimensional and "dynamic" constructions.

In literature, the stream-of-consciousness style was introduced by Marcel Proust, and taken forward by James Joyce. TS Eliot, Ezra Pound, WB Yeats, and Rainer Maria Rilke were great names in poetry, and poets Wilfred Owen and Siegfried Sassoon were directly inspired by the war. Jazz music, a fusion of different traditions but primarily African American, began to develop in America.

A portrait in the Cubist style (1912) by the artist Juan Gris (1887–1927).

1906–1912

1906 France and Spain gain control in Morocco.
1907 New Zealand becomes a separate dominion.
- Hans Kuzel adapts existing technology to create tungsten filament lamps.
- Maria Montessori develops Montessori method of education for young children.
- French physicist Pierre-Ernest Weiss develops theory of ferromagnetism.
- International Peace Conference with 44 participants held at The Hague, Netherlands.

1908 Austria annexes Bosnia-Herzegovina.
- Belgium occupies Congo in Africa.
- First Model T car produced by Henry Ford.
- Oil first discovered in the Middle East.
- Young Turk revolution in Turkey.
1909 American explorer Robert Peary reaches North Pole.
- Russian-born mathematician Hermann Minkowski develops concept of space-time.
1910 Union of South Africa formed.

WORLD WAR I: MAJOR BATTLE SITES

Arras, France September–October, 1914, and July, 1915, France vs Germany; April–May, 1917, Britain and Canadian and Australian troops vs Germany; March, 1918, Britain vs Germany; August–September, 1918, Britain, and Canadian troops vs Germany.

Ardennes, France August, 1914, France vs Germany.

Heligoland Bight, Frisian Islands August, 1914, Britain vs Germany (naval battle).

Marne, France September, 1914, France, Britain vs Germany; July–August, 1918, Germany vs France.

Ypres, Belgium October–November, 1914, Britain, France, Belgium vs Germany; April–May, 1915, Belgium, France, Britain, Canada vs Germans; July–November, 1917, Britain vs Germany (also known as Battle of Passendale or Passchendaele).

Gallipoli campaign 1915–16, British empire forces, France vs Ottomans, Germany.

A British trench during the Battle of the Somme.

Verdun, France February–December, 1916, France vs Germany.

Jutland, Denmark May–June 1916; Britain vs Germany (naval battle).

Somme, France July–November, 1916, Britain, France and Allies vs Germany.

Caporetto, Austria October–December, 1917, Germany, Austria–Hungary vs Italy.

Argonne, France September–November, 1918, France, USA vs Germany.

ANZAC DAY

Australia sent over 330,000 volunteers to fight in the war. Their worst losses were at Gallipoli, where the Australian and New Zealand Army Corps (Anzac) landed on April 25, 1915, and fought against Turkish troops. Anzac Day (April 25) remains a national holiday in Australia and New Zealand, commemorating the losses in this and other wars.

WORLD WAR I
1914–1918
Allied nations
Central Powers
--- Farthest advance by Central Powers
—— Trench line

- German Ferdinand Graf von Zeppelin develops first airship.
- Revolution in Portugal.
- Sri Aurobindo, spiritualist, philosopher, nationalist, sets up ashram in Puducherry, India.
- Wilhelm Ostwald, German physical chemist, wins Nobel Prize for chemistry; had developed method of producing nitric acid.
- **1910–13** Bertrand Russell (1872–1970) and Alfred North Whitehead (1861–1947) complete the

three-volume *Principia Mathematica* on logic and mathematics.
- **1911** Chinese Revolution.
- First Hollywood studio founded.
- Norwegian Roald Amundsen reaches South Pole.
- Morocco becomes French protectorate; France cedes territory to Germany in French Congo.
- **1912** New Mexico and Arizona become U.S. states.

REVOLUTION

While the World War was taking place, revolutions and struggles for independence continued across the world. Perhaps the most drastic changes took place in China and Russia.

Sun Yat-sen

Sun Yat-sen.

Ruled by the Manchu Qing dynasty, China was conservative and resistant to change. Sun Yat-sen was among many who believed that the Manchu government needed to be overthrown and a republic established.

In 1905 he founded the Tongmenghui (United Revolutionary League) in Tokyo, based on three principles: Nationalism, democracy, and people's well-being. A revolution took place in 1911, and the Republic of China came into being on 1 January, 1912. Sun Yat-sen was made provisional president. In March, he was replaced by Yuan Shikai, the former military governor. Though the monarchy ended, China was not politically united.

Vaslav Nijinsky.

RUSSIAN ARTS AND CULTURE

This was a particularly productive period of artistic endeavor, much of it inspired by the Russian Revolution. Aleksandr Aleksandrovitch Blok (1880–1921) composed one of his greatest poems, *The Twelve*, an account of a Red Army patrol that was actually led by Jesus Christ. Ivan Alexseyvitch Bunin (1870–1953) wrote realistic stories and novels based on Russian life, and was the first Russian to win the Nobel Prize for Literature, in 1933, although Maxim Gorky (1868–1936) is perhaps the best known writer of this time. Vladimir Mayakovsky (1893–1930) explored new styles in poetry. Sergei Diaghilev (1872–1929) encouraged and revived ballet, and established the Ballet Russes (1909–29) company, with dancers such as Vaslav Nijinsky (1890–1950) and Anna Pavlova (1881–1931). The musician Igor Stravinsky (1882–1971) created ballets especially for Diaghilev, apart from other compositions.

1912–1920

1912 African National Congress founded in Union of South Africa to promote civil rights.
- British ocean liner *Titanic* sinks; about 1500 die.
- Polish-born American biochemist Casimir Funk identifies the function of vitamins in the body.

1912–13 Balkan Wars.

1913 Young Turks organize coup in Turkey.
- South Africa reserves 87 per cent land for whites.
- Rabindranath Tagore of India wins Nobel Prize for Literature.

1913–21 Woodrow Wilson is president of USA.

1914–18 World War I.

1914 Britain and France occupy German colonies in West Africa.
- Panama Canal opens.

1915 Italy, Bulgaria join World War I.

1916 The 5175-mile-long Trans-Siberian railway, from Moscow to Vladivostok, completed.
- Husain ibn Ali of Mecca declares himself king of the Hejaz and caliph of all Muslims.

The Russian Revolution

During 1894–1917, Russia was ruled by the autocratic tsar Nicholas I. Peter Stolypin, prime minister during 1906–11, tried to improve the conditions of peasants and workers, but widespread unrest and a desire for change persisted and intensified. Russia's participation in World War I created further economic problems. Meanwhile the power of the revolutionary parties was growing. The Bolsheviks and Mensheviks were the two main ones. Both believed in Marxist ideas and revolution, but the Bolsheviks (meaning "the majority"), led by Vladimir Lenin, insisted that peasants and workers should be involved, whereas the Mensheviks ("the minority") believed in cooperation with the middle-classes.

Two revolutions took place in March and November 1917 (February and October, according to the Julian calendar then followed in Russia). Nicholas I abdicated and the Russian monarchy came to an end. A provisional government was set up, but it was overthrown by the Bolsheviks in November. This made Russia the first communist state in the world. After the Revolution, four socialist republics were established on Russian territory: The Russian, Transcaucasian, Ukrainian, and Belorussian. However, for the Bolsheviks or Communist Party to establish control over the whole of Russia was not simple, as there were several contending forces.

Russia withdrew from the First World War, and by the Treaty of Brest Litovsk (March, 1918) lost a number of her western territories, including Poland, Georgia, and Finland. Civil war followed between the Bolsheviks and a mixed group known as the Whites, who included the Mensheviks. Foreign troops aided the Mensheviks, but by the end of 1920 the Bolsheviks had established power. The building of a new country began. The four newly formed socialist republics came together to form the Union of Soviet Socialist Republics (USSR) in 1922, to which other republics were later added. Vladimir Lenin headed the party and the country until his death in 1924.

Lenin speaking at the Second Soviet Congress on October 26, 1917.

- Romania joins World War I.
- **1917** Ras Tafari (Haile Selassie) is regent of Ethiopia.
- Russian Revolution.
- Balfour Declaration promises homeland to Jews.
- **1918** Oilfields opened in Venezuela.
- Salote becomes queen of Tonga.
- Women over 30 years of age granted conditional vote in Britain.
- **1919** Kloet volcano erupts in Java, killing 16,000.
- First airplane crosses the Atlantic Ocean.

- Jallianwala Bagh massacre in India.
- Worldwide flu epidemic kills millions.
- **1919–1923** Weimar Republic in Germany.
- **1920** Women in USA granted the vote.
- In India, Mahatma Gandhi (1869–1948) leads Non-cooperation movement against the British.
- First radio station begins broadcasting from Pittsburg, Pennsylvania, USA.
- Right-wing Kapp Putsch (revolt) in Germany.
- **1920–33** Prohibition in the U.S.

THE INTERMEDIATE YEARS

The War had ended, peace treaties had been signed, but the world was still reeling from its debilitating effects. European countries had to come to terms with the tragic loss of people and destruction of property. Industries that had grown to meet war needs were in decline. Unemployment rose as soldiers returned to civilian life. Inflation soared. It was a period of turbulence and transition. The Russian Revolution had provided hope to millions who struggled with economic hardships. Perhaps because of this, communist movements and trade union activities were on the rise. General strikes took place, unrest was widespread. European colonies in Asia and Africa were seeking independence and change.

Franklin Delano Roosevelt (1882–1945).

Huge sums of money borrowed by the Allies during the war were owed to the USA. The USA itself was relatively unaffected by the war, and remained prosperous till 1929, when the Great Depression, a severe economic crisis, took place. The Depression's effects

A road-building program, part of the New Deal.

soon spread to other parts of the world. In 1933, president Franklin Roosevelt introduced policies known as the New Deal, which helped to revitalize the U.S. economy. Among various measures introduced were the temporary takeover of banks by the government, and acts to help farmers and to stimulate industry.

Of the European countries already facing an economic crisis before 1929, Germany had to make massive reparations, leading to a collapse of its economy. In 1923, inflation rose to such an extent that the German mark became totally worthless. A search for strong leadership, and a desire to reassert German power, led to the rise of Adolf Hitler, leader of the fascist Nazi Party.

France was exhausted by the war and remained economically backward, while political instability caused a rapid change in governments.

On the whole, Great Britain weathered the changes with her democracy intact, though there were several internal problems, including unrest in Ireland, the decline of industry, a general strike in 1926, and unemployment during the Great Depression. However what

1920–1927

1921 Albert Einstein receives Nobel Prize for physics.
- Swiss psychiatrist Carl Jung writes *Psychological Types*; founds analytical school of psychology.
- Treaty of Nystadt; Sweden cedes Baltic provinces to Russia.
1921–28 New Economic Policy introduces period of economic liberalization in the USSR; policy ended by Stalin.
1922 Fuad becomes king of Egypt with nominal independence under the British protectorate.

- First radio broadcast by the British Broadcasting Corporation.
- Irish Free State formed.
- Literary classic *Ulysses* written by Irish writer James Joyce.
- Poet TS Eliot completes *The Wasteland*.
1923 Earthquake at Kwanto, Japan, destroys Yokohama and Kyoto; about 140,000 dead.
- Three-light traffic signals invented by American Garett Morgan.

was notable was the rise of the Labour Party, which was able, for the first time, to form two governments during this period.

Spain was a constitutional monarchy ruled by Alfonso XIII from 1885, but general Primo de Rivera seized power as a dictator in 1923. Also affected by the economic crisis, Spain was beset by unemployment. Alfonso abdicated in 1931, and a republic was proclaimed. However a fierce civil war was fought between 1936 and 1939, ending in a victory for the right-wing nationalists. General Franco then took control of the government.

Adolf Hitler and Benito Mussolini in Venice, 1934.

Italy's economy had been strained during the war and she had not benefited from the post-war treaties. The difficult circumstances caused five governments to rise and fall between 1919 and 1922. Meanwhile, in 1919, Benito Mussolini formed the Italian Fascist Party. In 1922 Italian king Victor Emmanuel III invited Mussolini to form the government, and he gradually assumed dictatorial powers.

Art and design

The Bauhaus school founded in Weimar, Germany, by Walter Gropius (1883–1969) in 1919 pioneered new trends in architecture and interior design. Industrial design, commercial printing, graphics, and innovative furniture also began to develop. In the 1920s, surrealism rejected traditional art forms, and looked to symbolism and the subconscious for inspiration. The Art Deco style used stylized and decorative natural and geometric forms.

Right: The Bauhaus building in Dessau, Germany.
Far right: The Art Deco spire of the Chrysler building in New York, built in 1928–30.

- Adolf Hitler leads Beer Hall Putsch, a revolt that fails, in Munich.
- **1924** Ramsay Macdonald leads the first Labour government in Britain.
- German novelist Thomas Mann's major work, *The Magic Mountain*, published.
- **1925** F Scott Fitzgerald, one of the greatest American novelists, writes *The Great Gatsby*.
- **1926** John Logie Baird invents system for television in Britain.

- Erwin Schrödinger, Austrian physicist, develops mathematical theory of wave mechanics.
- Gertrude Ederle, American Olympic swimmer, becomes first woman to swim the English Channel.
- **1927** Canberra is made federal capital of Australia.
- American Charles Lindbergh makes non-stop flight across Atlantic in his monoplane.
- *The Jazz Singer*, first feature-length film integrating sound, made.

Joseph Stalin.

The War had benefited Japan economically since it supplied the Allies and countries in Asia with various products. However after 1921 European production began to recover, and Japan's exports suffered. The country experienced an economic crisis from 1929, and in 1932 the powerful army virtually took over.

Following the death of Lenin in 1924, Joseph Stalin assumed power in Russia in 1929. He ruled as an absolute despot. Key Communist Party members became the new rich elite in the USSR. Thousands who had participated in the 1917 Revolution were killed.

China was engaged in a struggle between the Kuomintang, the Nationalist People's Party, and the communists.

In Turkey, Mustafa Kemal Atatürk, a young general, denounced the Treaty of Sevres signed after the war, by which his country suffered huge losses. He negotiated the more favorable Treaty of Lausanne (1923). The last

Mustafa Kemal Atatürk.

Ottoman sultan abdicated, and Kemal became first president of the Turkish Republic, modernizing the country and curbing the social and legal role of Islam.

Positive results of the war

Welfare schemes were expanded, and more groups were granted the right to vote. Many women had started working in the war years, and their social and economic position improved. The telephone and telegraph spread through the world. Production of cars increased and commercial flights started. Consumer goods, such as washing machines, became widespread in Europe.

The Citroën Traction Avant car that began production in the 1930s.

1928–1939

1928 Briton Alexander Fleming discovers penicillin.
- First version of Oxford English Dictionary completed, in 10 volumes.
- President of Albania, Ahmed Zogu, makes himself king; known as Zog I.
- All women in Britain above the age of 21 gain voting rights.

1928–29 Erich Maria Remarque's *All Quiet on the Western Front* describes World War I through the eyes of a German soldier.

1929 American astronomer Edwin Hubble puts forward theory of expansion of the universe.
- First Oscar Awards presented in the USA.
- Samoa revolts against New Zealand.
- New York stock exchange crashes, triggering the Great Depression.

1930 Civil Disobedience movement led by Mahatma Gandhi in India.
- Gerulio Vargas becomes president of Brazil; rules as dictator from 1937.

The colonies

Britain, with the most territories, as well as the dominions of Canada, Australia, New Zealand, and South Africa, promised that independence would gradually be granted to her colonies. Meanwhile, southern Ireland gained dominion status (1922), Egypt semi-independence (1922), and Iraq independence (1931). France, with the second largest possessions, as well as most of the other colonizers, suppressed nationalist movements.

A poster for the movie *Battleship Potemkin*.

The media

The 1930s saw literature from other languages translated into English. Paperback books were introduced and more newspapers were published. But the greatest media revolutions were in radio and cinema. Radio became widespread in developed nations. Its reach enabled music of different regions to be accessible to the world. News broadcasts, however, gained popularity only during World War II.

Both art films and popular cinema were produced. Of the former, the Soviet director Sergei Eisenstein's (1898–1948) *Battleship Potemkin* (1925) is considered a masterpiece, while Charlie Chaplin (1889–1977), an Englishman settled in the U.S., was one of the greatest personalities of avant-garde films.

THE LEAGUE OF NATIONS

Created on January 10 1920, the League aimed to maintain peace in the world, and encourage international cooperation. There were some successes in the 1920s as the League settled several conflicts. The dispute between Finland and Sweden over the Aaland Islands (1921) was resolved. So were conflicts in Upper Silesia (1921); over the port of Memel (renamed Klaipėda) in Lithuania (1923), and between Bulgaria and Greece (1925). However, the League was unable to resolve the crises of the 1930s. For instance, it could not prevent the Japanese invasion of Manchuria (1931), or the Italian invasion of Abyssinia (1935). Finally, it was unable to prevent World War II. The League was dissolved in 1946, but had laid the foundation for its successor organization, the United Nations.

1931 102-story Empire State Building inaugurated in New York.
- Trans-African railway from Angola to Mozambique completed.

1932 American Amelia Earhart is the first woman pilot to fly across the Atlantic.

1932–35 Chaco War fought between Bolivia and Paraguay.

1933 Franklin D Roosevelt is president of USA.

1934 Oil pipeline from Kirkuk, Iraq, to Tripoli, Syria, opened.

1936–39 Civil war in Spain.
- *Fallingwater*, a residence and an icon of modern architecture, built by Frank Lloyd Wright.

1937–45 Sino-Japanese conflict.

1938 Hungarian George Biro invents ball-point pen

1939 American novelist John Steinbeck writes *Grapes of Wrath*.

1939 Robert Menzies is prime minister of Australia.

AT WAR AGAIN

World War II

The seeds of World War II were sown in the peace treaties following World War I and in the economic crisis that then hit almost all the world. The immediate cause was the policies followed by Germany, under Adolf Hitler's (1889–1945) Nationalist Socialist German Workers (Nazi) Party. In 1933 Hitler was appointed chancellor, and, in 1934, he became Führer, the leader of Germany. Hitler gained popularity as he restored national pride, rebuilding Germany's economy and the army. However he focused on the so-called "Aryan" racial superiority, and blamed Jews for the country's ills.

Preceding events

Hitler signed defensive pacts, while at the same time convincing European powers of his peaceful aims. In 1936, Germany and Italy formalized a pact known as the Rome-Berlin Axis, giving rise to the name "Axis powers" for Germany and her allies. 1937 Germany and Japan signed the Anti-Comintern pact. Hitler's troops took possession of the Rhineland, the demilitarized zone on the German

The "big three" Allied leaders: (from left) Churchill of Britain, Roosevelt of the USA, and Stalin of the USSR .

border near France, in 1936. In March 1938, he united Austria with Germany. Following this, in September 1938, he was allowed by Britain and France to occupy Czechoslovakia's Sudetenland. Keen to avoid a war, the Allied powers (Britain and France) did little to oppose German expansion in Czechoslovakia and Lithuania—this policy of "appeasement" is considered a major factor responsible for the war.

Germany and the USSR agreed to divide the territory of Poland between them. Then, on September 1, 1939, German armies invaded Poland. In defense of Poland, France and Britain declared war on Germany on September 3. World War II had begun.

The city of Wieluń, in Poland, burning on September 1, 1939, the first day of World War II.

1939–1945

1939 World War II: Australia, Belgium, Canada, New Zealand, South Africa are among many countries that declare war on Germany following its initial outbreak.

1940 Radar developed by British scientists.
- Winston Churchill becomes British prime minister.
- World War II: British and French forces are evacuated from Dunkirk, France.
- American writer Ernest Hemingway writes *For Whom the Bell Tolls*.

1941 American chemist Glenn Seaborg discovers plutonium; **1951** wins Nobel Prize.
- World War II: German General Erwin Rommel attacks British forces in Africa. German battleship *Bismarck* sunk in the Atlantic Ocean.
- Ethiopia regains independence.

1941–79 Muhammad Reza Pahlavi is shah of Iran.

1942 In India, Quit India movement against British.
- World War II: U.S. forces bomb Tokyo. Germany defeated at Battle of El Alamein, Egypt.

Allied ships near the Normandy coast on D-day, (June 6, 1944), the invasion of German-occupied France.

The course

The war lasted for six years. The turning point came when Hitler invaded the USSR (June, 1941), breaking his pact with them, and Japan bombed Pearl Harbor (December, 1941), an American naval base, leading to the USA's entry into the war. From mid 1942, Axis powers began to suffer defeats. Hitler committed suicide in April 1945, Germany surrendered in May, and Japan in August of the same year.

The cost

Prisoners in Mauthausen labor camp, in Austria, liberated on May 5, 1945 by the U.S. army.

Sixty-one countries participated in World War II. At least 110 million people were mobilized for military service. Huge amounts of money were spent on the military: $341 billion by the USA alone. A total of 19 million military personnel from both sides died in Europe. Japanese killed numbered six million. In addition, Allied civilian losses are estimated at 44 million, and Axis at 11 million. Another 21 million were displaced.

During the war, Jews were subject to a planned extermination campaign. They were shot, gassed and murdered in concentration camps, or held in sub-human conditions. By the end of the war, six million Jews had been killed.

BOMBING OF HIROSHIMA AND NAGASAKI

The war ended with the use of the latest and most horrific weapon of the time: The atomic bomb. On August 6 and 9, 1945, U.S. aircraft dropped one bomb each on the Japanese cities of Hiroshima and Nagasaki, killing around 84,000 and 40,000 people respectively. An equal number were injured, and those exposed to radiation suffered serious health problems. The USA justified it as a means to end the conflict, but it remains the most controversial action of the war.

The mushroom cloud at Hiroshima.

- Indian National Army founded.
- Russian Dmitri Shostakovich composes *Leningrad* symphony during the German siege of that city.
- **1943** French writer Jean Paul Sartre writes his philosophical work *Being and Nothingness*.
- World War II: Allies take Tripoli in Africa from Italy. Soviet forces win Battle of Kursk. Mussolini resigns.
- **1944** World War II: Allied troops begin reconquest of Europe and Asia. Anglo-American forces enter Rome. French Resistance helps liberate Paris.

- Synthesis of quinine marks breakthrough in treatment of malaria.
- Ukrainian-born American biochemist Selman Waksman discovers streptomycin.
- First nuclear reactors built.
- **1945** World War II: U.S. army enters Germany.
- World Zionist Conference held.
- Benito Mussolini killed.
- United Nations established with 51 member states.

INDEPENDENT NATIONS

European countries were exhausted by World War II. Germany and Italy had been crushed, and the center of power had shifted to the USA. Economically and militarily depleted, Britain did not feel strong enough to hold on to her colonies, which were at the same time clamoring for independence. In addition, world ideology was shifting towards the belief that nations had the right to govern themselves.

France, the Netherlands, Spain, and Portugal gradually gave up their possessions. During the war Japan had wrested territories such as Burma, Malaya, Singapore, the Dutch East Indies, and Indochina from European colonial powers. These had seen the myth of European supremacy destroyed, and had no wish to return to colonial rule.

In the East, India, Israel and Vietnam typified different problems faced by newly independent nations.

Jawaharlal Nehru (1889-1964) and Mahatma Gandhi (1869–1948) led India's struggle for independence.

India and Pakistan

In 1947 the British agreed to grant independence to India, dividing the country into two states, India and Pakistan, based on religious differences. Pakistan was fragmented, its western and eastern halves separated by Indian territory, and overall the partition resulted in savage riots, between Hindus and Sikhs on one side, and Muslims on the other. Around one million were killed, and 10 million displaced, as refugees frantically attempted to cross the borders in order to reach safety. The two new nations were hostile to each other from the beginning of their creation.

POST-COLONIAL IDEOLOGY

New ways of writing history, fiction, and films emerged, expressing themes of independence and struggle, division and strife.

Edward Said (1935–2003), a key intellectual who re-examined Western approaches to history, particularly of the Middle East.

1945–1951

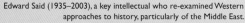

- **1945–81** Life of Bob Marley, Jamaican reggae singer and song writer.
- **1946** First electronic computer invented by John Mauchly and John Eckert.
- Juan Peron becomes president of Argentina.
- Republic established in Italy.
- USA tests new types of atomic bombs at Bikini Atoll, on Marshall Islands.
- Felix Bloch, Swiss-born U.S. physicist, develops analytical technique of nuclear magnetic

resonance, used in medical diagnostics (magnetic resonance imagery, or MRI).
- **1947** Edwin Herbert Land, American physicist, develops Polaroid camera.
- Russian Mikhail Kalashnikov designs AK-47 assault rifle.
- By the Truman Doctrine, the USA promises aid to any country resisting communism.
- USA's Marshall Plan offers economic help to countries in need.

Vietnam

Indochina (Laos, Cambodia, and Vietnam) was under French rule before the Japanese occupied the region during World War II. Ho Chih Minh (1890–1969), a communist, organized a revolutionary organization and declared Vietnam independent in 1945. War with France began, and the French were decisively defeated at Dien Bien Phu (May 1954). Laos and Cambodia gained independence, but the USA, determined to prevent the spread of communism, became the decision-maker in Vietnam. The country was divided into two halves, with Ho Chih Minh's communists in the North, while South Vietnam had a separate government. A civil war started in South Vietnam, with the Viet Cong, guerrillas supported by North Vietnam, trying to unite the North and South. Pouring in troops and weapons, the USA became involved in fighting the Viet Cong. The land was devastated and thousands of civilians killed. Finally, public opinion forced American withdrawal, and Vietnam was officially united in 1976.

A burning Viet Cong camp in Vietnam (1968).

Ho Chih Minh.

Israel

From 1917, there was a move to create a state for Jews, who had suffered persecution for centuries. Palestine, their ancient homeland, was an Arab state under a British mandate, but Jews had begun settling there. After World War II, it was decided that Palestine be divided between Arabs and Jews. When the British left on May 15, 1948 the first Arab–Israeli War broke out immediately. Several other wars were fought in succeeding years, and hostilities continue to this day.

ISRAEL

Israeli state, as proposed by UN, November, 1947.

Land conquered by Israel, 1948–49.

Land occupied by Israel after Six-Day War, June, 1967.

Beirut
LEBANON
Damascus
SYRIA
Golan Heights
Akko
Haifa
Tiberias
Sea of Galilee
Tel Aviv
West Bank
Jordan River
Ramallah
Jerusalem
Jericho
Amman
Bethlehem
Mediterranean Sea
Gaza
Hebron
Dead Sea
Beersheba
JORDAN
EGYPT
Sinai Peninsula
Eilat • Aqaba

- Transistor invented.
- General Agreement on Tariffs and Trade (GATT) signed by 23 countries.

1948 Mahatma Gandhi, Indian leader, assassinated.

- Burma (now Myanmar), Ceylon (now Sri Lanka), gain independence from Britain.
- State of Israel formed; thousands of Palestinians displaced.

1949 East Indies (now Indonesia) gains independence from Netherlands.

- Konrad Adenauer becomes first chancellor of West Germany, after establishment of the country following World War II.
- Independent state of Irish Republic declared.
- USSR tests its first nuclear bomb.

1951 European Economic Community or Common Market formed.

- Libya gains independence from Italy.
- Japan, USA, and 48 other countries sign peace treaty.

INDEPENDENT NATIONS

Independence brought a number of problems. Colonial boundaries had cut across territories of different ethnic groups, so as colonial powers withdrew, people's loyalties veered towards their own tribes and groups regardless of national boundaries. Although some states were able to provide good government and a sound economic system, military coups and civil wars occurred in others. After independence, there was such widespread resentment towards immigrants that thousands of Asians had to leave Africa in the late 1960s. In Rhodesia and South Africa, which had a large number of white settlers, there was resistance to granting independence to blacks.

Zimbabwe created

Robert Mugabe.

Northern Rhodesia won independence as Zambia in 1964, but Southern Rhodesia, led by Ian Smith's white-minority government, declared independence from Britain in 1965. After a long civil war, it became independent in 1980 as Zimbabwe, led by Robert Mugabe. Internal problems and conflicts between political and ethnic groups continued.

POST-COLONIAL AFRICAN LITERATURE

With 53 different countries in Africa, literature is extremely diverse, with authors writing in English, French, and Portuguese, as well as African languages. The Nigerian Wole Soyinka (b.1934) was the first African to win the Nobel Prize for Literature. Books were also written by white settlers: JM Coetzee (b.1940), originally from South Africa, and now an Australian citizen, received the Nobel Prize for Literature in 2003.

Wole Soyinka.

1952–1962

- American author JD Salinger wins acclaim with his book *The Catcher in the Rye*.
- **1952** Elizabeth II crowned queen of UK.
- **1953** Edmund Hillary of New Zealand and Tenzing Norgay of Nepal are first to summit Mt Everest.
- DNA discovered.
- Egypt declared a republic; gains freedom from British influence.
- **1955** Argentine president Juan Peron overthrown.
- **1956** Egyptian government takes over Suez Canal.

- Morocco, and Spanish Morocco, gain independence from France and Spain.
- Tunisia gets independence from France.
- Sudan achieves independence from Britain.
- **1957** Malaysia, and Gold Coast (Ghana), win independence from Britain.
- First satellite, *Sputnik I*, sent into space by USSR.
- **1958** French West Africa (Guinea) attains independence.
- First Grammy awards presented in the U.S.

Apartheid in South Africa

The Union of South Africa became virtually independent from Britain in 1931. Its white population was divided into Afrikaners and English speakers. In 1948, the National Party came to power and followed a policy of apartheid: Complete political and social separation of blacks and whites, with the latter dominating. The government tried to move blacks into separate "homelands," and in 1961, though South Africa became a republic, apartheid continued. Nelson Mandela led a movement for black rights which ultimately resulted in the African National Congress coming to power through multi-racial elections in 1994.

NELSON MANDELA

Born in 1918 in Transkei, South Africa, Mandela became involved in politics when a student. In 1943 he joined the black rights group the African National Congress, and in 1944 was one of the founder members of its Youth League. As a leading spokesman for black rights, Mandela was imprisoned for almost 27 years. He received the Nobel Peace Prize in 1993, along with FW de Klerk, South Africa's last white president. From 1994 to 1999, Mandela was the president of South Africa.

A signboard from South Africa's apartheid days.

FW de Klerk (b. 1936).

1959 Fidel Castro takes control in Cuba.
- Dalai Lama of Tibet flees to India with his followers.
1960 Cameroon wins independence from France and Britain.
- Nigeria and Cyprus achieve independence from Britain.
- Congo gains independence from Belgium.
- French West Africa (Mali and Senegal) acquires independence.
- Pop music group, The Beatles, become famous.

1961 Tanganyika independent from Britain; 1963 Zanzibar; 1964 unite as Tanzania.
- John F Kennedy is 35th president of USA.
- U.S. invades Bay of Pigs in Cuba.
- Yuri Gagarin of Russia is the first man to travel in space.
1962 China invades India.
- Rolling Stones, British rock music group, formed.
- Algeria obtains independence from France.
- Uganda achieves independence from Britain.

PEACE AND WAR

After the devastation caused by World War II, there were efforts to sustain peace so that a similar war would not take place again, particularly since a catastrophic nuclear war was a frightening new possibility. Some degree of stability was maintained, though there were still numerous wars: Perhaps 19–20 million were killed in over 100 wars and military actions in the developing world between 1945 and 1983.

Communist states, and power blocs

The Cold War, a period of hostility and suspicion, dominated the world during 1945–85. Its major players, the USA and the USSR, did not actually fight a war with each other, but took opposing sides on various issues. Communism, with the USSR as the dominant power, was spreading. Between 1945 and 1948, the East European countries Poland, Hungary, Romania, Bulgaria, Yugoslavia, Albania, and Czechoslovakia became communist states. After World War II Germany was initially divided among the Allied powers into four occupation zones, but in 1949 it was split into two: The Federal Republic of Germany (West Germany) and the communist German Democratic Republic (East Germany). In Asia, communist governments were established in North Korea (1948), China (1949) under Mao Zedong, and North Vietnam (1954).

Two major defensive alliances were formed: In 1949, Britain, France, Belgium, Holland, Luxembourg, the USA, Canada, Portugal, Denmark, Ireland, Italy, and Norway formed the North Atlantic Treaty Organization (NATO), joined by West Germany in 1955. The Soviets responded with the Warsaw Pact in 1955, consisting of their satellite communist states in Europe.

The USA, quick to take action against potential communist states, became involved in wars in Korea (1950–53) and in Vietnam (1965–75). The USSR wanted her satellites in East Europe to follow policies chalked out by her. This led to an invasion of Czechoslovakia in 1968.

A section of the Berlin Wall that separated East and West Berlin.

1962–1968

- Ruanda-Urundi (Rwanda and Burundi) gains independence from Belgium.
- **1962** American John Steinbeck wins Nobel Prize for Literature.
- First communications satellite, *Telstar*, launched in space.
- Cuban Missile Crisis.
- **1963** Kenya gains independence from Britain.
- Thirty African nations join together to form Organization of African Unity.

- John F Kennedy assassinated.
- **1964** U.S. passes Civil Rights Act to end discrimination based on race, color, or religion.
- Malta, Nyasaland (Malawi), Northern Rhodesia (Zambia), British Guiana (Guyana), win independence from Britain.
- Martin Luther King awarded Nobel Peace Prize.
- Palestine Liberation Organization formed to represent the rights of Palestinian Arabs.
- **1964–91** Kenneth Kaunda is first president of Zambia.

Thaw, détente, and the end of the USSR

With the death of Stalin in 1953 there was some reduction in hostilities. But tensions revived in the late 1950s, and in 1961 the Berlin Wall was erected by East Germany, cutting off the West German half of the city. In 1962 the USSR placed nuclear missiles in Cuba within striking distance of the U.S., sparking off the Cuban Missile Crisis that almost led to a nuclear war. From 1969, the USSR and USA attempted to limit weapons stockpiles through the Strategic Arms Limitation Talks (SALT) and a period of détente began. However, the Soviet invasion of Afghanistan in 1979–80 heightened tensions once again.

Mikhail Gorbachev (b. 1931).

Mikhail Gorbachev became leader of the Soviet Union in 1985 and attempted to transform the country through a more democratic structure and a move towards a market economy. Elections in 1989 and 1990 brought in some democracy and reduced the power of the Communist Party, and in 1988–89 the USSR withdrew from Afghanistan. Gorbachev also gave autonomy to the USSR's East European satellite countries. Relations with the USA and the West improved dramatically, and change swept through the region. The Berlin Wall was opened in 1989, and East and West Germany were reunified the next year. By the end of 1991 the USSR had dissolved, replaced by the Commonwealth of Independent States (CIS), which consisted of many of its former republics.

LITERATURE OF THE COLD WAR

The Cold War spawned a vast number of books and films. Ian Fleming (1908–64) created the British secret service agent James Bond, while John Le Carré (pseudonym of David John Moore Cornwell, b. 1931) wrote fiction on the dark world of espionage. The problems of Germany and the Soviet era were other topics.

Gunter Grass, awarded the Nobel Prize for Literature in 1999, wrote both fiction and non-fiction on themes including German reunification.

1965 Gambia obtains independence from Britain.
- Big Bang theory of the universe developed.
- Minimalist and Conceptual American artist Sol LeWitt begins his "open cube" sculptures.

1966 Basutoland (Lesotho) and Bechuanaland (Botswana) achieve independence from Britain.
- Cultural Revolution begins in China.
- American surgeon Michael DeBakey develops artificial heart.

1967 Six-Day War between Israel and Arab states.

- Aden (S. Yemen) independent from Britain.
- Pulsars (pulsating radio stars) discovered by British astronomers Jocelyn Bell Burnell and Antony Hewish.
- British engineer Godfrey Hounsfield develops computerized axial tomography (CT scanning).

1967–70 Civil war in Nigeria.

1968 French mathematician Rene Thom develops catastrophe theory, showing how gradual changes can trigger a catastrophic change.

PEACE AND WAR

As the world recovered from World War II, many different international organizations were formed with the aim of preserving peace and increasing cooperation among countries. Some groupings were regional but the most ambitious, the UN, embraced every country on earth.

The United Nations

Founded on October 24, 1945, the UN, though not always successful, has played a major role in world affairs, providing peace-keeping forces, helping new nations emerge from colonialism, encouraging disarmament, and keeping a check on nuclear proliferation. It has several secondary organizations, such as its Development Programme and Children's Fund. Its role in the world was recognized by the award of the Nobel Peace Prize in 2001. However, the permanent members of its Security Council (USA, Russia, Great Britain, France, and China) have the power to veto its decisions, leading to some imbalance and inequality among its members.

United Nations headquarters in New York, USA.

UN INITIATIVES

1947–49
Persuades Dutch to grant independence to Indonesia.

1956
• USSR sends troops into Hungary; Security Council's call to withdraw is vetoed by USSR.
• Asks Israel to withdraw from Egypt; vetoed by France and Britain.

1960–64
Sends 10,000 troops to help stabilize recently independent Belgian Congo.

1966–80
Imposes economic sanctions on Rhodesia due to its apartheid policy.

1974
Maintains peace in Cyprus between Greek and Turkish Cypriots.

1979–88
USSR occupies Afghanistan; vetoes Security Council resolution asking it to withdraw.

2003
Security Council backs U.S.-led administration in Iraq.

1968–1977

1968 Mauritius and Swaziland acquire independence from Britain.
• Spanish Guinea (Equatorial Guinea) gains independence.
• British rock group Led Zeppelin formed.
• Martin Luther King assassinated.
1969 Woodstock music and art fair held in Bethel, USA; attended by 60,000 people.
• U.S. astronauts Neil Armstrong and Edwin Aldrin are the first men to reach the moon.

1972 USA passes the Equal Opportunity Act.
• Sheikh Mujibur Rahman is first prime minister of Bangladesh.
• Managua, capital of Nicaragua, destroyed by earthquake; thousands killed.
1973 110-story Sears Tower opened in Chicago, USA; it is the tallest building of the time.
• Salvador Allende, president of Chile, assassinated.
1974 Guinea (Guinea-Bissau) wins independence from Portugal.

The Commonwealth of Nations

The British Commonwealth was established in 1931 as a group of nations that owed allegiance to the British empire. Later, the word "British" was dropped as more colonies became independent. The Commonwealth promotes cooperation and friendship among member nations, and encourages human rights and good government.

Non-Aligned Movement

Many Asian and African countries refused to join either of the two Cold War blocs. This Non-Aligned Movement (NAM) was formed in 1961 with 25 members. The key leaders were Jawaharlal Nehru of India, and Tito (Yugoslavia), Nasser (Egypt), Nkrumah (Ghana), Sekou Toure (Guinea), and Sukarno of Indonesia. Though Yugoslavia was part of the Warsaw Pact, the general aim of NAM was to take decisions independently, without pressure from the Cold War powers. After the end of the Cold War, NAM redefined its aims to reflect modern needs.

European Union

Various European organizations merged in 1965 (formally 1967) to create the European Economic Community (EEC), an association aiming to strengthen eonomic cooperation. In 1993, it was renamed the European Union. The Euro, a common unit of currency for many of its member states, was introduced.

Flag of the European Union (EU).

- Watergate scandal leads to resignation of president Nixon of USA.
- **1975** Mozambique and Angola gain independence from Portugal.
- Khmer Rouge communists take over Cambodia; their leader Pol Pot is prime minister.
- Bill Gates and Paul G Allen found Microsoft Corporation.
- USA, Canada, and 35 European countries sign Helsinki Accords; recognize World War II boundaries and promise to maintain friendly relations.
- **1976** American writer Alex Haley explores the black experience through his family saga, *Roots*.
- Supersonic jet Concorde makes its first flight from London to Bahrain.
- **1977** British biochemist Frederick Sanger, with Paul Berg and Walter Gilbert, develops DNA sequencing technique; **1980** they are awarded Nobel Prize for chemistry.

DEVELOPMENT AND GROWTH: ECONOMY

In general, capitalist countries experienced a "golden age" in 1950–73. The numbers of homeless and unemployed also increased, though welfare and social security systems provided some support for them.

The U.S. economy

American students take to the streets in protest against the Vietnam war in 1968.

The USA had not suffered economically during the war, since defense production revitalized industry and created new jobs. The aircraft and shipping sectors were booming. Moreover, the war inspired technological and scientific innovations, which led to lifestyle improvements. By 1945 the U.S. accounted for almost two-thirds of the world's industrial production, and had a gross domestic product greater than any other country. The U.S. Marshall Plan facilitated 13,000 million dollars of aid to western Europe over four years from April 1948, helping to revitalize that region.

President Truman attempted to introduce welfare schemes, but Congress only approved social security benefits and an increase in the minimum wage. The U.S. had to deal with civil rights problems and opposition to the Vietnam war, as well as economic problems aggravated by the war. Periods of recession during 1973–75, 1981–82, and 1990–91 were followed by a long period of growth and development in the 1990s.

Martin Luther King, Jr, (1929–68), civil rights leader for the cause of African Americans.

U.S. president Harry Truman.

1978–1986

1978 Louise Brown, first "test-tube" baby, born.
- Camp David Accords, a peace settlement, signed between Israel and Egypt.

1979 Ayatollah Khomeini overthrows the Shah; establishes Islamic republic in Iran.
- Saddam Hussein is president of Iraq.
- SALT II treaty signed.
- Zulfiqar Ali Bhutto, president and prime minister of Pakistan (1971–77), is executed.
- Smallpox eliminated from the world.

1980 Iraq declares war on Iran.
- In Poland, Solidarity trade union formed under Lech Walesa.

1981 First personal computer, the IBM PC, launched.
- AIDS disease detected in New York and California, USA.

1982 Peruvian writer Mario Vargas Llosa writes his classic *La Guerre del Fin del Mundo* (The War of the End of the World), on the history of Brazil.

The British economy

Margaret Thatcher (b. 1925).

The Labour government began state direction of the economy and nationalization of industries in order to recover from the effects of World War II. Decolonization added to economic problems, and though economic growth was slow, welfare policies were put in place. The Thatcher era (1979–90) saw privatization of major sectors, with a reduction in the role of the state. During the 1980s, Britain experienced a boom, but along with this, there was increasing social conflict and unemployment.

Russian reforms

Russia rebuilt itself rapidly through a planned economy. As growth slowed down, Mikhail Gorbachev began to introduce economic reforms in the mid 1980s. With the dissolution of the USSR in 1991, the economy declined sharply. Real GDP dropped by 40 per cent between 1990–96, and inflation and unemployment rose. In the late 1990s the economy began to stabilize.

WORLD ECONOMIC SYSTEMS

The complexities of the post-war world required new means of cooperation.

Even before World War II ended, a method of monetary management was put in place, which came into operation in 1945. Known as the Bretton Woods system, it set up rules and regulations for the functioning of the international monetary system. All currencies were linked to the U.S. dollar, which in turn was linked to gold, and thus there was a fixed exchange rate regime. The International Monetary Fund and the World Bank were also created at this time. In 1971 the link between the dollar and gold was cut, and the world moved towards a floating exchange system.

Among other important organizations, the World Trade Organization, an international entity to oversee and liberalize world trade, came into being on January 1, 1995.

The Organization of the Petroleum Exporting Countries (OPEC) was founded in 1960. It was once able to manipulate world oil prices, but with oil now found in many other places, it has less influence. However, its 12 member countries—from the Middle East, Asia, Africa, and South America—account for two-thirds of world oil reserves, so OPEC still has a major role in the oil economy.

- First operation to implant an artificial heart in a human being in Utah, USA.
- Audio compact discs first introduced commercially; later adapted to hold electronic data.
- 1983 First modern cellular phone introduced in Chicago.
- 1984 Indira Gandhi, prime minister of India, assassinated.
- 1985 Microsoft Corporation introduces Windows Operating System software.

- 1986 U.S. unmanned spacecraft *Voyager 2* is the first to fly past Uranus; 1989 past Neptune.
- *Mir*, Russian space station and laboratory, launched.
- President Ferdinand Marcos of Philippines overthrown; replaced by Corazon Aquino.
- Accident at Chernobyl nuclear power plant in the Ukraine kills 32, infects thousands with radiation.
- U.S. bombs government and military bases in Libya.

DEVELOPMENT AND GROWTH: ECONOMY

Shinzuku, in Tokyo, is one of Japan's most important commercial centers, where some of its biggest corporations have their headquarters.

As a communist nation, China was influenced by Russia, but soon embarked on her own path. Agricultural productivity was increased by land redistribution, cooperative farms, and communes. After Mao's death in 1976, a gradual introduction of market reforms began. By 2000, China was a major economic power, with one of the fastest growing economies in the world.

U.S. funds helped restore Japan's economy, which had been ruined by the war, and Japan soon became the second largest economy in the world. Hong Kong, Singapore, South Korea, and Taiwan, were among the fastest growing economies between the 1960s and 1990s, known as the Four Asian Tigers. Thailand, Malaysia, Indonesia, and India after the 1990s, were other rapidly expanding Asian economies. However, an Asian crisis in 1997 spread from Thailand to South Korea to Japan, and had an impact across the world.

In 1945, Latin America (South and Central America and some Caribbean islands) was underdeveloped. Many economies were dependent on a small range of products, while population growth and unstable governments also created problems. Foreign ownership of industry and agriculture drained money out of many countries. However, with new initiatives, the situation began to improve. For instance, Venezuela nationalized its oil industry in 1976, and created a huge refining and marketing system. During the 1980s, a debt crisis affected much of Latin America. Good growth began to be registered from the 1990s, but inequalities continued to be rampant in the region.

Wars and coups in Africa hampered growth. The discovery of oil in some countries, such as Equatorial Guinea, in 1996, led to high growth rates, but these did not translate into overall human development.

FOOD

On the whole, world food production began to increase. Calories available per capita showed an increase of 24 per cent from 1961 to 2000, with individual countries showing huge growth rates: The highest were in China (73 per cent), Indonesia (69 per cent), South Korea (44 per cent), USA (32 per cent), Thailand (27 per cent), Italy (26 per cent), India (20 per cent). However, the consumption of the richest fifth of the population was 16 times that of the poorest fifth. Eight-hundred and forty million people continued to be malnourished.

1987–1993

1987 Palestinians begin Intifada ("shaking off") resistance against Israelis.

1988 Seikan tunnel opens, connecting Honshu and Hokkaido islands of Japan; out of a total length of 34.46 miles, 14.5 miles is undersea.

1989 Berlin wall falls.
• Emperor Hirohito of Japan dies after 53 years of rule; succeeded by his son Akihito.
• First proposal for World Wide Web put forward by British scientist Tim Berners-Lee; further developed in **1990**; made available to public from **1991**.
• Student demonstration in Tiananmen Square, Beijing; hundreds killed.

1990 Nelson Mandela released from prison.
• Namibia gains independence from South Africa.
• Hubble Space Telescope launched.
• Yemen unified.
• Schengen Agreement promotes removal of internal border controls of European Community states.

INEQUALITIES PERSIST

In 1997, 1.3 billion people in the world were living on less than one dollar a day. Though there was an increase in global wealth and income, as well as an improvement in health, education and standards of nutrition, these had not reached the world's poor. The richest fifth of the world had a total income 74 times that of the poorest fifth. Vast inequalities permeated all areas of life.

Above: A slum in Mumbai, India (top right). Though India's economic growth from the 1990s onward was one of the fastest in the world, in 1999–2000, 26 per cent of the population was estimated to be below the poverty line. In contrast, Luxembourg (above) is one of the richest countries in the world in terms of per capita income.
Left: Valéry Giscard d'Estaing, president of France (1974–81), hosted the first G8 (then G6) summit, in Rambouillet.

WORLD GROUPS

There are numerous international groups. G77 was established in 1964 by 77 developing countries to promote their common economic interests. The G8 are a group of industrially advanced countries. The Group was founded as G6 in 1975, joined by Canada in 1976 and Russia in 1997. The G8 represent about 14 per cent of the world population but 60 per cent of the Gross World Product. G20, founded in 1999, consists of a group of finance ministers and central bank governors of 19 countries, plus the EU. There are several other regional groupings, such as ASEAN (Association of South East Asian Nations), established in 1967.

- Germany reunified.
- Iraq annexes Kuwait.
1990s Microprocessors made by Intel (founded **1968**) dominate the computer industry.
1991 Gulf War follows Iraqi invasion of Kuwait, between American-led coalition forces and Iraq; civil wars and ethnic cleansing follow.
- Boris Yeltsin becomes Russian president.
1991–92 Socialist Federal Republic of Yugoslavia breaks up into separate states.

1992 Maastricht Treaty establishes economic and monetary policies in the European Union; comes into force in **1993**.
- Rio Earth Summit: representatives of 178 countries meet in Brazil to discuss the world's environmental problems.
- North American Free Trade agreement (NAFTA) signed between U.S., Canada, and Mexico.
1993 Bill Clinton becomes U.S. president.
- Eritrea attains independence from Ethiopia.

DEVELOPMENT AND GROWTH: TECHNOLOGY

A radical revolution swept people's lives through vast strides in science and technology. Yet, unequal distribution of resources and lack of access to basic facilities did not allow the benefits to percolate down to the entire spectrum of humanity.

Production processes

Agricultural productivity grew, mainly due to better machinery and fertilizers and the development of new plant varieties, including genetically modified crops.
Industrial output increased through Henry Ford's factory system—breaking down manufacturing into separate stages—but eventually work forces needed more skills and adaptability. The batch production system, where each worker has a larger share in the final product, allowed for greater diversity. Companies also took an international view, using factories in countries where labor was cheaper, and outsourcing service industries. Flexible working hours and home-working were introduced.

Surge in electronics

Color televisions, personal computers, laptops, mobile phones, Internet, email, video conferencing, microwave ovens ... Consumer demand for electronic goods rose quickly. Between 1980 and 1995 the number of televisions per 1000 people worldwide nearly doubled, from 121 to 225. Videos began to be used in teaching. Computerization revolutionized transport, finance and banking, stock markets, credit card shopping, and the control of machine tools in industry. In 1970, only 50,000 computers existed in the world; by 2000, there were over 500 million. In 1995, 50 million people used the Internet; by 2000, this had risen to 450 million. However, 91 per cent of Internet users belonged to developed countries.

NEW MATERIALS

Nano technology, the development of extremely small devices, led to micro-chips. New high-strength materials were manufactured. Concrete, wood, and glass were reinvented in new forms such as fibre optics. Bionics or biomimetics was another emerging field, exploring aspects of the natural world, such as the strength of certain sea-shells, and attempting to recreate them in material form.

1993–2000

1993 Middle-East peace accord between Yitzhak Rabin of Israel and Yasser Arafat, chairman of PLO.

1994 Zapatista uprising in Mexico.

• Civil war in Rwanda; 800,000 estimated killed.

• Channel Tunnel under English Channel connects England and France.

• First multi-racial elections in South Africa.

1995 Global Positioning System (GPS) becomes fully operational.

• Dayton Peace Accord ends Bosnian-Croatian-Serbian war (began **1991**).

• Bose-Einstein condensation, a state of matter predicted to arise at low temperatures, observed for the first time by physicists in USA.

• Sub-atomic particle known as top quark discovered.

1996 First cloned animal, Dolly the sheep, born.

• Taliban, an Islamic political group, captures Kabul.

1997 Hong Kong returned by Britain to China.

Aviation

In 1945 aircraft capable of carrying 400 passengers were unheard of. Twenty-five years later, the Boeing 747 "jumbo jet" had that capacity, and by 1976, supersonic aircraft such as Concorde reached 1450 mph. However, supersonic passenger jets were not economical and were later discontinued, so average cruising speeds for passenger planes were 540–570 mph. Humanity landed on the moon in 1969 and space exploration continued.

The Boeing 747 passenger jet was certified for commercial service in 1969.

Medicine

In the last 50 years, genetic research has revealed that all heritable characteristics are carried by chemicals known as deoxyribonucleic acid (DNA). From the 1990s there were breakthroughs in genetic engineering, and brain-mapping is another area that has helped in health care.

James D Watson, who with Francis Crick discovered the double-helix structure of DNA

Energy

With world energy consumption constantly rising, nuclear power, natural gas, geothermic energy, solar heating, and wind power complemented coal, oil, gas, and hydro power.

STEPHEN HAWKING

This brilliant British astrophysicist (b. 1942) has tried to develop a "theory of everything." One of his great contributions has been to make science available to general readers through books such as *A Brief History of Time* (1988), *The Universe in a Nutshell* (2001), *A Briefer History of Time* (2005), and, along with his daughter, a children's book, *George's Secret Key to the Universe* (2007).

- Labour Party led by Tony Blair wins elections in Britain.
- U.S. spacecraft *Mars Pathfinder* lands on Mars.
- Kyoto Protocol agreement to reduce industrial emissions that lead to global warming.

1998 Akashi-Kaikyo bridge, the longest suspension bridge in the world, opened in Japan.

- Good Friday Agreement; founds Northern Ireland Assembly; regulates relations with the Republic.

1999 Euro currency introduced.

- Bill Clinton, president of USA, acquitted of all charges after his impeachment in **1998**.
- Nunavut, a self-governing homeland for the Inuit, created in Canada.
- Western nations, led by NATO, intervene in Kosovo, in southwest Serbia.
- Complete sequencing of a human chromosome completed for the first time.

2000 Scientists announce first draft mapping of the entire human genome.

Tackling terrorism

The attack on the twin towers of the World Trade Center (September 11, 2001).

A defining aspect of the 21st century is the "war on terror" that followed "9/11," when on September 11, 2001, hijackers flew two airplanes into the twin towers of the World Trade Center in New York, a third plane into the Pentagon, and crashed a fourth in a field in Pittsburgh. At least 3000 people died, and it was believed that Osama bin Laden, leader of the Al Qaeda Islamist group, had directed the attacks from Afghanistan. A U.S.-led coalition attacked Afghanistan in October 2001, and in 2003, U.S.-led forces invaded Iraq to remove alleged weapons of mass destruction. The USA is the only foreign nation to still maintain troops in Iraq, although British/Nato forces still accompany U.S. troops in Afghanistan.

Globalization

Political, economic, and social boundaries are being transcended, and the world is becoming more interdependent. Cities across the planet look similar, with high-rise buildings and "international" architecture. Through media connectivity and real-time television images, distances have been reduced. Hundreds of inter-governmental international organizations, and thousands of non-governmental ones, have been created. Trade and cultural exchanges are ever increasing. Globally-linked foreign exchange and capital markets operate 24 hours a day. More than one-fifth of goods and services produced each year are traded across the world. Some multinational companies control budgets larger than those of several sovereign countries. Despite the shrinking world, the relative gap between rich and poor nations, or the rich and poor within nations, is greater, as income disparities have increased.

2000–2003

2001 Laurent Kabila, president of the Democratic Republic of Congo, shot dead; replaced by his son, Joseph Kabila.
- Ariel Sharon becomes prime minister in Israel.
- Albanians organize rebellion in Macedonia; peace signed in August after six months of fighting.
- George W. Bush becomes 43rd U.S. president.
- Abandoned Russian space station *Mir* crashes down to earth.

- Netherlands becomes the first country to legalize same-sex marriages. Later, Belgium 2003; Spain 2005; Canada 2005; South Africa 2006; Norway, Sweden 2009; also currently legal in four U.S. states.
- In Nepal, King Birendra and four members of his family are massacred.
- USA is target of a deadly terror attack through hijacked aircraft; known as 9/11.
- VS Naipaul wins Nobel Prize for Literature.

Profusion of the Internet and electronics

Computers and the Internet have revolutionized the way the world functions.

Rapid technological progress has taken place in computing and the Internet. In 2009 an estimated one billion personal computers were in use. New softwares are constantly developed, and there is a growing use of Internet broadband, along with a host of new facilities: YouTube, a website for uploading videos; blogs, where anyone can write anything; Twitter and other micro-blogging platforms; social networking sites such as MySpace and Facebook. In 2007 Facebook alone had 55 million active members, but trends change every year.

Digital technology is applied in almost every kind of electronic products: Cameras, televisions, audio players (referred to as MP3/MP4), portable media players, and mobile phones with music, video, camera, and Internet facilities. Data storage capability is a fundamental aspect of everyday life; devices range from compact discs, versatile or video discs (DVD), blue-ray discs, tiny flash memory drives, and hard disk drives with huge capacity. Satellites are being used to generate and transmit data: Global Positioning System technology is increasingly used for navigation and fixing location. Robotics is developing for medical and domestic use.

INFORMATION SOCIETY

This term defines the current age, due to the availability of information which can be used for economic, scientific, cultural, and political activity. The "knowledge economy" generates wealth through the use and manipulation of information, and is the economy of the future, replacing manufacturing and industry. The information revolution of the last few years is as significant as the Industrial Revolution.

ADVANCES IN GENETIC RESEARCH

The Human Genome Project, founded in 1990 to sequence the three billion chemical letters in DNA, was completed in 2003. DNA can now be taken apart, recombined, or even moved from one organism and placed in another. The Project has identified more than 1800 disease genes. In 2005 another major step was the development of the HapMap, a catalog of common genetic variations, or haplotypes, in the human genome. Cloning, stem cell research, the preservation of endangered species—and even the possible revival of extinct species—are all aspects of genetic science.

- Temporary government headed by Hamid Karzai established in Afghanistan.
2002 Tamil Tigers, an insurgent group in Sri Lanka, sign cease-fire agreement with the government.
- Hindu-Muslim riots in Gujarat, India.
- U.S. and Russia agree to reduce nuclear weapons by two-thirds over the next 10 years.
- Timor-Leste, formerly East Timor, gains independence from Indonesia.
- First solo balloon flight round the world.

- Terrorist attack on nightclub in Bali, Indonesia; over 200 die.
- Chechen rebels hold 763 people in Moscow theater; rescued by troops, but 116 die.
- Hu Jintao succeeds Jiang Zemin as general secretary of the Communist Party in China.
2003 Ariel Sharon reelected in Israel.
- U.S. space shuttle *Columbia* disintegrates in flight. All seven astronauts aboard killed.

THE NEW MILLENNIUM AND THE FUTURE

Ecology and natural resources

Economic growth is draining the limited natural resources of the world. Fossil fuels such as petroleum, natural gas, and coal remain the primary energy sources, accounting for about 86 per cent of energy resources in 2006. There is a move towards nuclear, solar, and other renewable and non-polluting forms of energy, along with measures to improve fuel efficiency. Biofuel is getting attention, although growing it takes up land often needed for food crops. Soil erosion has affected fertility, while water resources are imperiled. Forests everywhere are being depleted, and wildlife is declining. The world population, 2.5 billion in 1950, is more than 6.8 billion now, and is estimated to stabilize at 9.3 billion in 2050. This will lead to a further strain on resources.

Due to warming temperatures, the Bering glacier in Alaska, America's largest, has retreated 7.5 miles since 1900. Other glaciers in Alaska are also steadily retreating. One side effect has been an increase in earthquakes.

A stranded ship on Central Asia's Aral Sea, which has shrunk to 10 per cent of its size between 1960 and 2007.

2003–2007

2003 U.S. and Britain launch war in Iraq, capture Baghdad and Saddam Hussein.
- Mahmoud Abbas becomes first Palestinian prime minister; resigns in a few months.
- Membership of Non-Aligned Movement rises to 116.
- Major earthquake in Algeria, North Africa; more than 2000 killed, 9000 injured.
- Libya agrees to pay compensation for bombing of plane over Lockerbie, Scotland.

- Shirin Ebadi of Iran wins Nobel Peace Prize for promoting rights of women and children.
2004 Terrorist attack on trains in Madrid, Spain; 200 killed, 1400 wounded.
- Seven new countries from East Europe join NATO.
- Ten new states join the EU.
- Floods in Bangladesh, Nepal, and north India; thousands killed, millions homeless.
- School children held hostage in Beslan, Russia, by Chechen rebels; several killed during rescue.

Climate change

Fossil fuels produce huge amounts of carbon dioxide, contributing to greenhouse gases and global warming. While the use of coal, the most polluting fuel, has declined in some countries such as the UK, it has increased in others. In 1973, it was discovered that chlorofluorocarbons (CFCs) used in refrigeration, air-conditioning, and other products were depleting the ozone in the earth's atmosphere, and allowing excessive ultra-violet radiation to reach the earth. The use of CFCs has been reduced, but climate change and global warming is increasingly becoming evident, and is a real threat to fundamental aspects of life on the planet. Despite international forums on these issues, disagreements between countries have hampered significant progress.

Right: Aerial view of the Amazon rainforest around the headwaters of the Xingu river in Brazil shows how much forest has been lost due to pressure from agriculture on its fringes.
Below: Entrance to a small coal mine in Shanxi, China. The Asian country is the largest producer of coal in the world.

- Palestinian leader Yasser Arafat dies.
- Earthquake off coast of Sumatra, followed by tsunami; over 200,000 killed across 11 countries bordering Indian Ocean.
2005 Mahmoud Abbas becomes president of Palestinian Authority; first presidential election since 1996.
- Benedict XVI becomes pope after death of pope John Paul II.
- Bomb attacks in London.

- Baku-Tbilisi-Ceyhan oil pipeline opens, connecting Caspian Sea to the Mediterranean Sea.
- Hurricane Katrina causes flooding in New Orleans, USA.
2006 Ehud Olmert becomes prime minister of Israel.
- Muhammad Yunus of Bangladesh and his Grameen Bank win Nobel Peace Prize for creating economic development from below.
2007 Romania and Bulgaria join EU; expands to 27.
- Nicholas Sarkozy becomes French president.

Rights for all

An important modern concern is to ensure rights for individuals, communities, and nations, and even animals. Fundamental human rights include non-discrimination based on race, religion, gender, physical or mental ability, and sexual orientation. Children have their own rights. Rights also pertain to intellectual property, education, and health care while civil liberties include freedom of speech and expression. Generally, these are granted most liberally in developed countries, and are severely restricted in others. The right of countries to govern themselves without interference from major powers remains unfulfilled, and many countries do not have democratically elected governments.

A monument to victims of the terrorist train bombings in Madrid, Spain in 2004.

Fundamentalism and new sects

In some countries, fundamentalism is a growing trend. Fundamentalists are resistant to change, to freedom for women, to education, and generally, to any activities that could bring about a different way of thinking. They emphasize a strict observance of religious and social laws and customs, and attempt to impose these on others, sometimes through violent means. In the Western world, there are new Protestant churches and new religious sects, as well as a revival of "pagan" religions.

Identity politics

The growing emphasis on national, religious, and ethnic identities is perhaps a reaction to globalization, but religious and political movements that arouse mass emotions have led to genocide and warfare. Political observers and intellectuals now believe the concept should be replaced with more inclusive policies.

2007–2010

2007 Intergovernmental Panel on Climate Change confirms global warming, with rising temperatures and seas.
- Earthquake and tsunami hit Solomon Islands.

2008 Fidel Castro resigns as president of Cuba after 49 years.
- Kosi river changes course in north India, causing floods; hundreds die, over two million displaced.
- Conflict between Russia and Georgia.

- Maoist prime minister elected in Nepal.
- Iraq and USA agree on timeframe for troop pullout.
- Eleven mountain climbers die on K2, the worst accident on this mountain since **1986**.
- Anti-government protests escalate in Thailand.
- G 8 nations pledge funds to fight disease in Africa; agree on the need to cut greenhouse gases in half by **2050**.
- U.S. banking crisis leads to global recession.

Science and technology

France's TGV train, currently in service, is one of the world's fastest, capable of reaching speeds in excess of 300 mph.

Humankind continues to explore the universe. Private spaceflights and space tourism have begun. Biological research suggests that a complete overview of the brain will be possible in the future. The search for the elusive particle known as the Higgs bosun, that endows others with mass, continues. Innovations in transportation include giant planes such as the Airbus 380 commercial airliner, introduced in 2007, which can carry up to 850 people. Automobiles that drive themselves are a future possibility.

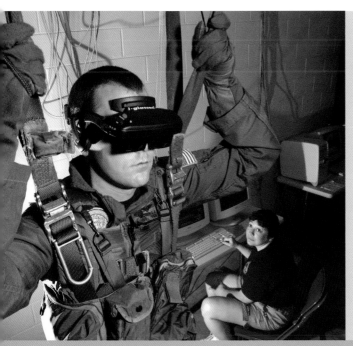

VIRTUAL WORLDS

As life becomes increasingly complex and stressful, people have sought solace in computer-simulated worlds. Virtual worlds can include games, text-based chatrooms, and computer conferencing. A popular software is Second Life, in which users, known as residents, can create a make-believe life for themselves and interact with other residents through a fictional persona.

A virtual reality (VR) parachute trainer used by the U.S. navy. The VR glasses create computer-generated scenarios, which help aircrew learn how to handle a parachute.

- Terrorists kill 173 people in Mumbai, India.
2009 G 20 leaders pledge $1.1 trillion to encourage world trade and stimulate economies of developing countries,
- Earthquake in Italy affects 26 towns.
- North Korea conducts second nuclear test.
- Barack Obama becomes U.S. president.
2010 Suicide bombers kill 40 in Moscow subway.
- U.S. and Russia agree to reduce nuclear arsenals.

- European air traffic is grounded by ash from a volcano under the Eyjafjallajokull glacier, Iceland.
- Oil spill in Gulf of Mexico threatens wildlife and coastlines.
- Israeli forces storm flotilla carrying aid to Gaza; kill nine activists.
- Thai army disperses "Red Shirt" protestors.
- Tropical storms cause a huge sinkhole to open up in Guatamala City; swallows 3-story building.

WORLD MAP

Africa is the second largest continent in the world, covering an area of approximately 11,720,000 square miles, with 53 independent countries as well as the disputed region of Western Sahara. Africa's coastline stretches 18,952 miles, and the equator crosses the continent, the equatorial region being one of high rainfall and dense forest. The African Union, founded in 1963, is an important regional organization.

Found only in equatorial Africa, the gorilla is an endangered species.

PORTUGAL Madrid FRANCE ITALY Istanbul Baku
Lisbon SPAIN Rome Ankara
Algiers Tunis GREECE TURKEY
Tetouan Oran Annaba Athens SYRIA Tehran
Casablanca Rabat TUNISIA Tripoli
MOROCCO Misratah Benghazi Alexandria Cairo IRAQ IRAN
ALGERIA Ghadames JORDAN
WESTERN In Salah LIBYA El Faiyum SAUDI
SAHARA Marzuq Asyut ARABIA Riyadh
EGYPT Aswan OMAN
MAURITANIA Port Sudan
Nouakchott MALI ERITREA YEMEN
Dakar NIGER CHAD Kassala Asmera
SENEGAL Bamako Ouagadougou Niamey Khartoum Djibouti
Bissau BURKINO FASO Kaduna Ndjamena Wad Medani Berbera
GUINEA BENIN SUDAN Addis Ababa SOMALIA
Conakry GHANA NIGERIA CENTRAL
Freetown IVORY TOGO Ibadan AFRICAN ETHIOPIA
Monrovia COAST Lome Lagos REPUBLIC
LIBERIA Abidjan Accra Yaounde Bangui UGANDA Mogadishu
CAMEROON Libreville Mbandaka Kisangani Kampala KENYA
GABON DEMOCRATIC Kigali Kisumu Kismayu
CONGO CONGO Nairobi INDIAN OCEAN
Brazzaville Kinshasa Bujumburo Mwanza Mombasa
Matadi Kananga Dodoma Zanzibar
ATLANTIC OCEAN Luanda TANZANIA Dar-es-Salaam
Likasi
ANGOLA Lubumbashi Antsiranana
Lobito Huambo Ndola MALAWI
Namibe ZAMBIA Lilongwe Mozambique Mahajanga
Lusaka Blantyre
NAMIBIA Livingstone MOZAMBIQUE Antananarivo
Windhoek ZIMBABWE Beira MADAGASCAR
Bulawayo Fianarantsoa
BOTSWANA
Gaborone Pretoria
Johannesburg Maputo
Maseru Mbabane
SOUTH AFRICA Durban
East London
Cape Town Port Elizabeth

HISTORY

Africa has a unique place in the history of the world, as the first human beings are believed to have developed here million of years ago, and, according to one theory, spread from here to the rest of the world. Around 3500 BCE, one of the oldest civilizations in the world developed in Egypt along the river Nile. Later, there were other powerful kingdoms and empires, including the Aksum empire. In the nineteenth and twentieth centuries, European nations colonized almost all of Africa. From the mid-twentieth century onwards, African nations gradually attained independence, yet most of the independent nations have

Priest of the Yoruba religion, Nigeria, in traditional dress.

faced coups, military dictatorships, conflicts over territory, and civil wars. Uneven or poor development, environmental concerns, and health issues are all matters of concern.

AFRICAN LANGUAGES

More than 2000 languages are spoken in Africa (including Arabic and colonial languages), although only 50 have at least 500,000 speakers. Swahili or Kiswahili is widely spoken in East Africa and some parts of Central Africa. The first script came from Arabic, and works were written in the Swahili–Arabic script from the seventeenth century on. Hausa, another widely spoken language, spread from the Hausa people to several others in west and north Africa.

RELIGION

Christianity reached North Africa as early as the first century CE, and soon spread to regions in Ethiopia and Sudan. Coptic Christianity survived to some extent in Ethiopia and Egypt. Christianity experienced a resurgence in the continent with the advent of European missionaries in the eighteenth century.

Islam is the other major religion, spreading through the continent from the seventh century. Indigenous religions, often involving ancestor worship, are practised exclusively by about 15 per cent of the population, but underlie other religions since some traditions and rituals have crossed over. Falasha Jews were once prominent in Ethiopia, and there are other small minority groups across Africa.

ART AND CULTURE

Traditional arts, music, and oral literature were revived by nationalist movements, although the ideas and culture of the west have also permeated Africa, particularly among the young.

Royal Bafokeng Stadium, one of the venues for the 2010 Soccer World Cup in South Africa—the first in an African nation.

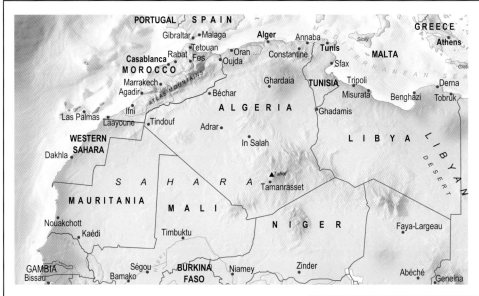

Algeria

Algeria
Area: *919,595
sq miles* •
Population:
34,178,188 •
Capital: *Algiers*
• System of
government:
Republic

Algerian Civil War cemetery.

Algeria, the second largest country in Africa, is largely part of the Sahara desert. It gained independence from France in 1962 after a long and violent liberation struggle, led by the FLN (Front de Liberation Nationale). Even after independence war and conflict continued between various factions. Ahmad Ben Bella was elected first president, but was overthrown by Houari Boumediene in 1965. The 1976 constitution made Algeria a socialist state, but from 1992 to 1998 there was a struggle between the Islamic Salvation Front, an extremist political group, and the government.

Algeria has large natural gas and oil reserves. The country has a rich literature in both Arabic and French, and the archaeological sites of Tipasa and Timgad are World Heritage sites.

Milestone Events

BEFORE 1200 BCE Berbers live in the region.

***c.* 1200 BCE** Phoenicians set up trading ports on Mediterranean coast.

42 CE Roman provinces are founded.

533 Region is part of Byzantine empire.

682 Arabs invade. Arab and then Berber dynasties rule.

1400–1600 Portugal and Spain gain control of some coastal areas.

1518 Ottoman rule begins in Algeria; extends to Libya.

1830 France occupies Algeria.

1881 France occupies Tunisia.

1911 Italy conquers Libya from Ottomans.

1912 Morocco becomes a French protectorate.

1942–3 During World War II, Britain and France occupy Libya.

1951 Libya becomes independent.

1954–62 Algerian War of Independence.

1956 Morocco, Tunisia gain independence from France.

Libya

Ninety per cent of Libya's land is desert. Muammar al-Gadhafi, who has been its leader from 1969, devised a new political ideology, a combination of socialist and Islamic ideas known as the Third Universal Theory.

Libya has a high GDP (PPP) per capita due to its petroleum reserves and its comparitively low population. There are several historic sites among which are Cyrene and Leptis Magna, while the capital Tripoli has monuments from ancient to modern days.

Libya
Area: *679,362 sq miles* •
Population: *6,324,357* •
Capital: *Tripoli*
• System of government: *Jamahiriya, local self-government; authoritarian in practice*

Morocco

Morocco
Area: *172,414 sq miles* •
Population: *31,285,174* •
Capital: *Rabat*
• System of government: *Constitutional monarchy*

Morocco, with a mountainous interior, and access to both the Atlantic and Mediterranean coastlines, has 75 per cent of the world's reserves of phosphate rock. The country gained independence from France and Spain after a long struggle. The sultan's palace at Meknes is called the Moroccan Versailles, and Moroccan culture is a mix of Berber, Arab, west African, Spanish, and French. Moroccan art and literature is rich and varied.

The Saharawi (or Saharan) Arab Democratic Republic

This disputed region of Western Sahara is recognised as an independent state by several nations, although most of the area remains under Morocco

Tunisia
Area: *63,170 sq miles* •
Population: *10,486,339* •
Capital: *Tunis*
• System of government: *Republic*

Tunisia

Tunisia, the smallest of the northern African states, is located along important shipping routes in the Mediterranean. It became a republic in 1957. Tunisia is unique among Arab countries since women form over 20 per cent of the bi-cameral legislature, and have been granted equal rights by law. Tunisia is known for its liberal and innovative cinema.

Egypt
Area: 386,700 sq
miles • Population:
83,082,869 (July
2009 est.) • Capital:
Cairo • System of
government: Republic

Lying across Northeast Africa and the Sinai Peninsula—the meeting point of Africa and Asia—with the Mediterranean Sea to the north and the Red Sea to the east, Egypt has a strategic location. The country is headed by a popularly elected president, who shares power with the prime minister, the leader of the majority party. In modern times, Egypt has a central role in Middle East politics, having made peace with Israel after several wars. Egypt has a wide variety of natural resources including petroleum and natural gas

EARLY AND MEDIEVAL PERIOD

On the fertile plains of the Nile river rose one of the most ancient civilizations of the world, around 3500 BCE. The monumental art, grand pyramids, and tombs of this period are one of Egypt's greatest heritages. Ancient Egypt had periods of Persian, Greek, Roman, and Byzantine rule. These were followed by the Arabs in the seventh century, who introduced Islam and the Arabic language. They were succeeded by the Mamluks in c. 1250, who, in turn, came under the nominal rule of the Ottomans in 1517.

Sailing boat on the Nile.

Milestone Events

17,000–15,000 BCE Late Paleolithic sites.
7000–4500 Neolithic cultures.
3100 King Menes unites Upper and Lower Egypt; ancient civilization develops.
332 Conquest by Alexander the Great.
1517 CE Egypt becomes part of the Ottoman empire
1859–69 Construction of Suez Canal.
1913 First modern Egyptian novel, *Zaynab*, by Muhammad Husayn Haykal, published.

1914 Egypt becomes a British protectorate; ties with Turkey severed.
1922 Gains independence; King Fuad I rules; Britain retains right to intervene in Egyptian affairs.
1948 Joins invasion of the newly-created State of Israel; is defeated but retains Gaza Strip.
1952 Gamel Abdul Nasser leads coup, overthrows King Farouk I; Muhammad Naguib installed as president and prime minister.
1953 Naguib declares Egypt a republic.

BRITISH RULE

In 1882, the British occupied Egypt, retaining the Ottoman ruler as the nominal head until 1914. After World War I, an Egyptian nationalist movement began, compelling Britain to grant independence to the country in 1922. However, Britain continued to have a role in Egyptian politics. This led to a military coup in 1952, following which a republic was established in 1953.

Al-Azhar mosque in Cairo.

POST INDEPENDENCE

Abdul Gamel Nasser (1918–70), a leading figure in the nation's early years of independence, promoted Arab unity and played a major role in the Non Aligned Movement. He also centralized the economy.

Abdul Gamel Nasser.

Three wars with Israel damaged the economy, but Egypt made peace with that country in 1979–80. In the 1990s, privatization and major economic reforms were introduced, and tax rates reduced, leading to substantial economic growth. Further reforms were initiated from 2004. Though Egypt has the second largest economy in the Arab world, after Saudi Arabia, living standards of the average citizen remain inadequate. The country has begun developing nuclear energy for peaceful use

CULTURE

Egypt's culture is a mix of different strands. Though Islam predominates, Christianity coexists peacefully and both Sufi and Christian saints are revered. More than a hundred motion pictures a year are produced in the country known as the "Hollywood of the Middle East;" an International Film Festival is held annually.

Egyptian novelists and poets are prolific: Naguib Mahfouz (1911-2006) was the first Arabic language writer to win the Nobel Prize in Literature, in 1988. Art and music are a mixture of indigenous, Mediterranean, African, Arab, and Western elements.

- Nasser becomes prime minister; **1956** president.
- **1956** Suez Canal nationalized; UK, France, Israel invade Egypt; are repelled.
- **1967** Six Day War with Israel.
- **1970** Nasser dies; is succeeded by Anwar al Sadat.
- **1971** Treaty of friendship with Soviet Union; Aswan Dam inaugurated.
- **1973** Yom Kippur War; **1974** Peace agreements.
- **1977** Egypt becomes first Arab country to recognize Israel.

1978 Camp David accords signed between Israel and Egypt; **1979** peace treaty signed.
1981 Sadat assassinated; Hosni Mubarak is new president.
1992–96 Egyptian Boutros Boutros Ghali is secretary general of the UN.
2005 Constitutional amendment changes the form of presidential election to direct election, allowing multiple candidates; Mubarak reelected for fifth term.

AFRICA

Djibouti

O ne of the tiniest African nations, Djibouti won independence in 1977, with Hasan Gouled Aptidon the first president. Djibouti's strategic location at the mouth of the Red Sea accounts for transit trade, and has also led to it being used as a base for military operations. Both the U.S. and France have troops stationed here.

Djibouti
Area: 8,958 sq miles •
Population: 724,622
• Capital: Djibouti city
• System of government: Republic

Eritrea

E ritrea gained independence from Ethiopia in 1993 after a long struggle. Economic progress has been hampered by military conflicts with Yemen and Ethiopia.. Eritrea has some of the oldest human fossil remains.

Ethiopia

E thiopia was free from colonial rule except during 1936-41. With the independence of Eritrea in 1993, Ethiopia lost her coastline along the Red Sea. The country's economic position is poor, due to the long-drawn-out conflict with Eritrea (1999–2000) along with frequent droughts.

Ethiopia is known for cultivating coffee, which may have originated there. Ethiopia's ability to resist European power, and the long rule of the emperor Haile Selassie from 1930–74, led to the emergence of the Rastafarians, a religious sect who saw Haile Selassie as a symbol of freedom, a messiah, and an incarnation of Christ.

Ethiopia
Area: 426,373 sq miles •
Population: 85,237,338
• Capital: Addis Ababa
• System of government: Federal republic.

Eritrea
Area: 45,406 sq miles •
Population: 5,647,168
• Capital: Asmara •
System of government: Transitional, republic.

Milestone Events

6–2 MILLION YEARS AGO Early hominid remains in Ethiopia.
c. 150 CE Aksum kingdom is powerful in the region.
4th CENTURY Coptic Christianity introduced in Ethiopia.
7th CENTURY onwards Arabs and Islam dominate the area.
1887 Britain proclaims protectorate over Somaliland.
1888 French colony of Somaliland established in region (included Djibouti).

1889 Italy sets up protectorate in central Somalia.
1899–1956 Sudan is known as Anglo-Egyptian Sudan, and is in effect under the British.
1936 Italy merges territories in Somaliland, Eritrea, and Ethiopia into Italian East Africa.
1941 Eritrea, Somaliland occupied by UK.
1946 Djibouti becomes overseas territory of France.
1953 Sudan granted self government.
1958 Military coup in Sudan led by Ibrahim Abboud.
1962 Eritrea occupied by Ethiopia.

Somalia

Somalia
Area:
246,201
sq miles •
Population:
9,832,017
• Capital:
Mogadishu
• System of
government:
Transitional,
parliamentary.

Located on the Horn of Africa, in ancient days Somalia was an important centre of commerce, but today is wracked by civil war. In 1960, the two separate areas of Somalia under Italy and Britain were granted independence and merged. In 1991 the Somali National Movement gained control of former British Somaliland, and declared independence. It remains separate, but does not have international recognition. There were many more civil wars with several areas declaring independence or autonomy. Somalia is also known for its pirates, who flourish along the coast. The country has several historic sites with early pyramidal structures and remains of ancient city states such as Opone and Malo

Sudan

Sudan is the largest country in Africa, dominated by the river Nile and its tributaries. Its ancient history as the kingdom of Kush was entwined with that of Egypt and it was often united with it politically. There were a succession of short-lived regimes after independence. Civil wars (1955–72, 1983–2005) as well as conflicts in the western region of Darfur proved disastrous for the country, although the economy has been helped by exports of crude oil from 1999. A coalition government was set up in 2005, and Sudan's first multi-party presidential elections since 1986 were held in April 2010.

A river boat on the Nile in Sudan.

Sudan
Area:
967,500
sq miles •
Population:
41,087,825
• Capital:
Khartoum •
System of
government:
Republic

1969 Colonel Gaafar Muhammad al-Nimeiry sets up military government in Sudan; 1971 is elected president; 1983 reelected for 3rd term; 1985 ousted in coup.

1970 Major-General Muhammad Siad Barre, who seized power in 1969, declares Somalia a socialist state.

1974 In Ethiopia the Emperor Haile Selassie (1892–1975) is overthrown by a military coup; socialist state set up.

1977 Djibouti gains independence from France.

1991 President Barre of Somalia overthrown.

1993 Eritrea gains independence.

1998 Nuruddin Farah (b.1945) of Somalia wins Neustadt International Prize for literature.

2004 Transitional Federal Government set up in Somalia.

2005–7 Conflict between Sudan and Chad.

2009 Sheikh Sharif Sheikh Ahmad elected president of transitional government in Somalia.

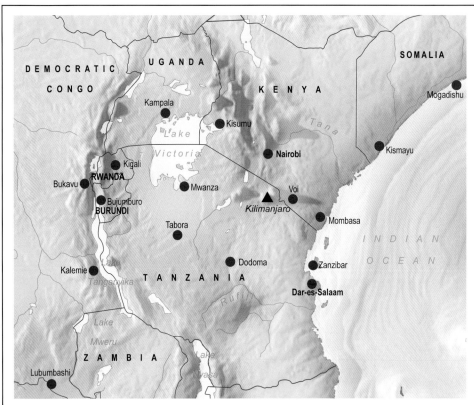

Burundi and Rwanda

Rwanda
Area: *10,169 sq miles* • Population: *10,746,311* • Capital: *Kigali* • System of government: *Republic*

Burundi
Area: *10,745 sq miles* • Population: *9,511,330* • Capital: *Bujumbura* • System of government: *Republic*

Burundi and Rwanda were colonized by Belgium and attained independence in 1962. Since then both countries suffered from civil war and conflicts between the two main ethnic groups, the Hutus and Tutsis, though they have been more peaceful from 2003.

Milestone Events

3-2 MILLION YEARS AGO Early hominids in Kenya and Tanzania.

11th CENTURY Arabs control coastal trade, establish Zenj city states in Kenya.

1800s Buganda (in Uganda region) becomes a large kingdom.

1832 Sultan Sayyid Said from Oman establishes his capital in Zanzibar.

1885 Tanganyika comes under Germany; after World War I under UK.

1890 Kenya becomes British protectorate.

• Rwanda–Burundi becomes part of German East Africa.

• Zanzibar becomes British protectorate.

1894 Buganda becomes a British protectorate; 1896 name Uganda adopted.

1902–62 Life of Shaaban Robert, Tanzanian author called the "poet laureate of Swahili."

1916 Belgium occupies the territory of Rwanda–Burundi.

Tourists visiting safari parks are a new source of income for Kenya.

Kenya

Kenya
Area: *224,081
sq miles* •
Population:
39,002,722 •
Capital: *Nairobi*
• System of
government:
Republic

After independence in 1963, the nationalist leader Jomo Kenyatta became prime minister then president the following year when Kenya became a republic. Kenya initially had a high economic growth rate, but this was not sustained.

Tanzania
Area: *365,755
sq miles* •
Population:
41,048,532
• Capital:
*Dodoma (Dar
es Salaam
till 1974)* •
System of
government:
Republic

Tanzania

Tanzania includes the former region of Tanganyika on the mainland, and the islands of Zanzibar and Pemba. In 1961, Julius Nyerere, "the father of the nation," became the first president after independence and attempted to develop the country.

Uganda

Uganda
Area: *93,065
sq miles* •
Population:
32,369,558
• Capital:
Kampala •
System of
government:
Republic

The army commander Idi Amin seized power in 1971 and began eight years of misrule, during which between 100,000 and 300,000 Ugandans were tortured or murdered. Since his removal in 1978 rebel movements have continued to hamper development.

Idi Amin.

1961 Tanganyika gains independence.
1962 Burundi, Rwanda, Uganda win independence.
1963 Kenyan independence.
1964 Tanganyika and Zanzibar merge.
1980–85 Milton Obote (1925–2005) is president of Uganda (earlier prime minister from 1962–65, president 1966–71).
1994 Rwandan Genocide, mass murders of Tutsis.
2001 Tanzania, Uganda, Kenya, inaugurate a regional parliament and court of justice in Arusha.

• Rwanda adopts new flag and national anthem.
2004 Kenyan ecologist Wangari Maathai wins Nobel Peace Prize.
2005 New constitution in Burundi; peaceful general election.
• Customs union introduced in Tanzania, Uganda, Kenya.
• Jakaya Kikwete is elected president of Tanzania.
2009 Rwanda and Burundi join the East African Community Customs Union.

All these countries were once colonized by European powers, and most gained independence in the 1950s to 1970s. Liberia (originally Monrovia) is unique because the colony was set up by Americans as a homeland for freed slaves from the USA, who were transported to Monrovia from 1822 onwards.

Since independence Cape Verde, a small group of islands, has maintained a relatively stable democracy, and Senegal, following the

Cape Verde
Area: *1,557 sq miles* • Population: *429,474* • Capital: *Praia* • System of government: *Republic*

Cote d'Ivoire
Area: *124,504 sq miles* • Population: *20,617,068* • Capital: *Yamossoukro* • System of government: *Republic*

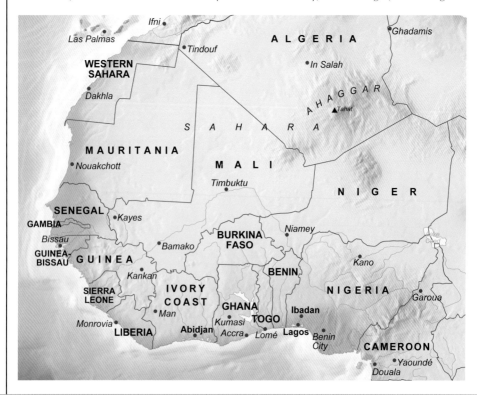

Milestone Events

5000 BCE Farming and cattle domestication begin.

400 BCE The first city-states emerge in the region; were involved in trade across the Sahara.

500–1000 CE Various peoples including Wolof, Serer, Tukolor, Berbers settle in the region.

15th–16th CENTURIES Arabs reach the area, resulting in a mixed Berber–Arab culture.

1444–45 Portuguese reach Senegal and Cape Verde for trade.

1600–1700 Dutch and French dominate trade.

1842–44 France establishes a protectorate in Cote d'Ivoire; 1893 it becomes a colony.

1894 The Gambia becomes a British protectorate.

1895 Senegal becomes French colony.

1903 Mauritania becomes French protectorate; colony in 1920.

1958 Ahmed Sekou Toure is first president of independent Guinea, rules till 1984.

Gambia, The
Area: *4,361 sq
miles* • Population:
1,778,081 •
Capital: *Banjul*
• System of
government:
Republic

Guinea
Area: *94,926 sq
miles* • Population:
10,057,975 •
Capital: *Conakry*
• System of
government:
Republic

**Guinea-
Bissau**
Area: *13,948 sq
miles* • Population:
1,533,964 • Capital:
Bissau • System
of government:
Republic

Liberia
Area: *43,000 sq
miles* • Population:
3,441,790 •
Capital: *Monrovia*
• System of
government:
Republic

Mauritania
Area: *397,955 sq
miles* • Population:
3,129,486 •
Capital: *Nouakchott*
• System of
government:
Republic

Sierra Leone
Area: *27,699 sq
miles* • Population:
5,132,138 •
Capital: *Freetown*
• System of
government:
Republic

Léopold Sédar Senghor of Senegal.

path laid down in 1960 by the first president Léopold Sédar Senghor (1906–2001), a poet, philosopher, and intellectual, is considered a model democracy in Africa.

The other nations in this group have suffered from coups or devastating civil wars. The conflicts have prevented countries from gaining the full benefits of natural resources whether minerals such as bauxite or plants such as the cocoa bean. Discoveries of oil and natural gas in the region may help to improve some economies.

Senegal River at Saint Louis, Senegal.

**Senegal (Republic
of Senegal)**
Area: *75,955 sq
miles* • Population:
13,711,597 •
Capital: *Dakar*
• System of
government:
Republic

1959 Cote d'Ivoire, Burkina Faso, Niger, Benin, form Conseil de l'etente; **1966** joined by Togo.

1961 Moktar Ould Daddah elected first president in Mauritania; reelected **1966, 1971, 1976**.

1982 Senegal and The Gambia form federation known as Senegambia; dissolved **1989**.

1984 Léopold Sédar Senghor, former president of Senegal, named to Academie Francais, first black person to receive highest French honour for contribution to French life and letters.

1993 In Guinea, Lasana Conte elected head of the civilian government, reelected **1998, 2003**; dies **2008**.

2000 Abdoulaye Wade elected president of Senegal; reelected **2007**.

2002 Sierra Leone's 10-year civil war displaces one-third of its population.

2007 Mauritania parliament outlaws slavery that had continued despite a **1981** ban.

2008 Military coup in Guinea.

Benin

Earlier known as Dahomey, Benin gained independence from France in 1960, and was renamed in 1975. From 1991 it became a multi-party democracy headed by a president. Benin began a program of economic reforms in 2001, and offshore oil was discovered in 2009.

Benin
Area: *43,484 sq miles* • Population: *8,791,832* • Capital: *Porto Novo* • System of government: *Republic*

Burkina Faso
Area: *105,869 sq miles* • Population: *15,746,232* • Capital: *Ougadougou* • System of government: *Republic*

Burkina Faso

Burkina Faso, meaning the land of upright people, was earlier known as the Republic of Haute Volta or Upper Volta. It gained independence from France in 1960, and was renamed in 1984. The country has faced several military coups, though it is now a democracy. Burkina Faso hosts the Panafrican Film and Television Festival of Ougadougou (FESPACO) every two years, considered the most important film festival in Africa.

Ghana

Three years after attaining independence, Ghana became a republic in 1960. The first prime minister and later the president, Kwama Nkrumah, was a charismatic leader, but was overthrown by a coup in 1966. There were other coups and civil strife, but the country stabilized from 2000. Agriculture remains important in the economy, though gold, timber, and cocoa are exported. Offshore oil reserves were discovered in 2007.

Ghana
Area: *92,098 sq miles* • Population: *23,887,812* • Capital: *Accra* • System of government: *Republic*

Milestone Events

c. 300 BCE Bantu peoples live in the region.
c. 500 CE Townships in the region.
7th CENTURY Islam spreads through trade.
1471 Portuguese explorers reach Ghana area, name it Gold Coast.
1874 Gold Coast becomes British colony.
1884 German protectorate of Togoland established.
1905 Mali is part of French Sudan.
1906 Region of present Nigeria comes under British rule.

1919 Region of present Burkina Faso becomes separate territory of French Upper Volta (Haute Volta); **1932** Divided among other French states; **1947** separate colony revived.
1920 Togoland divided between France and Britain.
1958 Benin granted autonomy.
1960 Modibo Keita is first president of independent Mali.
• Niger gains independence from France.
1963 President Sylvanus Olympio of Togo assassinated.

Mali

After gaining independence from France in 1959, Mali has had periods of turmoil and military dictatorship. Though a civilian government was established from 1992, unrest continued. Once a rich empire, today Mali's economy is largely based on agriculture.

Mali
Area: *478,841 sq miles* • Population: *13,443,225* • Capital: *Bamako* • System of government: *Republic*

Nigeria

Nigeria
Area: *356,669 sq miles* • Population: *149,229,090* • Capital: *Abuja (Lagos up to 1991)* • System of government: *Federal republic*

Nigeria gained independence in 1960 and from 1966 onwards has had long periods of military rule, though civilian rule was restored in 1999. During 1967–70, Igbo people attempted to set up a separate state, the Republic of Biafra, leading to a civil war and blockade: One million Biafrans starved to death during the war.

Oil became a major source of Nigeria's income from the 1970s, and as one of the world's largest oil producers, Nigeria has immense growth potential.

Niger

Niger
Area: *489,191 sq miles* • Population: *15,306,252* • Capital: *Niamey* • System of government: *Republic*

Niger has faced several coups and military governments, the latest being in February 2010. It also faces rebellion from the Tuareg ethnic group. Niger has diverse mineral resources but the majority of people are agriculturalists.

Togo

Togo
Area: *21,925 sq miles* • Population: *6,031,808* • Capital: *Lome* • System of government: *Republic*

In 1956, the British area of Togoland was merged with the Gold Coast, and became independent as Ghana. French Togoland became an independent country in 1960 as Togo. The economy is based mainly on agriculture and Togo is also a regional center for commerce and trade. Riots and civil war have affected the economy.

1967 Gnassingbe Eyadema leads coup in Togo.
1968–73 Severe drought affects Niger.
1972 Mathieu Kerekou leads military coup in Benin, sets up Marxist government.
1995 Writer and activist Ken Saro-Wiwa, along with eight others, executed in Nigeria.
1996 Kerekou elected president in Benin, reelected **2001**.
1999 Olusegun Obasanjo wins presidential election in Nigeria; civilian rule restored.

• Niger approves new constitution.
2000 John Kufuor elected president in Ghana; reelected **2004**.
2005 In Togo, president Gnassingbe Eyadema, dies, son Faure Gnassingbe seizes power.
2007 Floods cause devastation in Ghana.
2009 In Burkina Faso, law passed that 30 per cent candidates standing for election should be women.
2010 President Mamadou Tandja of Niger overthrown in coup.

All these countries were once colonized by European powers. Since independence Cameroon, a culturally diverse country, has had a diversified economy and a relatively stable political system. Gabon is another peaceable country, although political conditions are not ideal. All the other countries have seen coups, assassinations, and civil wars that have hindered their development, even though many have plentiful natural resources including gold and oil. Equatorial Guinea is exploiting its oil reserves, but

Joseph Mobutu of the Democratic Republic of Congo.

Cameroon
Area:
183,553 sq miles •
Population:
18,879,301
• Capital:
Yaounde •
System of government:
Republic

Chad
Area:
495 755 sq miles •
Population:
10,329,208
• Capital:
N'Djamena
• System of government:
Republic

Republic of Congo
Area: *132,047 sq miles* •
Population:
4,012,809
• Capital:
Brazzaville
• System of government:
Republic

Central African Republic (CAR)
Area: *240,535 sq miles* •
Population:
4,511,488 •
Capital: *Bangui*
• System of government:
Republic

Democratic Republic of the Congo (DR Congo)
Area: *905,355 sq miles* •
Population:
68,692,542 •
Capital: *Kinshasa*
• System of government:
Republic

Equatorial Guinea
Area:
10,8301 sq miles •
Population:
633,441 •
Capital: *Malabo*
• System of government:
Republic

Milestone Events

6th–15th CENTURY Sao civilization in part of the area.

c. 1000 Bantu peoples live in the region.

1910 Areas of Chad, Gabon, Congo (Later Republic of), CAR become part of French Equatorial Africa.

1960 Joseph Kavubu is president of Democratic Republic of Congo, Patrice Lumumba prime minister.

• Francois Tombalbaye becomes first president of Chad; assassinated **1975**.

1960–65 David Dacko is president of CAR; overthrown by Jean Bedel Bokassa.

1961 Patrice Lumumba assassinated in Democratic Republic of Congo.

1963 Abbe Fulbert Yulou is first president of Republic of Congo.

1965–97 Joseph Mobutu holds power in Democratic Republic of Congo.

1968 Francisco Macias Nguema is first president of Equatorial Guinea.

Sao Tomé and Principe
Area: *372 sq miles* •
Population: *212,679* •
Capital: *Sao Tomé* • System
of government: *Republic*

Gabon
Area: *103,347 sq
miles* • Population:
1,514,993 • Capital:
Libreville • System of
government: *Republic*

the income from this is not equally distributed.

One of the region's most infamous dictators was Jean Bedel Bokassa of the Central African Republic (CAR). President in 1966 after a coup, he proclaimed himself emperor in 1977, ruling for two years before being overthrown, and was accused of eating the flesh of his enemies.

Above: A family from one of Congo's pygmy peoples.
Below: Craters on Mount Cameroon.

1971–97 Democratic Republic of Congo
renamed Zaire.
1975 Sao Tomé and Principe gain independence
from Portugal.
1982 Paul Biya elected president of Cameroon.
1986 Poisonous gas from Lake Nyos in Cameroon
kills more than 1700.
1992 Cameroon holds first multi-party
presidential elections.
1995 Principe gains self-government.

1997 Mobutu ousted by Laurent Kabila; Zaire
renamed Democratic Republic of Congo.
2000 World Bank approves funds for oil and
pipeline project in Chad and Cameroon.
2001 Kabila shot dead; son Joseph Kabila becomes
president of DR Congo.
2003 General Francis Bozize takes power in a
militray coup in CAR; 2005, elected president.
2006 Idriss Deby reelected as president of Chad.
2009 National unity government formed in CAR

After World War II some countries under direct British rule achieved independence relatively peacefully, such as Botswana (one of the world's biggest diamond producers), Malawi, and Zambia, all fairly stable multi-party democracies; and Lesotho and Swaziland, tiny kingdoms surrounded by South Africa.

Elsewhere in southern Africa, Namibia won independence from South Africa, where the white minority government repressed blacks through its policy of separate development or apartheid. The movement for black equality, led by Nelson Mandela, achieved democratic elections in 1994.

Milestone Events

3 MILLION YEARS AGO Hominid fossils found in the region.

c. 1100 Great Zimbabwe settlements built.

1814 Cape Colony (South Africa) ceded to Britain by Netherlands.

1834 Boers begin leaving Cape Colony, South Africa, establish republics in Natal, Orange Free State, Transvaal.

1859 Scottish explorer David Livingstone reaches Malawi.

1899–1902 Boer War; Britain annexes Transvaal and Orange Free State.

1948 National Party in South Africa begins policy of apartheid.

1953 British government creates Federation of Rhodesia and Nyasaland.

1958 Hastings Kumuzu Banda returns from U.S. and U.K to lead Nyasaland African Congress.

1977 Anti-apartheid activist Steve Biko "martyred;" killed by South African police.

Botswana
Area: 224,607 sq miles • Population: 1,990,876 • Capital: Gaborone • System of government: Republic

Lesotho
Area: 11,720 sq miles • Population: 2,130,819 • Capital: Maseru • System of government: Constitutional monarchy

Malawi
Area: 45,747 sq miles • Population: 15,028,757 • Capital: Lilongwe • System of government: Republic

Namibia
Area: 318,261 sq miles • Population: 2,108,665 • Capital: Windhoek • System of government: Republic

South Africa
Area: 470,671 sq miles • Population: 49,052,489 • Capital: Pretoria • System of government: Republic

Swaziland
Area: 6,809 sq miles • Population: 1,337,186 • Capital: Mbabane; Lobamba is royal and legislative capital • System of government: Monarchy

Southern Rhodesia's white minority government seceded from Britain in 1965 as Rhodesia. It gained majority rule and independence as Zimbabwe in 1980. Since then it has been dominated by Robert Mugabe, who has led the country into poverty.

Portugal's former colonies, Angola and Mozambique, each fought long wars of independence before gaining their freedom.

Nelson Mandela, freedom fighter and former president of South Africa.

Zambia
Area: 290,587 sq miles • Population: 11,862,740 • Capital: Lusaka • System of government: Republic

Zimbabwe
Area: 150,872 sq miles • Population: 11,392,629 • Capital: Harare • System of government: Republic

Angola
Area: 481,354 sq miles • Population: 12,799,293 • Capital: Luanda • System of government: Republic

Mozambique
Area: 308,642 sq miles • Population: 21,669,278 • Capital: Maputo • System of government: Republic

Comoros
Area: 863 sq miles • Population: 752,438 • Capital: Moroni • System of government: Republic

Madagascar
Area: 226,657 sq miles • Population: 20,653,556 • Capital: Anatananarivo • System of government: Republic

1980–87 Robert Mugabe is first prime minister of Zimbabwe; from **1987**, president.

1984 Protests against apartheid spread through South Africa.

1986 Mswati III becomes king in Swaziland.

1986–2004 Joaquim Chissano is president of Mozambique; launches economic development and stabilises country.

1990 Nelson Mandela, leader of African National Congress, freed from prison in South Africa.

1991 New constitution makes Zambia a multi-party democracy.

1993 Nelson Mandela and FW de Klerk awarded Nobel Peace Prize for their role in creating democratic South Africa.

1994 Nelson Mandela becomes president of South Africa after first free elections.

• First multi-party elections held in Malawi.

2008 Botswana sets up own diamond trading company.

North America covers Canada, the USA, and Mexico—9,540,000 square miles altogether. Although the countries of Central America and the Caribbean islands are technically part of the North American subcontinent, they have their own culture and history. The name America probably derives from that of an Italian explorer, Amerigo Vespucci, who visited the region between 1499–1502.

North America has a diverse landscape, ranging from the temperate grasslands of the prairies to arid deserts in the southwest of the USA and in Mexico, and the ice and snow wilderness of Alaska to the north, where the highest mountain in the United States, Denali (formerly Mt. McKinley) rises 20,320 feet. Mineral resources include coal, iron ore, oil and natural gas, and gold and silver deposits.

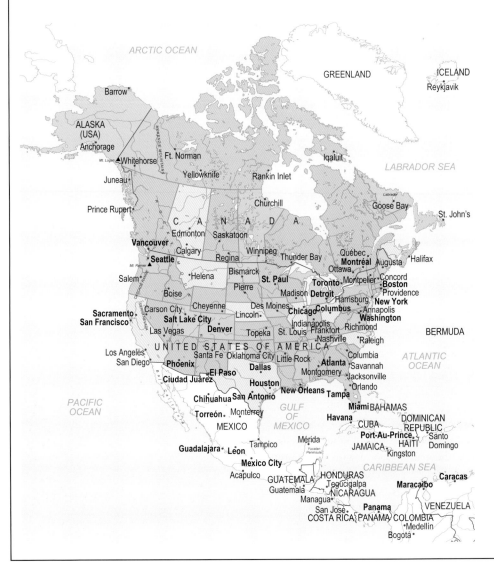

The Seattke skyline.

HISTORY

Sometime between 30000 and 13000 BCE, humans migrated into North America, either across the Bering Straits which once formed a land bridge with Siberia, or by sea, then spread through the continent. The Inuit are believed to have arrived in the region much later than other groups.

The Vikings reached North America in the late tenth century although their settlement in Canada did not survive for long, and Europeans later began to explore and settle from the late fifteenth century. Up to this time there were numerous farming cultures, some of which were advanced civilizations. In the sixteenth century Spain conquered Mexico and Central America, while north of Mexico the English and French were prominent. Gradually the English dominated the region of modern Canada, while the USA declared its independence from Britain in 1776, which was confirmed by 1783 after the Revolutionary War. In the USA, the Native American groups were almost wiped out by disease or in a series of wars, and in Canada, too, the First Nations were gradually displaced. From around 1650 African slaves were imported; the move to abolish slavery was the main reason for the American Civil War in 1861–65, in which the northern union defeated the southern Confederacy that supported slavery. Eventually the USA expanded to reach 50 states.

Canada became a self-governing dominion of the British empire in 1867, then in 1882 took formal control over its constitution from Britain, although it remains a member of the British Commonwealth of Nations. The twentieth century saw the countries survive two world wars, followed by the Cold War, and in the twenty-first century Canada and the USA are prosperous, technologically advanced, and world leaders in international affairs. At the same time Mexico is facing challenges from violent, powerful drug gangs.

CULTURE

English is the main language, though French is spoken in parts of Canada, and Spanish is the language of Mexico and of people throughout the region of Hispanic origin. Inuit and Native American languages are also spoken. Christianity is the main religion, but there are major Jewish communities, especially in New York. American music, movies, and television shows influence popular culture around the world.

The Polar bear, found in Alaska and Canada, is an endangered species.

NORTH AMERICA

Area: *3,855,106 sq miles* •
Population: *33,487,208* •
Capital: *Ottawa* •
System of government: *Constitutional monarchy and federal parliamentary democracy*

Canada is the second largest country in the world, occupying most of the continent of North America, to the north of the United States. It has a strategic location between Russia and the U.S. via the north polar route.

Canada is a federation with ten provinces and three territories, each with its own symbols and some amount of autonomy. The chief of state is the British monarch, represented by a governor general, while the head of government is a prime minister. The legislature is bicameral.

Canada has rich natural resources, including iron ore, nickel, zinc, copper, gold, lead, molybdenum, potash, diamonds, silver, coal, petroleum, and

Milestone Events

15000–11000 BCE Early settlements in Canada in the Yukon area.

1100–9000 BCE Palaeo-Indian settlements spread to many parts of Canada including Nova Scotia, Québec, Ontario, British Colombia.

8000 BCE Amerindian people live in St.Lawrence river valley; Clovis people occupy region around Niagara Falls.

6000 BCE Neolithic farming begins.

5000–4000 BCE Earliest petroglyphs.

3500 BCE Haida culture flourishes on northwest coast of Canada; known for its art and potlatches, or ceremonial distribution of goods.

2000 BCE–1000 CE several settlements in various parts of Canada.

1000 CE Vikings reach coast of Newfoundland.

1300–1500 Iroquois people live in villages in present southwestern Québec and Ontario.

1497 John Cabot of England reaches Newfoundland.

natural gas. It is the world's largest producer of zinc and uranium, and rich diamond deposits were discovered in 1989 in a remote area of Canada known as the Barren Lands. Its river and lake systems provide hydropower. Forests cover about 49 per cent of the area, and are

Yukon river, northern Canada.

partly used for timber. Commercial fishing dates back to the first European occupation. Crops include wheat, barley, oilseed, tobacco, fruits, and vegetables. Major industries consist of transportation equipment, chemicals, petroleum and natural gas, minerals, food products, and wood and paper products. Huge oil reserves in Alberta are now being exploited.

Wildlife is varied and Canada is a world leader in ecological and environmental concerns.

Canada is economically and technologically well developed. It has a market-oriented economy and high living standards. It has a trade surplus with the U.S., which accounts for almost 80 per cent of Canadian exports. The U.S. and Canada are the largest trade partners in the world. Canada had good economic growth from 1997 to 2007, but in 2008 was affected by the global economic downturn. However, Canada's major banks remained stable.

The population of Canada is multi-ethnic and diverse, with a large number of immigrants especially from Asia. Though the country is largely united, it faces a separatist tendency in French-speaking Québec. In 2006 the Parliament agreed that Québec would be recognised as a "nation" within Canada, though this is not a legal or constitutional provision but simply a symbolic recognition.

Canada claims the Arctic region, though other countries, including the U.S., Denmark, and Russia have territorial claims in the area.

Totem pole carved by the Tlingit native Canadians, British Columbia.

INUITS

Inuits have their own unique culture and art including the building of igloos for homes. They exist in several regions, and in Canada, the separate territory of Nunavut has been created for them. Inuit traditional religion includes belief in spirits, animism, and shamanism, though many of them have converted to Christianity. Intricate Inuit carvings are known from ancient times. Sculpture and art prints are now marketed to improve their economy.

An Inuit family in traditional fur parkas.

1534 Jacques Cartier (1491–1557) of France reaches the Straits of Belle Isle on the east coast of Canada.

1604 French found their first settlements in Canada in present area of Nova Scotia; develop fish and fur trade.

1625 Jesuits arrive in Québec to begin missionary work.

1670 English Hudson's Bay Company opens its first fur-trading posts in Canada.

1740–44 War of Austrian Succession in Europe leads to French–English conflict in Canada.

1758 British forces defeated by French in Fort Ticonderoga in Canada.

1760 English capture Montréal during Seven Years' War.

1763 France surrenders its Canadian lands to England.

1775 U.S. invasion of Canada ends in failure.

1791 Britain divides Canada into predominanatly French Lower Canada and English Upper Canada.

CANADA IN THE PAST

The Algonquin, Huron, Iroquois, Kwaikutl, Nutka, and Inuit were amongt the Native American tribes who established early settlements in Canada. By 1600 the First Nations population numbered around 250,000. In 1627 France founded the colony of New France along

Parliament building, Ottawa.

the St. Lawrence river, and British settlers later colonized the eastern seaboard. By the Treaty of Paris in 1763, after the Seven Years' War, New France came under the British. In 1867 the British North American Act made Canada a self-governing dominion of the British empire. At this time Canada was a federation of Nova Scotia, New Brunswick, Québec (Lower Canada), and Ontario (Upper Canada). With the opening of the transcontinental Canadian Pacific Railway in 1885, British Columbia joined the federation, and provinces and territories were later created in the northwest. The Constitution Act of April 17 1882 transferred formal control over the constitution from Britain to Canada.

ARTS

Canada has more than 2100 museums, archives, and historic sites. Among the major events of a flourishing theater scene are the Stratford Festival and the Shaw Festival in Niagara On The Lake. The Canadian film industry, once strongly dominated by Hollywood, has begun to develop independently. The Toronto International Film Festival (TIFF) is considered one of the most important in the world. Various styles of traditional music exist. These include French, Irish, the Scottish-derived Cape Breton music, and the Franco–Celtic styles of Québec.

Canadian literature has a dual heritage of French and English. In the twentieth century, Margaret Atwood (b.1939), poet and novelist, is one of the great names in Canadian literature and won the Booker Prize in 2000 for *The Blind Assassin*. Other Booker Prize winners from

Milestone Events

1806 *Le Canadien*, a Québec nationalist newspaper is founded.

1818 49th parallel is accepted as boundary between U.S. and Canada from Lake of the Woods to the Rockies.

1837 There are failed revolts that take place against British rule in Upper and Lower Canada.

1840 Britain unites Upper and Lower Canada.

1867 The British North American Act makes Canada a self-governing dominion of the British empire.

1885 Canadian Pacific Railway opens linking West and East.

1905 Alberta and Saskatchewan provinces formed.

1908 Lucy Maud Montgomery (1874–1942) writes classic children's story, *Anne of Green Gables*.

1931 Statute of Westminister provides more autonomy to Canada.

1939-45 Almost 1.5 million Canadians participate in World War II; after the war more immigrants settle in Canada.

Canada are Yann Martel in 2002 for *The Life of Pi* and novelist and poet Michael Ondaatje (b.1943 in Sri Lanka), best known for his novel *The English Patient*, co-winner of the Booker (1992).

Early Canadian works in French were accounts of explorers and missionaries. Among later writers, the French Canadian Marie Claire Blais (b.1939) is well-known.

Regional cultures also find literary space. Acadian history and folklore as well as native dispossesion and a search for identity are among literary themes.

A 1908 tipi used by native Canadians of the prairies.

Early Canadian artists were influenced by European trends. Among notable nineteenth-century artists were the Dutch-born Cornelius Krieghoff (1815-72) who painted scenes from the lives of French–Canadian farmers in Québec, as well as portraits and landscapes. The Irish-born Paul Kane (1810-71) is known for depicting Native American life in western Canada. In the twentieth century, a distinctly Canadian style of painting developed, but after the 1930s, Canadian painters explored individual styles.

From the 1970s newer styles of avant garde art including Conceptual Art, Performance Art, and Video Art developed. Performance art includes music, dance, or theater along with visuals; video art uses television and video technology.

The Toll Gate, by Dutch-born Canadian painter Cornelius Krieghoff, 1859.

1949 Canada is among the countries that form a defensive pact, the North Atlantic Treaty organisation (NATO).

1975 USA, Canada, and 35 European countries sign Helsinki Accords; recognise World War II boundaries and promise to maintain friendly relations.

1976 Montréal hosts XXI Olympic Games.

1989 US–Canada Free Trade Agreement (FTA) is signed.

1990 Transatlantic Declaration on EU–Canada relations adopted.

1994 Canada joins North American Free Trade Agreement (NAFTA).

1997 Calgary declaration recognises unique nature of Québec society.

1999 Federal territory of Nunavut created for the Inuit; capital Iqaluit.

2003 Toronto is affected by SARS virus.

2005 Canada legalizes same-sex marriages.

NORTH AMERICA

DEPENDENT AREAS OF THE USA

American Samoa, Baker Island, Guam, Howland Island, Jarvis Island, Johnston Atoll, Kingman Reef, Midway Islands, Navassa Island, Northern Mariana Islands, Palmyra Atoll, Puerto Rico, Virgin Islands, Wake Island

The USA, located in the continent of North America, is a federal republic of 50 states and one district, along with some outlying areas. Covering a wide variety of terrain from arctic areas to deserts, the USA is the third largest country in the world. The capital, Washington DC, is the seat of the U.S. president, the head of the government. Each state has its own constitution, and shares powers with the Federal Congress, which is solely responsible for foreign affairs and defence. The president is indirectly elected for a period of four years, and the Federal Congress is bicameral consisting

Great Seal of the USA.

Area: 3,794,100 sq miles (includes only the 50 states and District of Columbia)
• Capital: Washington DC • Other major cities: New York, Chicago, Los Angeles •
Population: 307,212,123
• System of government: Federal republic

Milestone Events

30,000–13000 BCE Migration into America takes place, across Bering Straits or by sea.

9500 BCE Clovis stone tool-making culture emerges in North America.

1–1400 CE Several farming settlements and cultures in North America.

1492 Christopher Columbus reaches the island of San Salvador in the Bahamas. He is considered the European discoverer of America.

1607 English settle at Jamestown, Virginia.

1620 Mayflower Compact, a self-governing agreement, signed by English settlers in Plymouth in Massachusetts, considered first constitution of USA.

17th–18th CENTURIES Thousands of Africans transported to USA and used as slaves in plantations and elsewhere.

1756–1763 Seven Years' War (also known as the French and Indian War) between France and Britain. At the end of the war Britain

of the Senate, which has one hundred seats with two representatives from each state, and the House of Representatives with 435 popularly elected members.

There are two main political parties today, the Republicans, who tend to be more conservative, and the Democrats. The current president, from January 1, 2009, is Barack Obama, a Democrat, who is the first African-American president of the USA. In the twenty-first century the USA is politically the most powerful country in the world. It has a leading role in a number of international organizations, and influences political decisions in many other countries. Its economy is market-oriented, and the largest in the world. Overall, the population has a high standard of living.

The country has rich natural resources including the world's largest coal reserves as well as other minerals. Its industries include steel, motor vehicles, aerospace, telecommunications, chemicals, electronics, and a wide variety of consumer goods and food products. Though it has oil resources, they do not meet the needs of the country, and the USA is the world's largest importer of oil. It also has a large number of conserved forests and national parks.

The USA is involved in scientific, technological, biological, and space research, and is, in all aspects, technologically advanced.

Literature, arts, and music have flourished from the time of its foundation, while its cinema, centered at Hollywood, is known throughout the world. Despite its culturally diversity, with people from different ethnic groups, there is a merging together to create a unique American identity.

The Hollywood sign in Los Angeles.

obtains Canada, the Great Lakes, and the upper Mississippi Valley from France.

1775–83 American War of Independence; George Washington leads colonial army against British.

1776 Thirteen colonies of USA declare independence from Britain.

1783 Britain and the United States sign the Treaty of Paris, U.S. independence recognized.

1787 New Constitution for United States.

1789 George Washington becomes first president of the United States.

1791 Ten amendments (Bill of Rights) added to the U.S. Constitution, guarantees individual freedom.

1792 Democratic-Republican Party founded.

1803 Louisiana Territory bought from France; U.S. land area doubles.

1804–64 Life of American writer Nathaniel Hawthorne.

1808 Atlantic slave trade abolished.

NORTH AMERICA

The early days

Though the USA became a nation state only in the late eighteenth century, the region was occupied from the late stone age. Native American tribes were settled in various parts of the area. The first European settlement was founded by Spain at St. Augustine in present Florida. Other claimants to the region were France and England. By the treaty of Paris in 1763, France lost its North American possessions, which came under the British.

Chief Sitting Bull of the Sioux.

One of the "gold spikes" used to complete the transcontinental railroads.

Declaration of independence

The Declaration of Independence, affirming independence from Britain, was adopted on July 4, 1776, a day still commemorated as Independence Day. At this time there were thirteen states in the United States of America. The Revolutionary War with Britain begun in 1775, continued till 1783, when, by the Treaty of Paris, Britain recognized the USA as a separate nation. In 1789, George Washington became the first president of the United States, under a new constitution.

In 1823, the USA asserted its territorial integrity through a statement known as the Monroe Doctrine. Yet threats to the new nation came not from outside, but from within, as a Civil War was fought between 1861-65, mainly over the issue of slavery. Slaves had been imported from Africa into the country to work as unpaid labor from around 1650. In the war the northern union of states finally defeated the southern Confederacy of states that supported slavery.

Abraham Lincoln, president during the Civil War.

During these years, the American colonists also fought against Native Americans, finally defeating them and occupying their land.

Milestone Events

1812–14 War between United States and Britain.
1817–62 Life of Henry David Thoreau, influential American writer and philosopher.
1818 United States and Britain agree on an open border between Canada and the United States.
1819–92 Life of poet, Walt Whitman.
1823 Monroe Doctrine promulgated.
1826–64 Life of American songwriter Stephen Foster, considered "father of American music," whose songs are still popular.

1835–10 Life of great American novelist known as Mark Twain (Samuel Langhorn Clemens).
1846–48 War between the United States and Mexico; United States gains land from Texas.
1854 Republican Party founded.
1860 Abraham Lincoln of Republican Party elected 16th U.S. president; **1865**, assassinated.
1861 Confederate States of America formed by eleven southern states that secede from the Union.
1861–65 Civil War in USA.

The twentieth century: the first half

By 1900 the USA had forty-five states, spread across the country.

In the early twentieth century the USA became involved in World War I. At the end of the war, the Senate did not accept either the Treaty of Versailles or the League of Nations, despite the efforts of president Woodrow Wilson (a Democrat), and remained somewhat isolated from international events and policies. Three Republican presidents followed Wilson, Warren Harding (1921–23), Calvin Coolidge (1923–29), and Herbert C. Hoover (1929–33).

Until 1929 the country was generally prosperous. However, a stock market crash in 1929 led to the Great Depression, an economic crisis during which millions lost their jobs. In 1933, Franklin Roosevelt as president brought in the New Deal, a series of social and economic reforms that helped revitalize the USA. Though the New Deal was not entirely effective, Roosevelt was the only president to be elected four times, and remained in power till his death in April 1945.

The White House.

PROHIBITION

President Roosevelt revoked prohibition in 1933. It had been introduced in 1919, and instead of providing a safe and sober society as intended, it instead inspired gang warfare and crime. Al Capone (1899–1947), a noted gangster engaged in smuggling and bootlegging became the symbol for lawlessness related to prohibition in the 1920s and 30s.

1867 Alaska bought from Russia.
1876 U.S. troops defeated by Sioux Indians at Little Big Horn.
1890 U.S. massacres Sioux at Wounded Knee.
1897–1991 Life of Frank Capra, great film director.
1898 Spanish–American War fought; peace treaty gives independence to Cuba; Philippines, Puerto Rico, and Guam come under United States.
1906 President Theodore Roosevelt visits Panama, first visit by any president abroad.

1908 Henry Ford introduces mass production of low-cost car.
1914 Panama Canal across Central America opens, connects Atlantic and Pacific oceans.
1915 *Birth of a Nation* is pioneering U.S. movie.
1917 U.S. enters World War I.
1920 Women granted right to vote.
1935 Social Security Act passed.
1935–77 Life of great pop and rock singer Elvis Presley.

World War II and afterwards

The Statue of Liberty in New York.

The Second World War began in 1939, involving several countries across Europe. In 1941, the USA joined in the war after Japan attacked the U.S. navy base at Pearl Harbor.

Franklin Roosevelt died just before the end of World War II and was replaced by the vice president, Harry Truman, whose first task was to conclude the war. While Germany surrendered in May 1945, Japan surrendered in August after the controversial bombing of Hiroshima and Nagasaki. In his domestic policies, Truman introduced a 21-point programme, which included policies to control prices, increase employment, and guarantee civil rights.

CIVIL RIGHTS MOVEMENT

After the Civil War of 1861–65 laws were passed to provide voting and other rights to blacks. Despite this the southern states continued their discrimination against them. A long Civil Rights Movement followed, in which many groups and people participated. Among the main leaders was Martin Luther King. Many others were part of the movement, including Rosa Parks (1913–2005), and Malcolm X (b.1925; assassinated 1965). Martin Luther King's efforts were recognized in the award of the Nobel Peace Prize in 1964. However, he was assassinated in 1968.

Rosa Parks said "No" to discrimination in Alabama and launched the Mongomery Bus Boycott.

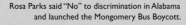

Milestone Events

1941 American film *Citizen Kane* is produced, considered one of the best ever made.
• Japanese attack naval fleet in Pearl Harbor, Hawaii; U.S. enters World War II.
1947 Marshall Plan announced to provide aid for Europe.
• Atomic Energy commission founded.
1949 United States, Canada, and 10 European nations form North Atlantic Treaty Organization (NATO).

1950–53 U.S. involved in war in Korea.
1951 J.D. Salinger (1919–2010) writes *Catcher in the Rye,* a cult novel on adolescence and alienation.
1955 U.S. begins 20-year involvement in Vietnam.
1958 National Aeronautics and Space Administration (NASA) founded.
1961 Alan B. Shepard is astronaut in first manned U.S. space flight.
1962 Cuban missile crisis.

In 1948 Truman won the presidential election, and initiated policies known as the Fair Deal, which incorporated social security programmes. Truman was followed by President Eisenhower (1953–61), and then by John F. Kennedy (1961–63).

Despite the inauguration of the United Nations after the war, hostility grew between the USA and USSR, known as the Cold War. Both countries headed defensive alliances opposed to each other. Within America communists were persecuted, and externally the country began to get involved in wars to suppress communism, mainly in Korea (1950–53) and Vietnam (from 1955). Finally, under president Nixon (1969–74), the Vietnam War ended. The war had proved a huge drain on resources, and had become extremely unpopular among liberals and students in the USA.

A thaw began between the two power blocs in the 1970s.

President Nixon's second term began in January 1973, but facing the "Watergate" scandal, when the Democratic Party's officies in the Watergate building were broken into by members of the Republican Party, he resigned. Succeeding presidents were Gerald Ford (1974–77), Jimmy Carter (1977–81), and Ronald Reagan (1981–89). Each took steps to strengthen U.S. defense systems while improving relations with other countries.

JOHN F KENNEDY

Young and charming, John F Kennedy of the Democratic Party became president in 1961 at the age of 43. In his foreign policy he faced a crisis in Cuba, and tried to improve relations with the USSR. In his internal policies, he did his best to ensure civil rights. Kennedy was assassinated on September 22, 1963, but his policies were incorporated in the Civil Rights Act of 1964.

John F. Kennedy.

1964 Civil Rights Act signed which bars discrimination in public places based on race or color.

1965 Voting Rights Act supplements Civil Rights Act of 1964; social welfare extended in education, health, housing.

• Immigration and Nationality Services act allows entry Into the U.S. of non-European people.

1968 Civil Rights Act bans discrimination in the sale or renting of housing.

1969 July 20, astronauts Neil Armstrong and Edwin Aldrin are first humans to land on moon in *Apollo 11* spaceship.

1974 President Nixon resigns after Watergate scandal; succeeded by vice president Gerald Ford.

1975 U.S. *Apollo* and Soviet *Soyuz* spacecraft linked together in space.

1977 First of *Star Wars* series of films released.

1978 U.S. organizes Middle East summit at Camp David; Israel and Egypt move towards peace.

NORTH AMERICA

1990–2010

President Barack Hussein Obama.

Presidents of the USA during these years, George H. W. Bush (1989-1993), Bill Clinton (1993-2001), George W. Bush (2001-09), and Barack Obama (b.1961), America's first black president, had to focus both on internal issues and world problems.

1991 saw a change in the world with the collapse of the USSR. The cold war ended, and the USA's relationship with the USSR, and later Russia, improved. Russia was no longer as powerful as the old USSR, and the USA became the greatest power in the world.

A new problem arose, of a rise in terrorism worldwide. Terrorism also directly affected the USA. Among the deadly attacks in the U.S. were the bombing in Oklahoma city in 1995, and the attacks on the World Trade Center and Washington D.C. on September, 2001. In retaliation, the USA invaded Afghanistan, as the chief suspect, Osama bin Laden, was believed to be hiding there.

The internal security system was also restructured. In 2002, a new post of Homeland Security (DHS) was created to protect against terrorism, combining various federal agencies. A new National Missile Defense programme was inaugurated. In 2003 immigration rules were tightened.

In 2003, the U.S. invaded Iraq, believing that they had "weapons of mass destruction" that could pose a threat to the world. U.S. troops still remain there.

U.S. troops in Afghanistan.

Milestone Events

1979 Diplomatic relations established between the U.S. and China.

1981 Sandra Day O'Connor is first female Supreme Court judge.

1983 U.S. invades Grenada, removes communist government.

1987 Intermediate Nuclear Force (INF) treaty signed by USA and USSR to reduce intermediate-range and shorter-range nuclear missiles.

1991 U.S. attacks Iraq after it invades Kuwait.

1993 North American Free Trade Agreement (NAFTA), to establish free trade between the United States, Canada, and Mexico, is signed.

• Toni Morrison (b.1931) wins Nobel Prize for Literature.

1997 Great American film, *Titanic*, produced.

1999–2003 *Matrix* futuristic film trilogy produced.

2001 September 11, terrorists hijack and crash U.S. commercial airliners into the twin towers of the World Trade Center in New York City and into

CINEMA

U.S. cinema, broadly known as Hollywood, is famous the world over. Among great American film companies are Walt Disney, founded in 1923, which is today one of Hollywood's biggest studios, and which also owns eleven theme parks and several television networks. Other great companies include Warner Brothers, founded in 1918, and Universal. Hollywood has gone through several different phases, recently focusing on futuristic and innovative films.

Marilyn Monroe and another famous actress Jane Russell.

Economic downturn and recovery

D uring these years there were several economic crises. 2001 saw the collapse of the energy company, Enron, and 2002 that of the telecommunications giant, WorldCom.

The economic problems of the U.S. came to a head in 2008, with the failure of important banks and financial institutions. This had repercussions all over the world, despite government attempts to rescue and revive the banks. However, the economy began to recover from 2009 onwards. A package for economic stimulus, the American Recovery and Reinvestment Act, was signed by the new president, Barack Obama, in February 2009. Another major achievement of Obama ws the Patient Protection and Affordable Care Act (March 2010) a comprehensive health-care act. On the international front, Obama has reduced and promised withdrawal of troops in Iraq, while stepping-up efforts in Afghanistan.

FAST FOOD

American fast-food chains are spread across the world. Though there are several of them, McDonald's typifies the ubiquitous fast-food culture. Begun in 1940, McDonald's operates in 119 countries with over 31,000 restaurants worldwide. The signature Big Mac burger turned 40 in 2008 and sells over 550 million units a year.

---

the Pentagon in Washington, D.C., killing more than 3,000 people. A fourth plane crash lands.
- U.S. attacks Afghanistan.
2003 U.S. invades Iraq.
- U.S. space shuttle *Columbia* disentegrates killing all seven astronauts.
2005 Hurricane Katrina hits the Gulf of Mexico, flooding New Orleans; thousands flee.
2007 Nancy Pelosi of Democratic Party becomes first woman Speaker of the House.

- Harper Lee (b.1926) author of great novel *To Kill a Mocking Bird* (1960) is awarded Presidential Medal of Freedom, highest U.S. civilian award, for her contribution to literature.
2009 President Barack Obama wins Nobel Peace Prize.
2010 President Obama and Russian president Medvedev sign treaty to reduce nuclear arms.
- A massive oil spill in the Gulf of Mexico threatens several southern US states.

Mexico is a federal constitutional republic with thirty-one states and one federal district, the capital city. It has rich mineral resources and is an exporter of oil. Mexico had several early civilizations, including the Olmec, the Toltec, the Mixtec, the Maya, and the Aztec, and their ancient settlements are a major tourist attraction. Spanish settlers reached the area in the sixteenth century. After independence from Spain Mexico faced considerable instability. A revolution took place in 1910, which led to a new constitution in 1917, on which Mexico's current political system is based. This is a republican presidential system with three elected levels of government: the Federal Union, the state governments, and the municipal governments. There is a bicameral legislature.

Aztec vulture vessel

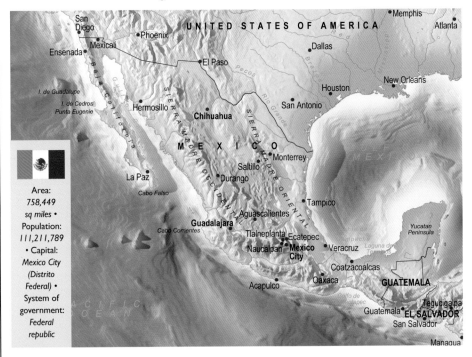

Area:
758,449
sq miles •
Population:
111,211,789
• Capital:
Mexico City
(Distrito
Federal) •
System of
government:
Federal
republic

Milestone Events

c. 1500 BCE–900 CE Early cultures including Olmec, Zapotec, Maya.

c. 1325 CE Aztecs found city of Tenochtitlan in region of present day Mexico City.

1521 Spanish conquest of Aztecs completed.

1810 Mexican independence proclaimed.

1821 Spain recognizes independence of Mexico.

1824 Mexico becomes a republic.

1846–48 Mexico loses war with United States, cedes large territory including Texas.

1863 French troops occupy Mexico city.

1864 French make Maximilian of Austria emperor of Mexico.

1867 Mexican forces regain control, Maxmilian is shot.

1910 Revolution begins in Mexico, led by Emiliano Zapata, Francisco Madero, and Pancho Villa.

1911 Francisco Madero is president.

1913 Madero assassinated, unrest in Mexico.

1929 National Revolutionary Party, later Institutional Revolutionary Party (PRI) is formed.

MEXICAN CULTURE

Mexico has numerous television networks. Mexican music includes traditional as well as classical, rock, and pop: Mexican ranchero and mariachi music is popular in many countries. Manuel Maria Ponce (1882–1948) and Carlos Chavez (1899-1978) were great classical music composers and conductors. Renowned artists include Frida Kahlo (1907–54), known for self-portraits, and Diego Rivera (1886–1957), a well-known mural painter. Among writers, Octavio Paz (1914–98) won the Nobel Prize in 1990. Other internationally recognized authors include Carlos Fuentes (b.1928); Alfonso Reyes (1889–1959); Juan Rulfo (1917–86); Elena Poniatowska (b.1932) of mixed Mexican and Polish descent who settled in Mexico; and Jose Emilio Pacheco (b.1939). Football and baseball are popular sports in Mexico, along with Charreada (rodeo events). Bullfighting takes place in most large cities. Masked wrestling is another popular sport. Mexican food is spicy and distinctive, and the country is also known for uniquely flavored chocolate.

La Princesa, female masked wrestling star.

The Institutional Revolutionary Party (PRI) was in power from the time of independence. A non-PRI candidate, Vincent Fox of the National Action Party (PAN) became the president for the first time in 2000, though the PRI had already faced losses in 1997. The PRI regained some ground in 2009.

Mexico is a mix of the old and the new, and faces a number of problems. Wealth distribution is unequal, and every year thousands of Mexicans try to illegally cross the border into the USA. Mexico also faces a problem of warfare between powerful drug dealers. Society is largely a mix of Native American and Spanish. Some of the Native American groups have an ongoing struggle for more rights.

Mexico is industrially well-developed, both in the manufacturing and service sectors, and has free trade agreements with a number of countries including the USA and Canada. It is known for its Native American crafts, including pottery, jewelry, and textiles.

Revolutionary general Pancho Villa.

1968 XIX Olympic Games held in Mexico City; student demonstration held, security forces open fire, kill or injure hundreds.

1976 Offshore oil reserves discovered.

1985 Earthquake hits Mexico city, thousands killed.

1994 North American Free Trade Agreement (NAFTA); comes into effect.

• Zapatista National Liberation Army, group of Native American rebels, start revolt in Chiapas.

1995 Government and Zapatista National Liberation Front (EZLN) reach agreement.

1999 Rains, floods, and earthquakes devastate Mexico.

2000 Vincent Fox of PAN party elected president, ends 71 years of PRI rule.

2006 Felipe Calderon elected president.

• USA decides to build fence along Mexican border to halt illegal immigration.

2007 Rains flood Tabasco state, over 500,000 homeless.

CENTRAL AMERICA

entral America, an isthmus that forms a bridge between North and South America, and is technically included in the continent of North America, includes the states of Belize, Costa Rica, El Salvador, Guatemala; Honduras, Nicaragua, and Panama. In ancient days this region had a number of settlements, of which the Maya civilization was the most important. On the eve of the Spanish conquest, the population in the region could have been as much as six million.

Belize

The spectacular coral reefs off Belize.

Belize
Area: 8,867
sq miles •
Population:
307,899
• Capital:
Belmopan •
System of
government:
Constitutional
monarchy
with
parliamentary
democracy

ormerly known as British Honduras, Belize has the world's second largest coral reef with 200 islands. Belize is the only country in Central America with English as its official language, though Spanish is increasingly being used. The British monarch is still the chief of state, with a governor-general as her representative in Belize. The prime minister is the head of state. Belize has an elected legislature, a bicameral National Assembly, and the leader of the majority party becomes the prime minister. Today the service sector is prominent in the economy, and agricultural and marine products are exported. Oil exploitation began in 2006, increasing the growth potential. Drug trafficking is one of its problems.

Milestone Events

c.1500 BCE–c. 1500 CE Maya and other indigenous cultures in the region.

16th CENTURY Spain occupies and conquers most of Central America.

1821–23 Spanish-controlled Central American states gain freedom from Spain.

1823 United Provinces of Central America established; includes Guatemala, Honduras, El Salvador, Nicaragua, Costa Rica; **1838–40** constituent nations proclaim independence.

1944 Guatemala educator Juan José Arevalo is elected president, new constitution introduced.

1961 Military coup by right-wing National Conciliation Party in El Salvador.

1963–4 Irazu volcano erupts in Costa Rica.

1967 Miguel Angel Asturias of Guatemala wins Nobel Prize for Literature.

1973 British Honduras changes name to Belize.

1980 Archbishop Romero killed in El Salvador by government death squads; civil war breaks out.

Costa Rica

Costa Rica is headed by an elected president. It has better living standards than its neighbors, and is a stable state with a well-developed welfare system. Costa Rica does not have a standing army. The economy is mainly dependent on agriculture, along with manufacturing industries, particularly electronics, and tourism. Though indigenous populations are few today, their culture survives in textiles, jewelry, and craft designs. More than 1000 species of orchids are found here.

Costa Rica
Area: 19,730 sq miles • Population: 4,253,877 • Capital: San José • System of government: Republic

El Salvador

Republic of El Salvador
Area: 8,124 sq miles • Population: 7,185,218 (July 2009 est.) • Capital: San Salvador • System of government: Republic

Though a tiny country, El Salvador is well industrialized, but has been affected by earthquakes and civil war. Its name means "the saviour," referring to Jesus Christ. El Salvador is headed by a president elected for a five-year term, and has a unicameral legislature. From around 1979, the left-wing Farabundo Martí National Liberation Front organized guerrilla activities, and protested against death squads backed by the army, which killed thousands. After a peace accord signed in 1991 between the government and the Farabundo, important military and political reforms have been introduced. El Salvador adopted the U.S. dollar as its currency in 2001.

Guatemala

Guatemala is headed by a president, elected for a four-year term, who is assisted by a council of ministers. The legislature is unicameral. Guatemala has had a series of military and civilian governments as well as 36 years of civil war, ended in 1996. After this the economy began to stabilize, but inequalities and poverty persist. The indigenous Maya descendents amount to about 50 per cent of the population.

Guatemala
Area: total: 42,042 sq miles • Population: 13,276,517 • Capital: Guatemala City • System of government: Republic

---

1981 Belize gains independence from UK.
1987 President Oscar Arias Sanchez of Costa Rica wins Nobel Peace Prize for role in ending regional conflict; reelected **2006**.
1991 Guatemala finally recognizes Belize after years of claiming its territory.
1992 Civil war in El Salvador ends after UN brokers peace.
1993 Guatemala resumes claims to Belize territories.
1996 Long-running civil unrest ends in Guatemala.

1998 Hurricane Mitch affects Guatemala, Honduras, Nicaragua; around 20,000 killed.
2005 Tropical storm Stan kills hundreds in Guatemala.
2006 USA–Central America Free Trade Agreement (CAFTA) comes into effect; most countries in region eventually join.
2008 Dean Barrow of the United Democratic Party becomes Belize's first black prime minister.
2009 Left-wing leader Mauricio Funes of FMLN wins elections in El Salvador.

CENTRAL AMERICA

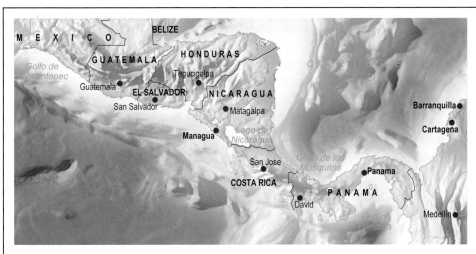

Honduras

Honduras today is headed by an elected president and has a unicameral legislature, but in the past the country saw a number of dictatorships and unstable governments. In the 1980s Honduras was a base for guerrillas fighting against the Nicaraguan government. However, the situation improved after 1993 with the election of Carlos Roberto Reina, who initiated economic and political reforms.

Carlos Roberto Reina of Honduras.

Honduras has rich mineral deposits, forests, and a variety of wildlife Bananas and coffee are important exports. The culture is primarily Spanish, its architecture reflecting a Native American and Spanish mix. There are several ancient Maya sites including the important ceremonial site, Copan. Honduras' main problems are inequality, street crime, and drug trafficking.

Honduras
Area: *43,278 sq miles* •
Population: *7,833,696*
• Capital: *Tegucigalpa*
• System of government: *Republic*

Milestone Events

c.1500 BCE–c.1500 CE Maya and other indigenous cultures in the region.
16th CENTURY Spain occupies and conquers most of Central America.
1821–23 Central American states gain freedom from Spain.
1822 Panama part of the Republic of Gran Colombia with Colombia, Ecuador, Venezuela; dissolves 1830, Panama remains with Columbia.

1823 Honduras, Nicaragua part of United Province of Central America; 1838–40 constituent nations proclaim independence.
1903 Panama gains independence from Columbia.
1914 Panama Canal completed and owned by USA.
1932–48 Tiburcio Carias is benign dictator of Honduras.
1961 Left-wing Sandinista National Liberation Front (FSLN) founded in Nicaragua.

Nicaragua

Nicaragua is headed by an elected president and has a unicameral legislature. The Somoza family of Spanish descent occupied the top posts in the country from 1937, and appropriated much of government revenue. Following a civil war, Sandinista guerrillas came to power in 1979, and, led by Daniel Ortega, began redistributing property and improving health and education facilities. However their leftist leanings led the U.S. to sponsor a counter-revolution and to impose trade sanctions. In elections from 1990 to 2001, the Sandinistas were defeated, but in 2006 former Sandinista President Daniel Ortega was reelected. Nicaragua's economy had been devastated by civil war and after a brief revival, was again wrecked by Hurricane Mitch in 1998. It is now being restored, and tourism is increasing, its forests and beaches among the main attractions.

Nicaragua
Area: *50,336 sq miles* •
Population: *5,891,199* • Capital: *Managua* •
System of government: *Republic*

Panama

Panama is strategically located between North and South America, while the Panama Canal links the Atlantic and Pacific oceans. The country is headed by a president, elected by popular vote, and has a unicameral legislature. Panama has disbanded its regular military forces, but special forces can be created when required.

Panama has been closely linked to the USA, which constructed the canal, and until recently, retained control of it. Revenue from the Panama Canal contributes considerably to the economy. Panama's Colon free trade zone, which houses at least 2000 companies, is the second largest in the world. In 2006 a free-trade agreement was signed with the U.S., though Panama is not part of CAFTA. Income distribution is unequal in the country, and Panama is also a transit point for drugs. Panama has about 400 coral islands, of which around 50 are inhabited by Cuna Indians, who have political autonomy. Cuna textiles are famous and tourism is increasing on these islands.

Republic of Panama
Area: *29,120 sq miles* •
Population: *3,360,474* • Capital: *Panama* •
System of government: *Republic*

1963 Coup by Osvald Lopez Arellano in Honduras.

1968–81 In Panama, General Omar Torrijos Herrerra, rules as dictator; **1981** dies in plane crash.

1972 Managua in Nicaragua is hit by earthquake, thousands killed.

1983 Manuel Noriega takes over Panama government, rules as dictator, deposed 1989.

1985–90 Daniel Ortega of the FSLN is president of Nicaragua; **2006** reelected.

1991 Panama disbands regular military forces.

1998 Hurricane Mitch affects Honduras, Guatemala, Nicaragua; around 20,000 killed.

1999 Mireya Moscoso becomes first woman president of Panama.

2000 Panama gains control of Panama Canal.

2004 Martin Torrijos Espino, son of former dictator Omar Torrijos, elected president in Panama.

2006 USA–Central America Free Trade Agreement (CAFTA); most countries in region eventually join.

2009 Military coup in Honduras.

CENTRAL AMERICA

The Caribbean islands are located east of Central America, mainly in three arc-shaped lines between Mexico and Florida. Early settlers in the Caribbean Islands were various American Indian groups including the Taino (Arawaks), Ciboney, and Carib among others. In the sixteenth century Europeans began to occupy the islands and exploit the gold resources there. The main occupiers were the British and French, but the Spanish, Portuguese, and Dutch also held territories, while Denmark and Sweden made brief inroads. Sugar and later cacao and other plantations were established in the islands, and proved lucrative, run with slave labor from Africa. After the abolition of slavery, labor was imported from India, China, and other countries.

Haiti was the first to gain independence, after a long struggle. Gradually, many other islands gained independence in the twentieth century, though some remain under various countries. Today the islands are grouped into 27 territories including thirteen independent nations. The largest Caribbean nation is Cuba, followed by the Dominican Republic. Cuba is the only communist state.

Antigua and Barbuda
Area: *171 sq miles* • Population: *85,632* • Capital: *St Johns* • System of government: *Constitutional monarchy with parliamentary democracy*

The Bahamas
Area: *5,282 sq miles* • Population: *307,552* • Capital: *Nassau* • System of government: *Constitutional monarchy with parliamentary democracy*

Barbados
Area: *166 sq miles* • Population: *284,589* • Capital: *Bridgetown* • System of government: *Constitutional monarchy with parliamentary democracy*

Cuba, Republic of,
Area: *42,803 sq miles* • Population: *11,451,652* • Capital: *Havana* • System of government: *Communist*

Dominica, Commonwealth of
Area: *290 sq miles* • Population: *72,660* • Capital: *Roseau* • System of government: *Republic*

Dominican Republic
Area: *18,792 sq miles* • Population: *9,650,054* • Capital: *Santo Domingo* • System of government: *Republic*

Milestone Events

2400 BCE Early settlements in Caribbean islands.
1492–94 Spanish reach the region, conquer Hispaniola (modern Haiti and Dominican Republic).
1511 Spanish conquer Cuba.
1627 British settle in Barbados.
16th–17th CENTURIES Sugar and tobacco plantations introduced in islands.
1655 British occupy Jamaica.
1697 Saint-Domingue, western part of Hispaniola, (now Haiti) ceded to France by Spain.

1763 Dominica comes under British.
1783 St Vincent and the Grenadines comes under British.
1804 Haiti gains independence.
1814 St. Lucia comes under British.
1834 Slavery abolished in British islands.
1843 Santo Domingo (eastern Hispaniola) proclaims independence as Dominican Republic.
1898 Cuba freed from Spanish, occupied by Americans.

Each island group has its own unique cultural heritage, with Native American culture overlaid by European influences, and blended with features of African and Asian (mainly Indian and Chinese) settlers. European as well as Creole languages — a mix of African syntax and European words—are spoken. Caribbean music has influenced music around the world.

The USA has been closely involved in the region, directly interfering in the affairs of some states such as Cuba, Haiti, and Grenada. Puerto Rico and the Virgin islands are under the USA.

Before gaining independence, ten former British territories formed the West Indies Federation between 1958 and 1962. Though this was dissolved, they still retain certain common aspects, including membership of the Commonwealth, and even a common West Indies cricket team.

The islands have different levels of development and economic growth. Among the more prosperous are the Bahamas, which is an international banking hub, and Trinidad and Tobago, which has oil resources. The strategic location of the islands makes them centers of trade, but at the same time has negative aspects, as some are bases for the transit trade in drugs. All the islands have great scenic beauty, and are popular with tourists.

St Vincent and the Grenadines
Area: 150 sq miles • Population: 104,574 • Capital: Kingstown • System of government: Constitutional monarchy with parliamentary democracy

St.Kitts and Nevis
Area: 101 sq miles • Population: 40,131 • Capital: Basseterre • System of government: Constitutional monarchy with parliamentary democracy

Haiti
Area: 10,714 sq miles • Population: 9,035,536 • Capital: Port-au-Prince • System of government: Republic

Trinidad and Tobago
Area: 1,980 sq miles • Population: 1,229,953 • Capital: Port-of-Spain • System of government: Republic

Grenada
Area: 133 sq miles • Population: 90,735 • Capital: St.George's • System of government: Constitutional monarchy with parliamentary democracy

Jamaica
Area: 4,244 sq miles • Population: 2,825,928 • Capital: Kingston • System of government: Constitutional monarchy with parliamentary democracy

St.Lucia
Area: 238 sq miles • Population: 160,267 • Capital: Castries • System of government: Constitutional monarchy with parliamentary democracy

Other territories
British territories: Anguilla, Cayman Islands, Montserrat, British Virgin Islands, Turks and Caicos
Dutch territories: Aruba, Netherlands Antilles
American territories: Puerto Rico, United States Virgin islands
French territories: Guadelope, Martinique, Saint Barthelemy, Saint Martin

1902 Tomas Estrada Palma is first Cuban president; USA retains right to intervene in Cuba.
1910 Oil is discovered in Trinidad.
1959 Fidel Castro seizes power in Cuba.
1961 Barbados gains internal self-government.
1962 Jamaica, Trinidad and Tobago gain independence from Britain.
1966 Barbados gains independence.
1967 Che Guevara, associate of Castro, captured in Bolivia and executed.

1973 Caricom, common market formed.
• Bahamas and most other British islands gain independence by 1983.
1983 Military coup in Grenada, USA and 6 other Caribbean nations intervene.
2004 Jean Bertrande Aristide, president of Haiti, deposed.
2008 Raul Castro succeeds Fidel Castro as president of Cuba.
2010 Earthquake devastates Haiti.

South America covers 6,890,000 square miles and is fourth in size among the continents, but fifth in population. It comprises twelve independent countries and three dependecies. The Amazon river with its thick rainforests flows through the region, and other features are Angel Falls in Venezuela, the world's highest waterfall; Lake Titicaca between Bolivia and Peru, the highest navigable lake; the dry Atacama desert

and the 5500-mile-long Andes mountains. There are several volcanoes in the ranges and earthquakes are common. South America has plentiful mineral resources, including petroleum, as well as diamonds and emeralds. It is home to some unique plant and animal species.

Che Guevara.

HISTORY

The region may have been occupied by migrants who crossed the Bering land bridge and reached North America between 30,000 and 10,000 BCE, or even earlier. By around 7000 BCE there were agrarian settlements in the region, and, in the Andes highlands, animals such as llamas and alpacas were domesticated by around 3500 BCE. There were numerous early cultures in the region, among them the Chico and Nazca, followed by the Chimu, Huari, and Inca civilizations.

After Christopher Columbus reached America in the sixteenth century, the Pope helped settle a dispute by Spain and Portugal over control of the area. Apart from Brazil, taken by Portugal, most of South America was under the Spanish. Guyana finally came under the British, while Suriname was under the Dutch. French Guyana remains with the French. From the sixteenth century African slaves were imported to the region as labor, and slavery was abolished only in the nineteenth century.

The majority of countries attained independence in the early nineteenth century, but afterwards there were several conflicts and revolutions in the region. By the late twentieth century the region had a large number of socialist leaders but at the same time had begun to follow free market principles, however, although economic growth has been considerable, there is uneven distribution of wealth, and a wide gap between rich and poor. Large cities generally have a better standard of living.

CULTURE

Spanish is the official language of nine of the twelve countries, while English is the official language in Guyana, Portuguese in Brazil, and Dutch in Suriname. In addition, a number of Native American languages are spoken, of which Guarani is an official language jointly with Spanish in Paraguay.

The Spanish and Portuguese heritage is reflected in religion, as most South Americans are Roman Catholic. Musical styles such as the tango and bossa nova are known all over the world, and there are some rhythms that are recognized as uniquely South American.

An Argentinian "cowboy" at work.

SOUTH AMERICA

Columbia

Columbia gained independence from Spain in 1810 as part of Gran Columbia. It became a separate republic in 1830. For forty years Columbia has faced serious problems from both left- and right-wing insurgent groups, particularly the Revolutionary Armed Forces of Columbia (FARC). Drug-trafficking and social inequality are other serious problems.

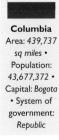

Columbia
Area: *439,737 sq miles* •
Population: *43,677,372* •
Capital: *Bogota*
• System of government: *Republic*

Guyana

Guyana
Area: *83,000 sq miles* •
Population: *752,940*
• Capital: *Georgetown*
• System of government: *Republic*

Once occupied by Native American tribes including the Arawik and Carib, and later settled by the Dutch, Guyana then came under Britain. It is the only south American state that is English-speaking and a member of the British Commonwealth. There are political and ethnic tensions between descendents of African slaves and descendents of laborers from India and other regions. The economy is poor, but offshore oil provides prospects of improvement. The country has abundant forests with some unique wildlife.

Milestone Events

13,000–7000 BCE Stone age settlements in region.

c.1000 BCE–1500 CE Numerous Native American settlements in the region.

1500 onwards Spanish, Dutch, and British establish settlements.

1809 Latin American revolutions against Spain begin; eventually win independence.

1814 Britain takes Guyana from the Dutch; **1831** declared British colony, British Guiana.

1819 Simon Bolivar (1783–1830) becomes president of the Republic of Gran Colombia, comprising modern states of Venezuela, Ecuador, Colombia, and Panama.

1829–30 Venezuela and Ecuador leave Gran Columbia; Columbia and Panama become New Granada; **1886** Republic of Columbia; **1903** Panama separates.

1870–88 Venezuela stable under Antonio Guzman Blanco.

Suriname

The Palm Gardens (Palmentuin) at Paramaribo, Suriname.

Suriname
Area: *63,251 sq miles* •
Population: *481,267* •
Capital: *Paramaribo*
• System of government: *Republic*

Suriname was occupied by the Dutch in the seventeenth century. After the abolition of slavery in 1863, labor was brought from India and Indonesia and there are political and ethnic tensions between descendents of these groups and descendents of Africans. There was civil war in 1986–91 following a coup. Suriname has tropical rainforests and rich wildlife. The economy is based on mining, particularly of bauxite, but Suriname was granted a share in an offshore oil region in 2007.

Venezuela

Venezuela
Area: *352,144 sq miles* •
Population: *26,814,843* •
Capital: *Caracas*
• System of government: *Federal republic*

As well as the mainland country, Venezuela includes eleven federally controlled island groups.

From 1959 governments have been democratically elected. There is a unicameral legislative assembly and the chief of state and head of government is a president elected by popular vote. The socialist policies of Hugo Chavez, who became president in 1999, aim to improve the standard of living. Chavez has raised the minimum wage, nationalized several industries, and centralized the economy. Venezuela has great natural beauty, with mountains, tropical forests, and beaches. It is rich in mineral resources, and its economy is largely based on oil.

Hugo Chavez during a visit to Brazil.

1885 Conservative Party rules Columbia for next 45 years; country centralized.
1908–35 Venezuela under dictator Juan Vicente Gomez becomes world's largest exporter of oil.
1954 Suriname gains limited self-government.
1960 Venezuela is a founding member of OPEC.
1966 British Guiana gains independence as Guyana.
1973 Guyana joins Caribbean Community and Single Market, Caricom; **1995** Suriname.
1975 Suriname becomes independent.

• Carlos Perez, president of Venezuela, wins Earth Care award for protecting the environment.
1982 Gabriel Garcia Marquez (b. 1928) of Columbia receives Nobel Prize in Literature.
1998 The left-winger Hugo Chavez (b. 1954) wins presidential election in Venezuela; reelected twice.
• Forest fires devastate Guyana.
1999 Floods and landslides in north Venezuela.
2010 About 300 cocaine-trafficking gangs are active in Columbia.

SOUTH AMERICA

Chile

Chile includes a mainland area and several islands, including Easter Island. Initially occupied by Araucanians, a Native American group, northern Chile came under the Incas in the fifteenth century. The Spanish next conquered the region before Chile attained independence in the early nineteenth century.

In 1970 Salvador Allende was elected president, and began a policy of nationalization and a controlled economy. He brought in higher wages and initiated a redistribution of income.

Salvador Allende.

He was overthrown and killed by General Pinochet in 1973. In 1989, the first presidential elections for 19 years brought in Patricio Alwyn Azocar as president, and Chile gradually emerged as a functioning democracy. Chile has a modern and cosmopolitan urban culture, while rural culture has an Araucanian base overlaid by Spanish traditions. Two great poets of Chile have won the Nobel Prize for Literature: Gabriela Mistral and Pablo Neruda.

Chile
Area:
*291,932
sq miles* •
Population:
16,601,707
• Capital:
Santiago •
System of
government:
Republic

Chile has rich mineral resources, particularly copper. There are some dense rainforests, which contrast with the Atacama desert region in the north. The high Andes mountains extend across the length of the country.

Milestone Events

8000 BCE Early settlements in the region.

c. 1450 Incas conquer part of the region.

1532 Spanish begin to occupy the region.

1563 Quito, Ecuador, becomes a seat of Spanish colonial government.

1569 In Peru, Spanish viceroy Francisco de Toledo's system of government lasts 200 years.

1821 José San Martin leads nationalist forces, enters Lima from Chile; Peru declared independent.

1824 Simon Bolivar defeats Spanish at Junin and Ayacucho; ends wars of independence..

1879–84 War of the Pacific, Chile defeats Peru and Bolivia, gains present northern regions.

1904 and 1942 Ecuador loses territories in a series of conflicts with neighbors.

1925 New constitution in Chile expands voting rights.

1945 Gabriela Mistral (pseudonym of Lucila Godoy Alcayaga, 1889–1957) Chilean poet,

Ecuador

Iguanas in the Galapagos Islands.

Ecuador includes a mainland area and the Archipielago de Colon (Galapagos Islands), known for its unique animals and ecosystem. Occupied from about 8000 BCE, Ecuador was later a part of the Maya civilisation and the Inca empire, before coming under the Spanish. Civil wars, revolutions, and rapid changes in governments were common after independence. In 2008, Ecuador's twentieth constitution came into force. The economy is largely dependent on its petroleum reserves. After facing economic problems in 1999–2000, reforms were introduced and the U.S. dollar adopted as the currency. In coastal areas, where there was slave labor, there is a Spanish–African culture.

Ecuador
Area: *109,483 sq miles* • Population: *14,573,101* • Capital: *Quito* • System of government: *Republic*

Peru

Peru has a varied terrain: An arid coastal region where most of the cities and industries are located; the sierra upland region, with the high peaks of the Andes ranges; and the montana, a less elevated region.

A traditional precarious bridge in the Andes.

Peru had several ancient cultures including the Chavin and Moche, before falling to the Incas around 1500 and the Spanish in 1533. Peru declared independence in 1821, though the Spanish were not defeated till 1824. The second half of the twentieth century saw instability, military coups, and guerrilla warfare by insurgent groups, among which was the Maoist Sendero Luminoso (Shining Path). With President Alberto Fujimori's election in 1990, there was an improvement in social stability, and the economy has improved in the new millennium.

Peru has numerous archaeological sites, including the famous remains at Machu Picchu. The country has rich mineral resources and tropical forests.

Peru
Area: *496,225 sq miles* • Population: *29,546,963* • Capital: *Lima* • System of government: *Republic*

scholar, and diplomat, wins Nobel Prize for Literature.
1960 Earthquakes and tidal waves cause damage in Chile.
1971 Pablo Neruda (pseudonym of Neftali Ricardo Reyes y Basoalto, 1904–73), Chilean poet, wins Nobel Prize for Literature.
1972 Ecuador begins export of petroleum; economy improves.

1980 Shining Path guerrillas begin armed struggle in Peru.
1990 Alberto Fujimori is elected president in Peru; reelected 1995, 2000, but resigns over corruption scandal.
1995–99 War between Peru and Ecuador.
2001 Alejandro Toledo becomes first Native American president of Peru.
2009 Peru enters into trade agreement with U.S.
2010 Major earthquake in Chile.

SOUTH AMERICA

Bolivian women in the bowler hats
they have adopted since the 1920s.

Bolivia
Area: 424,164 sq
miles • Population:
9,775,246 •
Capital: La Paz
• System of
government:
Republic

Bolivia

Bolivia, named after Simon Bolivar, who brought freedom to the region, has the high Andes Mountains running north–south, as well as plateaux and lowlands. After independence Bolivia had a turbulent history with a large number of coups and counter-coups. From 1982, conditions improved with democratic elections.

Bolivia's economy used to be largely dependent on tin exports, but in the early 1980s the collapse of this market led to economic problems. In 1985 Sanchez de Lozada, then minister for planning, used radical tactics to reduce inflation from a high of 25,000 percent. Lozada, of the MNR party, later became president (1992-97, and 2002-03) and introduced a number of reforms. However, problems of poverty, inequality, social unrest, and an illegal drug trade continue.

Bolivia has a large Native American population that maintains its languages and many of its traditional practices, overlaid by Spanish influence.

Milestone Events

1500 BCE Early settlements in the region.
300–1000 CE Tiahuanaco civilization flourishes in region of modern Bolivia.
14th–16th CENTURIES Bolivia under Inca empire.
1537 Spanish establish fort on Paraguay river.
1538 Hernando Pizarro of Spain conquers area of Bolivia.
17th–18th CENTURIES Spanish settlements in Bolivia increase; silver mines explored.

1620 Paraguay becomes part of viceroyalty of Peru under Spanish rule.
1726 Spanish take over Uruguay from Portuguese.
1776 Spain creates viceroyalty of La Plata, containing Argentina, Bolivia, Paraguay, and Uruguay.
1811 Paraguay becomes independent from Spain; **1825** Bolivia and Uruguay.
1812–20 Orientales, Uruguayans from the eastern side of the river Plata, fight against Argentinian and Brazilian invaders.

Paraguay

Paraguay
Area:
157,048
sq miles •
Population:
6,995,655
• Capital:
Asuncion •
System of
government:
Republic

The Trans-Chaco Rally, popular with auto drivers since 1971.

Paraguay is divided by the Paraguay river with the Gran Chaco, an alluvial plain, to the west, and a plateau to the east.

The original inhabitants, the Native American tribes of Paraguay, are known as Guarani, which is the language they speak. The Spanish began to occupy the area from 1537, and gradually gained control. In 1865, seeking to expand his territories, president Francisco Solano Lopez (1862–70), led the country into a war against Argentina, Brazil, and Uruguay, which ended in disaster for Paraguay, and prevented her economic development for the next fifty years. The country had 31 presidents between 1904 and 1954, when Alfredo Stroessner (1912–2006) became president, assuming dictatorial powers and remaining in office till 1989.

Paraguayan culture is a mixture of Guaranian and Spanish traditions, with Argentine and other influences.

Uruguay

Uruguay is mainly a region of plains with low hills and plateaux. In the nineteenth century Spain and Portugal vied for control of the area, ending in 1821 when Portugal annexed the territory and it became part of Brazil, though independence was soon achieved.

In the twentieth century there was considerable political instability. The Tupamaros, a revolutionary group, aimed to overthrow the government, and violence escalated in the early 1970s. In 1973 President Bordaberry handed over the government to the military in an attempt to control the situation. The Tupamoros were suppressed, but political conditions were repressive. Uruguay returned to civilian rule in 1985. The economy is largely based on agriculture, though manufacturing and tourism are gaining importance. The country is known for its advanced education and social welfare systems. José Mujica, former Tupamaro guerrilla fighter, was elected president on November 29, 2009.

Uruguay
Area: 68,037
sq miles •
Population:
3,494,382
• Capital:
Montevideo
• System of
government:
Republic.

1814–1840 José Gaspar Rodriguez Francia rules as dictator in Paraguay.
1828 Eastern Republic of Uruguay formed.
1865–70 War of the Triple Alliance fought by Paraguay against Argentina, Brazil, and Uruguay; Paraguay loses much of its territory and population.
1879–84 Bolivia defeated in War of the Pacific.
1903–15 President José Batlle y Ordonez of Uruguay brings in social reforms.

1930 Uruguay hosts first football World Cup.
1932–35 Chaco War between Bolivia and Paraguay; Paraguay wins territory.
1950s National Revolution in Bolivia.
1967 Che Guevara captured and killed in Bolivia.
2005 Evo Morales becomes president of Bolivia.
2008 Fernando Lugo wins presidential election in Paraguay.
2009 New constitution in Bolivia gives more rights to indigenous people.

SOUTH AMERICA

The statue of Christ the Redeemer overlooking Rio de Janeiro.

B razil, the largest country in South America, is a functioning democracy headed by an elected president with a bicameral legislature. The Brazilian federation contains 26 states, one federal district, and a number of municipalities. A country of mountain ranges, plateaux, and river valleys, Brazil also has lowlands in the basin of the river Amazon with tropical rainforests, and several islands. The country has abundant mineral resources including offshore oil, iron ore deposits, gold, and diamonds.

Originally inhabited by Native American groups, including the Arawak, Carib, and Tupi-Guarani, Brazil was occupied by the Portuguese from around 1500, and gained independence in 1822. Initially, Brazil was a monarchy but became a republic in 1889.

Over the years Brazil had a number of both popular and military governments. In 1985 the first elections were held for 21 years. In 1989 Fernando Collor de Mello became

Area:
3,287,612 sq miles •
Population:
198,739,269
• **Capital:**
Brasilia •
System of government:
Federal republic

Milestone Events

c. 8000 BCE Early occupation in the region.
1500 Portuguese explorer Pedro Alvares Cabral lands in the area and claims it for Portugal.
1530s Settlements established at present-day Recife and Salvador.
1580–1640 Brazil comes under Spain as Spanish king rules Portugal.
1763 Rio de Janeiro becomes capital.
1807 Portuguese regent, Prince John, moves to Brazil as Napoleon's army reaches Portugal.

1822 Pedro I, the son of the Portuguese king, declares independence, becomes Emperor of Brazil.
1853 Import of African slaves banned.
1888 Slavery abolished.
1889 Federal republic established.
1930 Military overthrows republic; Getulio Vargas is head of provisional revolutionary government.
1945 Vargas overthrown in another military coup.

president through direct elections, and began a program of privatization. Inequalities in wealth and income led to discontent, and in 2003 left-wing leader Luiz Inacio Lula da Silva became president, and was reelected in 2006. He retained progressive economic policies, but also raised the minimum wage and inaugurated a Zero Hunger program to see that basic food needs were met.

One of the spectacular displays during Rio de Janeiro's annual Carnivale.

Brazil faced an economic crisis in 1991 and again in the late 1990s, but currently the economy is booming, with all sectors well-developed. The country is predicted to become one of the top five economies in the world. Brazil is also a leading political power in the region.

CULTURE

Brazil has a rich culture influenced mainly by Native American, Portuguese, and African traditions. Literature in Brazil dates back to the 16th century, to the writings of the first Portuguese explorers in Brazil. In modern times Brazilian literature has flourished. Among notable names are novelists Jorge Amado (1912–2001), José Lins de Rego (1901–57) and Erico

Pelé, perhaps the world's most famous footballer, in 1960.

Lopes Verissimo (1905–75). In music Heitor Villa-Lobos (1887–1959) was an internationally renowned classical music composer. Specific Brazilian styles that have worldwide popularity include the music for Afro–Brazilian dance forms the samba and bossa nova. Among sports Brazil is known for football, and its national team has won the World Cup several times. Basketball, volleyball, auto racing, and martial arts are other popular sports. Brazilian drivers have won the Formula 1 world championship a number of times.

1946 New constitution introduced.

1950 Football World Cup held in Brazil.

1951 Vargas elected president; 1954 commits suicide when threatened by military.

1960 Capital moves from Rio de Janeiro to the newly built Brasilia.

1974 General Ernesto Geisel becomes president, allows some political freedom.

1992 Earth Summit with 100 world leaders is held in Rio de Janeiro.

1994 Fernando Henrique Cardoso elected president; 1998, reelected.

1998 Forest fires in Amazon basin.

2002 Tumucumaque National Park created, covering 3.8 million hectares, the largest tropical forest reserve in the world.

2004 Brazil's first space rocket successfully launched.

2007 XV Pan American Games held in Rio de Janeiro.

rgentina, the second largest country in South America, has a varied terrain of mountains, plateaux, and plains. Argentina is headed by an elected president serving a four-year term, and has a bicameral legislature.

In the sixteenth century the region was taken over by Spain. A revolutionary movement started in 1810, and in 1816 the United Provinces of South America (later of the Rio de la Plata), declared independence from Spain. Initially the provinces were not really united at all, but under General Juan Manuel de Rosas (1829–52) took the name the Argentine Confederation. By the early nineteenth century, Argentina emerged as a leading nation of South America, but was affected by the economic depression of 1929.

After World War II Juan Peron of the Peronist or Labor Party became president, helped in some areas of government by his popular wife Eva. Peron was overthrown in 1955 but was reelected in 1973 after a series of intervening governments, but he died in

Argentina (Argentine Republic)
Area: 1,073,518 sq miles •
Population: 40,913,584
• Capital: Buenos Aires
• System of Government: Republic

1974, and the military took control from 1976–83. Argentina faced a severe political and economic crisis which reached new depths in 2001–02. President Fernando de la Rua resigned on December 20, 2001, and was succeeded by four presidents within just ten days. An economic emergency followed as

Milestone Events

11,000 BCE First occupation of the region.
1480 Incas occupy part of Argentina.
1580 Spain establishes settlement at Buenos Aires.
1680 Portuguese establish trading post across the Rio de la Plata (River Plate) from Buenos Aires.
1800s Argentina becomes prosperous through exports.
1810 National Library set up in Buenos Aires.
1853 Argentina becomes a republic with confederation of states.

1874–1938 Life of Leopoldo Luhones, Argentine writer and journalist.
1908 Colon Theatre established in Buenos Aires.
1910 Roque Saenz Pena becomes the president.
1914–18 Argentine economy flourishes during World War I as it exports farm produce.
1916 Hipolito Yrigoyen of Radical Party is elected president; reelected **1928**.
1930–32 Military dictatorship takes control.
1939 Remains neutral at start of World War II.

bank accounts were frozen and the currency lost all value. However in 2003 agricultural exports rose, and debt was restructured. Offshore oil and natural gas are becoming increasingly important to the economy.

CULTURE

Argentine culture has been influenced by the large number of European immigrants. Its Spanish literature developed nationalistic

Jorge Luis Borges.

Juan Peron.

Eva Peron.

overtones in the nineteenth century, and in the twentieth century there were numerous internationally known writers, of whom the most acclaimed is Jorge Luis Borges (1899–1986). Argentina is also known for its cinema. The Argentinean cartoonist Quirino Cristiani made the world's first animated feature films in 1917 and 1918, and although the golden age of Argentine cinema is said to be from the 1930s to 1950s, recent films such as *The Official Story (La historia official)* and *The Motorcycle Diaries (Diarios de motocicleta)*, have gained international recognition.

The Buenos Aires Teatro Colon (Colon Theatre) is one of the world's great venues for classical music and opera, attracting top musicians, composers, and conductors. Alberto

Ginastera (1916–83) was one of Argentina's great classical music composers. Argentina has also contributed the Argentine tango, a ballroom dance, as well as its tango music, which has worldwide popularity. Football is the most popular sport, and Argentina is said to have the best polo players in the world.

The Colon Theatre, Buenos Aires, one of the world's finest opera houses.

1944 Argentina ends diplomatic relations with Germany and Japan.
1945 Argentina declares war on Germany and Japan.
1946 Juan Peron wins presidential elections.
1966 Military coup led by General Juan Cralos Ongania.
1974 Peron is succeeded by his third wife, Isabel Peron.
1976 Military government takes control.

1982 April War starts with the United Kingdom over the Falkland Islands; June, Argentina surrenders, but does not give up claim.
1983 Civilian rule restored.
1996 Administrative Reform Act passed.
2003 Nestor Kirchner elected president.
2007 Cristina Fernandez de Kirchner, wife of previous president Nestor Kirchner, becomes president.
2009 January, Emergency declared after severe drought.

ASIA

Asia, the largest continent, covers an area of 17,350,000 square miles, including several islands. The highest mountain in the world, Mt. Everest (29,035 feet) is in Asia, forming part of the great Himalaya range. Several other ranges extend from the Pamir Knot, a high plateau region. Rivers begin in the mountains, and flow through the lowlands, creating fertile alluvial plains. Among the main rivers are the Tigris and Euphrates, Indus, Ganges, Brahmaputra, Mekong, Yangzi, and Huang He (Yellow). Asia contains minerals of all kinds, including oil and natural gas deposits, though the distribution is uneven. The two countries with the highest populations in the world, China and India, are located here.

Statue of the Buddha, Belum Caves, Andhra Pradesh, India

HISTORY

Asia was occupied by early hominids at least 1 million years ago, although the earliest human fossil remains date to 700,000 to 500,000 years ago. The first towns are believed to have emerged in West Asia (Middle East), and in the continent's alluvial plains three great early civilizations arose: Mesopotamia from around 3500 BCE in and around today's region of Iraq; the Indus Valley (2500–1800 BCE) in northwest and west India, and a civilization along the Huang He river in northern China. Great empires followed, among them those of the Achaemenids of Iran or Persia, the Parthians, and Kushans. Meanwhile, following Alexander the Great's invasions across Asia, the Seleucid Greeks occupied part of the region. The seventh century CE saw the rise of Islam, and in the thirteenth century the Mongols arose as a great power under Gengis Khan and his descendants. After their decline the Seljuk and Ottoman Turks swept across the region. With the growth of industry and the need for raw materials, European powers stepped in and began to colonize Asia, and despite struggles for independence, colonialism continued into the twentieth century. Even areas not directly under the colonial powers, such as China, were influenced by the expanding European nations.

By the early twentieth century Japan was rivaling European powers. Soon after World War II ended, many Asian countries gained independence, and some countries such as China, North Korea, and North Vietnam turned to communist governments. In the Palestine region new problems were created with the formation of Israel.

Today China is recognized as a major economic power, and India too is poised for an economic breakthrough.

CULTURE

Numerous languages are spoken in the region including Persian, Arabic, Turkish, Hebrew, Russian, Sino-Tibetan languages, and Hindi, Tamil and many others in India.

All the major religions originated in Asia, including Judaism, Christianity, and Islam in southwest Asia; Zoroastrianism in Iran; Buddhism, Hinduism, Jainism, and Sikhism in India; Daoism and Confucianism in China; and Shinto in Japan. Today the three religions most prominent in Asia are Islam in southwest and central Asia, Buddhism in east and southeast Asia, and Hinduism in India.

Art, architecture, music, and literature are correspondingly diverse, and Asian cuisine also varies widely, though on the whole spices are more prominent than in the Western world.

Former British colonies such as India and Pakistan inherited the British addiction to cricket, though all games are popular and China has become a leading medal-winner in the Olympics.

Giant panda, Beijing Zoo.

These central Asian countries had long been ruled by Russia, but in the 1920s became autonomous republics of the USSR. All attained freedom in 1991 with the collapse of the USSR, since when both Russia and the USA have struggled to establish some influence in the region and to set up military bases.

Kazakhstan
Area:
1,052,090
sq miles •
Population:
15,399,437
• Capital:
Astana •
System of
government:
Republic

Kazakhstan

Practically the size of Western Europe, Kazakhstan has an elected president and a bicameral legislature. The Kazakh khanate was formed in the fifteenth century when the Kazakhs emerged as a distinct ethnic group but later split into three tribal groups. Between 1731 to 1742 all three joined Russia for protection from the Mongols The country has huge mineral resources, and oil exploitation has stimulated economic growth, however wealth distribution is unequal.

Modern developments in the
city of Almaty, Kazakhstan.

Milestone Events

1st CENTURY BCE Cities in Central Asia develop along Silk Road.

7th–8th CENTURIES CE Arabs invade and introduce Islam.

9th–10th CENTURIES Samanid dynasty of Persia controls Central Asia.

13th CENTURY Gengis Khan conquers Central Asia.

14th CENTURY Tajikistan and Uzbekistan part of Timur's empire.

15th–17th CENTURIES Part of Central Asia is under Persian rule; independent states elsewhere.

1822–1900 Tsarist Russia gains control of the region.

1921 Turkestan Autonomous Soviet Socialist Republic (ASSR) is formed, which includes present-day Uzbekistan, Kyrgyzstan, northern Tajikistan, part of northern Turkmenistan, and southern Kazakhstan.

Kyrgyzstan

Kyrgyzstan
Area: 77,202 sq miles • Population: 5,431,747 • Capital: Bishkek • System of government: Republic

Kyrgyzstan has towering mountain peaks and a beautiful landscape. After independence in 1991, the country became a democracy that initially functioned well, but later there were accusations of corruption. From 2005, with the "Tulip" revolution, it has faced waves of unrest, with riots leading to collapses of government. Kyrgyzstan is primarily agricultural.

Tajikistan

Tajikistan
Area: 55,251 sq miles • Population: 7,349,145 • Capital: Dushanbe • System of government: Republic

A mountainous region with valleys to the north and south, in the sixth century BCE the Tajikistan region was part of the Persian empire. The Tajiks emerged as a separate ethnic group in the eighth century CE, and the area came under Russia in the nineteenth century. Tajikistan's economy is poor and it was further damaged by civil war between 1992–97.

Turkmenistan

Turkmenistan
Area: 188,456 sq miles • Population: 4,884,887 • Capital: Ashgabat • System of government: Republic (single party)

Turkmens probably arrived in this mainly desert region in the eleventh century. Turkmenistan has large oil and gas reserves and is a major cotton producer. A new constitution was framed in 2008, two years after the death of president Saparmurat Niyazov who had created a cult around himself during his 21 years of autocratic rule.

Uzbekistan

Uzbekistan
Area: 172,742 sq miles • Population: 27,606,007 • Capital: Tashkent • System of government: Republic

In ancient days Uzbekistan had great cities such as Bukhara and Samarkand. Russians occupied it in the nineteenth century, and since independence the country has faced sporadic unrest, to which the government has responded with oppressive measures. Uzbekistan is one of the largest exporters of cotton, and also has reserves of gold, natural gas, and oil.

1925–36 The states become separate Soviet Socialist Republics in the USSR.

1940s Hundreds of thousands of other nationalities in USSR sent to Kazakhstan and Uzbekistan.

1948 Earthquake in Ashgabat, Turkmenistan kills over 100,000

1954–62 About 2 million Russians moved to Kazakhstan to develop virgin lands.

1991 All become independent.

2001 June: Kazakhstan joins China, Russia, Kyrgyzstan, Uzbekistan, Tajikistan in the Shanghai Cooperation Organisation. March: Caspian Consortium pipeline opens for transporting oil from Tengiz oilfield in Kazakhstan to Russian Black Sea port of Novorossiyik.

2005 Uzbekistan and Russia sign agreement for greater military cooperation.

2010 Ethnic clashes in Kyrgyzstan force thousands of minority Uzbeks to flee.

Afghanistan

Afghanistan
Area: *251,827 sq miles* •
Population: *28,395,716* •
Capital: *Kabul*
• System of government: *Republic*

Located in a strategic region between Iran and India, Afghanistan has a chequered history. From the earliest days invaders crossed through it to enter the rich land of India, yet the rugged landscape has always made it a difficult area to conquer or control. In recent years, beginning with the Soviet invasion of 1979, the country has been devastated by warfare. Development continues to be hampered by sporadic unrest, the presence of the Taliban, a fundamentalist Islamic group, and the ongoing American-led war against terrorism. Afghanistan is now headed by an elected president and has a bicameral legislature. The country is often classified as in the Middle East.

Armenia
Area: *11,484 sq miles* • Population: *2,967,004*
• Capital: *Yeravan* • System of government:
Republic

Armenia

A landlocked country, Armenia in the sixteenth century came under the Ottoman Turks. In the late nineteenth and early twentieth centuries, as Armenia sought a national identity, the people were ruthlessly suppressed by the Turks. After the Turkish defeat in World War I, Armenia declared its independence in 1918, but two years later was annexed by the Soviet army. The country was industrialized under the USSR, but in recent years, despite beginning to privatize industry, its economic growth was poor.

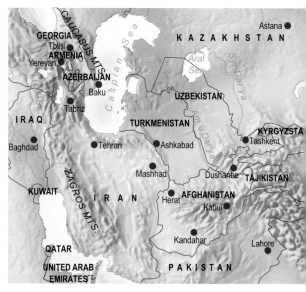

Milestone Events

6th CENTURY BC–651 CE Iran-based empires dominate the region.

636 Arabs invade the region.

13th CENTURY Mongols invade.

1828 Treaty of Turkmanchey divides region of Azerbaijan between Russia and Iran.

1936 Armenia, Azerbaijan, Georgia, become Soviet Republics.

1964 Afghanistan becomes constitutional monarchy.

1973 Muhammad Daud seizes power in Afghanistan and declares a republic; **1978** is killed.

1979 USSR invades Afghanistan, installs Babrak Karmal as ruler.

• Iranian Revolution.

1988 Major earthquake in Armenia kills 45,000.

1989 USSR troops withdraw from Afghanistan.

1994 Ceasefire between Azerbaijan and Armenia after dispute over Nagorno–Karabakh region.

Azerbaijan

Azerbaijan's ancient history is closely linked with that of Iran. In 1920 it came under the Soviet Union, and after independence it has initiated economic reforms. It has substantial petroleum and natural gas deposits, and oil production has increased in the late 1990s. The Nagorno–Karabakh region, formerly within the Azerbaijan Soviet Republic, has declared its independence but is claimed by both Azerbaijan and Armenia.

Azerbaijan
Area: *33,436 sq miles* • Population: *8,238,672* • Capital: *Baku (Baki)* • System of government: *Republic*

Georgia

Georgia
Area: *26,911 sq miles* • Population: *4,615,807* • Capital: *Tbilisi* • System of government: *Republic*

Georgian horsemen.

Located between Europe and Asia, Georgia is a transit region for goods, including oil and gas which pass through the region in pipelines. After independence from the USSR, Georgia faced coups and civil wars. Two regions, South Ossetia and Abkhazia, have seceded from Georgia and declared their independence.

Iran

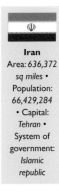
Iran's spiritual leader Ayatollah Khomeini.

The name Iran means "Land of the Aryans." Also called Persia, in ancient days Iran dominated the region of southwest Asia. In 1925, Reza Shah Pahlavi became the ruler of Iran, followed in 1941 by his son, Muhammad Reza Shah Pahlavi, who began a program of modernization. However, there was civil unrest in the 1970s, and in 1979 the Islamic leader Ayatollah Khomeini took over, with the shah going into exile. Since then Iran has remained an Islamic republic. Iran has considerable oil resources, but is attempting to diversify its oil-dependant economy. The country is often grouped in the Middle East.

Iran
Area: *636,372 sq miles* • Population: *66,429,284* • Capital: *Tehran* • System of government: *Islamic republic*

- Fundamentalist religious group, the Taliban, under Mullah Muhammad Omar, begins to emerge as a major power in Afghanistan.
- **1995** Eduard Shevardnadze elected president of Georgia; reelected 2000.
- **1996** Taliban seize Kabul in Afghanistan and introduce strict Islamic laws; President Burhanuddin Rabbani joins anti-Taliban Northern Alliance led by Ahmad Shah Masood.

- **1997** Mohammad Khatami appointed president of Iran.
- **2001** Hamid Karzai becomes head of interim government in Afghanistan.
- USA and UK invade Afghanistan to root out Osama bin Laden, leader of Al-Qaeda, the terrorist group suspected of masterminding "9/11."
- **2003** Rose Revolution in Georgia; Shevardnadze deposed.
- **2008** War between Georgia and Russia.

Iraq

Saddam Hussein.

Iraq
Area: *169,235 sq miles* •
Population: *28,945,569* •
Capital: *Baghdad* •
System of government: *Parliamentary democracy*

Iraq, a country near the Persian Gulf, once the center of the ancient Mesopotamian civilization, is today devastated by conflict.

After World War I, the territory of Iraq was given to the UK by a League of Nations mandate. Though Iraq gained independence in 1932, it was again occupied by the UK during World War II. In 1979 Saddam Hussein of the secular Baath Party became the Iraqi president. Though he modernized the country he was involved in a number of wars, including the wasteful Iran–Iraq War and the invasion of Kuwait leading to the First Gulf War, and he began a weapons build-up that threatened peace in the region. In 2003 a USA-led coalition invaded Iraq to destroy alleged weapons of mass destruction that were believed to be a threat to world peace. Although Iraq's economy has since been in tatters, the country has huge oil reserves, the third largest in the world.

Jordan

King Hussein of Jordan.

Jordan
Area: *34,495 sq miles* •
Population: *6,269,285* •
Capital: *Amman* •
System of government: *Constitutional monarchy*

The small state of Jordan has an important role in the Middle East struggles. After World War I and the end of the Ottoman Empire, Britain created the semi-autonomous region of Transjordan from Palestinian territories. It gained independence in 1946 and was known as Jordan from 1950. King Hussein (r. 1953-99) reintroduced parliamentary elections and permitted political parties. After his death, his son Abdullah took charge, and has introduced political, economic, and social reforms.

Milestone Events

10,000–5000 BCE Farming settlements in the region.
3500–800 BCE Urban centers in the region.
7th CENTURY Arabs occupy the area.
16th CENTURY Ottomans occupy the region.
1918 Britain, France control the area.
1922 Transjordan created under a British mandate.
1923–98 Life of Nizar Tawfiq Qabbani, Syrian diplomat, one of the most acclaimed contemporary poets of the Arab world.

1943 Lebanon gains independence from France.
1946 Syria gains independence from France.
• Transjordan independent from Britain.
1948 Lebanon, Syria, Transjordan among five states that invade Israel.
1967 Israel defeats Jordan, Syria, Egypt, in Six-Day War.
1970 Hafiz al-Asad seizes power in Syria.
1975 Lebanese civil war begins.
1979 Saddam Hussein becomes president of Iraq.
1980–88 Iran–Iraq War.

Lebanon

Lebanon on the Mediterranean coast was the land of the ancient Phoenicians. It was occupied by the Ottomans in the sixteenth century, and became part of a region known as Greater Syria. Along with modern Syria, it was given as a mandate to France after World War I. After independence, it became a relatively prosperous nation, then a series of civil wars between 1975 and 1991 devastated the country. The 2005 protests against Syrian troops in Lebanon, known as the Cedar Revolution, led to Syria's withdrawal, but Lebanon faces problems from the presence of the Hezbollah and from Israel's attacks on that Islamic organization.

Lebanon
Area: *4,015 sq miles* •
Population: *4,017,095* •
Capital: *Beirut* •
System of government: *Republic*

The Ummayad Mosque or Grand Mosque of Damascus.

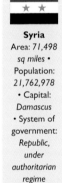

Syria
Area: *71,498 sq miles* •
Population: *21,762,978* •
Capital: *Damascus* •
System of government: *Republic, under authoritarian regime*

Syria

Syria, mainly consisting of a desert plateau, has played a major role in the conflict with Israel. The country was given as a mandate to France after World War I, and after independence saw several unstable governments until 1970. Syria has oil and natural gas reserves. Damascus, the modern capital, was also the capital of historic dynasties, and remains a major center of culture.

1982 Israel attacks Lebanon.
1988 King Hussein of Jordan gives up claims to the West Bank.
1990 Iraq invades Kuwait.
• U.S. imposes sanctions on Iraq.
1991 First Gulf War; coalition forces liberate Kuwait from Iraq.
1994 Jordan signs peace treaty with Israel.
1998 USA and UK bomb Iraq to destroy weapons (Operation Desert Fox).

1999 King Hussein of Jordan dies, succeeded by son, Abdullah.
2000 Bashar al-Asad Hafiz elected president in Syria, reelected 2007.
2003 Second Gulf War; invasion of Iraq; Saddam Hussein captured; 2006, is executed.
2005 Iraqi transitional government elected.
2006 Israel's attack on Hezbollah in Lebanon damages the country.
2009 Iraq holds elections to provincial councils.

ASIA/MIDDLE EAST

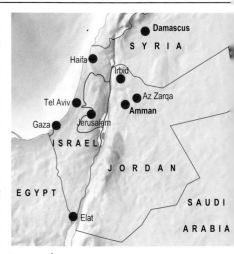

Palestine, located where long-distance routes crossed linking three continents, has a long history, beginning with the Canaanites, followed by the Hebrews or Jews. Later it was invaded and controlled by Assyrians, Babylonians, Persians, Greeks, and Romans, followed by several Arab and Turk dynasties. Jesus Christ lived and preached in the area, thus it is sacred to Christians. In addition, Jerusalem is the third holiest city of Islam.

Scattered throughout the world, many Jews in the late nineteenth century retained a yearning for their homeland, and with a rise in European nationism, the zionist movement began for a separate Jewish state in their ancient lands. After the Holocaust, the demand for a homeland for Jews increased.

Israel

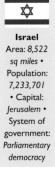

Israel
Area: 8,522 sq miles • Population: 7,233,701 • Capital: Jerusalem • System of government: Parliamentary democracy

In 1948 the British mandate over Palestine ended, and the Jewish population declared the state of Israel. The Palestinians and other Arabs refused to accept this new state, but after the resulting war, Palestinian Arabs were left with scarcely any territory. Of the 800,000 Arabs who lived in the region, only 170,000 remained. The rest became refugees in various Arab lands.

David Ben Gurion, the first Israeli prime minister, began the task of building the country. Jewish migrants came from all over the world, and Israel received aid from the USA and from overseas Jews in other parts of the world, building up a strong army and defense system. The kibbutz, or commune, helped develop agriculture and industry. After a period of high inflation in the 1970s and 80s the economy stabilized, and by 2004 Israel was a fast-growing economy. Israeli culture is diverse because of the different nationalities that occupy the country, but they draw together through their shared Jewish identity.

Milestone Events

1897 Theodor Herzl founds zionist movement in Basel, Switzerland, to develop a separate state for Jews in Palestine.

1917 Balfour Declaration supports foundation of a Jewish state in Palestine after World War I.

1922 UK receives mandate to administer Palestine.

1930s Jewish migration to Palestine increases.

1947 UN agrees to divide Palestine into separate Arab and Jewish states.

1948 Israel founded as a separate independent state; is attacked by Egypt, Syria, Lebanon, Iraq, Transjordan (Jordan).

1949 Israel wins war and takes over part of Arab Palestine, including West Jerusalem.

1956 Suez crisis: Israel, UK, France attack Egypt; repulsed.

1966 Shmuel Yosef Agnon (1888–1970) of Israel is joint winner of Nobel Prize for Literature.

Palestine

Palestine
Area: *1,958 sq miles in West Bank, 141 sq miles in Gaza strip*
• Population: *4.3 million*
• Intended capital: *East Jerusalem* •
System of government: *Elected council*

The Palestinian Liberation Organisation (PLO) was founded in 1964 to represent several Palestinian groups who were struggling to regain lands from Israel. Some groups engaged in terrorism, and after many years of attacks and reprisals from both sides, a peace agreement was made in 1993 at Oslo. This established some degree of autonomy for Palestinians in the West Bank and the Gaza Strip, administered by the Palestine National Authority (PNA). Israel later withdrew from some parts of these areas. Yasser Arafat (1929–2004), head of the PLO, was president of the PNA until his death in 2004. However, Hamas, a militant group, won the 2006 PNA elections, although its authority has not been recognized by Israel, the USA, and others. Hamas and Fatah have battled for supremacy, and conflict with Israel continues.

Israel's separation wall cutting through Ramallah in the West Bank.

1967 Six-Day War takes place, Israel defeats Arab forces; occupies Golan Heights.
1973 Yom Kippur War: Egypt and Syria's attack on Israel is defeated.
1987–93 First Intifada (Palestinian uprising), literally "shaking off."
1979 Israel and Egypt sign peace treaty.
1994 Palestinians begin self-rule in Gaza Strip and West Bank.
• Israel and Jordan sign peace treaty.

• Yasser Arafat, Yitzhak Rabin, Shimon Peres (of Israel) share Nobel Peace Prize.
2000 Second Intifada (Palestinian uprising) begins after peace talks break down.
2002 Israel begins building separation or security wall in the West Bank.
2008–9 Gaza War: Israel attacks Hamas in the Gaza Strip; uses phosphorus bombs.
2010 Israeli commandos kill 9 activists bringing aid to Gaza.

Bahrain

Bahrain, an archipelago in the Persian Gulf, has been ruled by the al Khalifah family from 1783, but surrendered its foreign policy and defense to Britain in 1861. It gained independence in 1971, and now has an elected parliament. Though the economy is largely based on oil, declining reserves have led it to diversify. Its population includes 235,108 non-nationals.

Bahrain
Area: 286 sq miles •
Population: 728,709
• Capital: Manama •
System of government:
Constitutional
monarchy

Kuwait

Kuwait has the fifth largest oil reserves in the world. Britain controlled Kuwait's defense and foreign policies from 1899 to 1961, while internal affairs were under rulers of the al Sabah dynasty. It now has an elected legislature.

Kuwait
Area: 6,880 sq
miles • Population:
2,692,526 • Capital:
Kuwait City • System
of government:
Constitutional
monarchy

Oman

Oman
Area: 119,499 sq miles
• Population:
3,418,085 • Capital:
Muscat • System of
government: Monarchy

On the southeastern corner of the Arabian Peninsula, Oman was once a large empire, known for its trade. Sultan Said bin Taimur was deposed by his son Qaboos bin Said in 1970, who introduced economic reforms and modernized the country, providing health-care and education. Oman's economy is largely dependent on oil.

Qatar

Qatar
Area: 4,473 sq miles •
Population: 833,285
• Capital: Doha •
System of government:
Monarchy

Qatar, a small peninsula on the larger Arabian Peninsula, is an oil-rich nation, and has the second highest GDP per capita in the world. The well-known Arab television station al Jazeera is based in Qatar.

The Hajj, annual Muslim pilgrimage to Mecca.

Milestone Events

c. 1200 BCE–525 CE Early kingdoms in the region.
7th CENTURY Islam is introduced by the prophet Muhammad; soon spreads throughout the region, unifying Arabs.
16th CENTURY Ottomans occupy most of the region.
1650 Portuguese occupiers expelled from Oman.
1756 Arab al Sabah clan begin rule in Kuwait.
1783 Al Khalifa family conquers Bahrain from Iran.
18th CENTURY Sultanate established in Oman.

1800–1900 Omani empire extends to east coast of Africa.
1902 Abdalaziz (ibn Saud) of al Saud family gains control of Riyadh.
1916–18 Arab revolt against Ottomans led by Hashemites of Mecca.
1918 North Yemen gains independence from Ottomans.
1922 Hashemites driven out of Mecca by Ibn Said, given Transjordan by Britain.

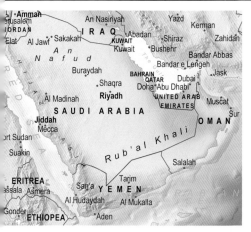

Saudi Arabia

Saudi Arabia occupies a large part of the Arabian Peninsula, and has a prominent role among Arab states since it is the guardian of the most sacred sites of Islam, Mecca and Medina. The al Saud dynasty came to power in the region in the eighteenth century, and in 1932 Abdalaziz (ibn Saud) conquered Mecca from the Hashemites and took over other territories in the Hijaz. The country has more than 20 per cent of the world's known oil reserves. Its population includes 5,576,076 non-nationals.

Saudi Arabia
Area: *830,000 sq miles* • Population: *28,686,633* • Capital: *Riyadh* • System of government: *Monarchy*

United Arab Emirates (UAE)

The UAE consists of seven emirates: Abu Dhabi, Ajman, Dubai, Fujayrah, Ras al Khaymah, Sharjah, and Um al Qaywayn. Formerly known as the Trucial States of the Persian Gulf (when their defense was controlled by Britain through a truce), the modern federation began in 1971. The heads of state act as a Federal Supreme Council and elect the president from among themselves; from the beginning he has been the ruler of Abu Dhabi.

UAE
Area: *32,278 sq miles* • Population: *4,798,491* • Capital: *Abu Dhabi* • System of government: *Federation*

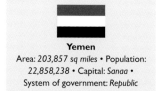

Yemen
Area: *203,857 sq miles* • Population: *22,858,238* • Capital: *Sanaa* • System of government: *Republic*

Yemen

In 1990, after decades of tension, North and South Yemen finally united. Unlike the rest of the region, Yemen has a great deal of fertile agricultural land.

1932 Abdalaziz (ibn Saud) founds Saudi Arabia after a 30-year campaign to unify the region.

1937–38 Oil first discovered in Arabia (Kuwait/Saudi Arabia).

1962–70 Civil war in North Yemen.

1967 South Yemen (Aden) gains independence from Britain.

1970 Qaboos bin Said becomes sultan of Oman, modernizes country.

1971 Trucial States (later UAE) and Bahrain attain independence from Britain.

1980s Dubai begins drive to make itself a major tourist destination.

1981 Six Persian Gulf states (except for Yemen) join together in Gulf Cooperation Council.

1990 North and South Yemen unite to form Republic.

• Iraq invades Kuwait, is expelled in First Gulf War.

1999 Oman and UAE sign border agreement.

2009 Rebellion in Yemen.

ASIA

China has the largest population in the world—one-fifth of the global total—and is the fourth largest country in area.

China includes some of the world's highest mountain ranges, including the Tian, Kunlun, and Himalaya. In addition there are mountainous plateaux and hilly regions, deserts, and fertile plains with some great rivers including the Yangzi and Huang

Milestone Events

c. 700,000–500,000 YEARS AGO Early human remains in China ("Peking man").

2700 BCE Tea known in China.

c. 1766 BCE Shang dynasty founded.

c.1050–479 BCE *Wu Ching*, or five classics of Chinese literature are composed.

551–479 BCE Life of Confucius.

221 BCE Qin dynasty established; first Great Wall built.

206 BCE Han dynasty founded.

c. 112 BCE Silk route opens.

c.105 BCE Paper invented.

c. 496 CE Shaolin temple established.

618–907 Tang dynasty period.

c. 920 Footbinding of women introduced.

1279 Mongols conquer China; Kublai Khan establishes Yuan dynasty.

1368 Ming dynasty established.

1404 Work begins on the palace complex, the Forbidden City, in Beijing.

He (Yellow). In the north, the Amur river forms the northeastern boundary with Russia. China has mineral resources including coal, petroleum, natural gas, and iron ore, as well as the world's largest hydropower potential. The natural world is rich and varied, and includes the giant panda that is unique to China.

Area: 3,705,407 sq miles • Population: 1,338,612,968 • Capital: Beijing • System of government: Communism

The country is divided into 22 provinces, as well as five autonomous regions in which ethnic minorities predominate (Guangxi, Inner Mongolia, Ningxia, Xinjiang, Tibet), and four special municipalities: Beijing, Chongqing, Shanghai, Tianjin.

Left: Empress Cixi. Above: The Forbidden City in Beijing.

1644 Manchus found Qing dynasty in China.
1839–42, 1856–60 Opium wars force China to open up to foreign trade and missionaries.
1851–64 Taiping rebellion.
1900 Boxer rebellion against foreign influences.
1911 Revolution, **1912** Nationalist Republic of China established, initially under Sun Yat-sen.
1927 Civil war
1931 Japanese invasion of Manchuria.
1949 Communist People's Republic of China founded.

1950 China supports North Korea in Korean War; Tibet officially becomes part of China.
1958 The "Great Leap forward," a system of planned economic development begins.
1962 China is involved in Indochina War between Vietnamese nationalists and France.
1966–76 Cultural Revolution.
1976 Death of Mao Zedong; "Gang of Four" politicians fail in bid for power.
1977 Deng Xiaoping becomes main leader.

In addition, Hong Kong and Macao are "separate administrative regions." China also considers that Taiwan is its 23rd province.

China's recorded history goes back 3500 years, and in the past it was one of the leading civilizations of the world, known for its scientific and technological inventions. By the early 20th century, however, the country was in decline, and, ending centuries of imperial rule, China became a republic in 1912 after a revolutionary movement led by Sun Yat-sen's Kuomintang (KMT) or Nationalist Party. In 1921 the

The Great Wall of China.

Chinese Communist Party was formed. At first the KMT under Sun's successor Chiang Kai-shek welcomed the communists as allies against Japanese invaders, but later Chiang turned on the Communist Party, and civil war began.

Mao Zedong emerged as leader of the communists during the Long March to escape KMT forces, and eventually he established the People's Republic of China (PRC) on October 1, 1949. Mao and his socialist, collective policies dominated China until his death in 1976.

Mao's successor Deng Xiaoping gradually introduced private ownership and market-oriented economic policies that made China the fastest developing country in the world and a leader in the global economy.

TIBET

Tibet's spiritual leader, the Dalai Lama, who fled from Chinese forces in 1959, leads a government in exile located in Dharamsala, India that disputes Chinese sovereignty over Tibet.

Tenzing Gyatso, the Dalai Lama.

Milestone Events

1979 "One child" policy aims to curb population growth.

1986 China begins "open door" policy allowing foreign investment; industries are privatized; private enterprise allowed.

1989 Tiananmen Square democracy protests broken up by army.

1990s Population shift from country to cities begins.

1992 Chinese government announces the country now has a "socialist market economy."

1997 Hong Kong is returned to China by Britain.

2000 Trade relations with the U.S. normalized.

2003 First manned space flight, by Yang Liwei.

• Hu Jintao becomes president of the PRC, reelected **2008**.

2006 Three Gorges dam on Yangtze opens.

• China is now the third largest trading nation in the world after the USA and Germany.

2007 China launches a missile into space, destroying an obsolete satellite.

MAO ZEDONG

Mao Zedong (1893–1976) was the leading figure in the PRC until his death. Maoism, though based on Marxist principles, encouraged rural peasants to support communism, whereas Russian communism believed in mobilizing urban industrial workers. Mao unified the country and greatly improved the lot of women and peasants, and his 1958 Great Leap Forward scheme introduced autonomous local communes and production targets. In the Cultural Revolution he attempted to bring in a new society through mobilizing youth and severing cultural links with the past. Some of his programs did not work, but his ideas were collected in the Little Red Book, *which influenced revolutionaries across the world.*

Communist China's propaganda posters showed proud, well-fed, and united workers.

- There are 100 million transient workers living on temporary, low-paid work.
- **2008** Hangzhou Bay Bridge, the longest trans-oceanic bridge in the world, opens linking Shanghai and Ningbo.
- Demonstrations against Chinese rule in Tibet.
- Earthquake in Sichuan province kills more than 69,000 people.
- 1.3 million people evacuated in south China for fear of floods and landslides.

- Baby milk in Gansu is contaminated.
- China wins most gold medals (51) at first Olympic Games in China, in Beijing.
- Restrictions on travel between the PRC and Taiwan are relaxed.
- Following the global recession, exports fall for the first time in 7 years.
- **2009** Hu Jintao takes part in the G20 Summit meeting which agrees to provide $1.1 trillion to support economic growth and jobs worldwide.

ASIA

Japan is an archipelago with a number of islands, the four largest of which—Honshu, Hokkaido, Kyushu, and Shikoku—cover 97 per cent of the land area. Japan is prone to earthquakes and tsunamis.

Japan adopted a constitution in 1947 and has a hereditary emperor and an elected bicameral parliament.

From around 1603 Japan began a conscious program of isolation in order to safeguard itself from foreign influence and the inroads of colonial powers, and only in 1854 did it open up to trade and modernization, soon becoming powerful enough to

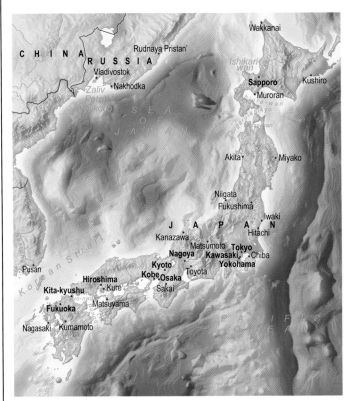

Emperor Akihito.

Area: 145,883 sq miles •
Population: 127,078,679 •
Capital: Tokyo • System of
government: Constitutional
monarchy

Milestone Events

30,000 BCE Upper Paleolithic sites in Japan.

c. 10,000 BCE–300 BCE Jomon Culture.

660 BCE Traditional date of founding of Japan, with accession of legendary Japanese emperor, Jimmu Tenno.

c. 550 Buddhism reaches Japan from Korea.

1603 Ieyasu founds Tokugawa shogunate, hereditary warlords ruling nominally under emperor (Edo period).

1639 Japan restricts contact with the outside world.

1854 The USA forces Japan to open to foreign trade.

1868 Meiji restoration reestablishes direct rule of the emperor.

• Samurai warrior caste abolished.

1904–5 Japan shows it is now a formidable power by defeating Russia in Russo-Japanese war.

1914–18 Japan supports Britain and Allies in World War I with limited role.

1923 Earthquake in Tokyo region kills more than 100,000.

Heian shrine, Kyoto, a typical idyllic Shinto shrine.

defeat China (1894–95) and Russia (1904–5). Japan was devastated after World War II, not least by the atomic bombs dropped on Hiroshima and Nagasaki, and only recovered with U.S. aid.

Japan is a leading economy of the world, known for new technology and electronics.

CULTURE

Flower arranging, origami or paper craft, theatre forms such as kabuki and noh, and formal tea ceremonies are among Japan's unique traditions, while modern manga comic-books have influenced film animation around the world.

A Kabuki dancer in traditional costume.

1931 Japan invades Manchuria.
1937 Japan conquers Nanjing, China.
1940 During World War II Japan signs the Axis Pact with Germany and Italy.
1941 Japan bombs U.S. naval base at Pearl Harbor.
1945 US drops atom bombs on Hiroshima and Nagasaki; Japan surrenders; end of World War II.
1947 New constitution introduced; establishes parliamentary system, emperor is only ceremonial head; Japan renounces war.

1952 Japan regains independence after Allied occupation following World War II; US retains some islands as military bases.
1950s Japan develops as an electronics giant.
1989 Akihito becomes emperor after death of Emperor Hirohito.
1997 Economic crisis as several banks and financial institutions collapse.
2004 Powerful earthquakes in north Japan.
2009 Democratic Party wins elections.

Mongolia

Mongolia contains contrasts such as the Gobi desert and the high Altai mountains in the southwest.

Gengis Khan united the Mongol tribes in the thirteenth century, but after its glory days as an empire, Mongolia came under Chinese sway, not becoming independent until 1911. In 1924, the Mongolian People's Republic was established with support from the USSR, but in 1992 the new constitution provided for an elected president with a unicameral legislature.

In 1997 Mongolia became the only country in the world to eliminate all taxes on trade.

Mongolia
Area: *603,909 sq miles* •
Population: *3,041,142*
• Capital: *Ulaanbaatar*
• System of government: *Republic*

The barren Gobi desert covers much of southern Mongolia.

Milestone Events

500–400 BCE Old Choson kingdom emerges in North Korea.

56 BCE–668 CE Period of three kingdoms, Koguryo, Paekche, Silla in Korea.

c. 350 CE Turkic tribes in Mongolia.

668 Unified Korean state established. 13th century Mongol empire established by Gengis Khan.

1259–1356 Mongols conquer Korea.

16th CENTURY Tibetan Buddhism gains popularity in Mongolia.

1650 Mongol Khan of Urga (now Ulaanbaatar) proclaimed "Living Buddha."

1696–1911 Mongolia controlled by China.

1910–1945 Japan occupies Korea.

1921 Mongolian People's Revolutionary party, helped by USSR, sets up provisional government.

1945 Allied forces free Korea from Japanese; Soviet Union occupies territory north of 38th parallel; U.S., south.

A South Korean market in Seoul.

**North Korea
(Democratic
People's
Republic of
Korea)**
Area: 465,340
sq miles •
Population:
22,665,345
• Capital:
Pyongyang •
System of
government:
Communist

North Korea (Democratic People's Republic of Korea)

After World War II, Korea was divided along the 38th parallel with a communist government in the North, and a nationalist government in the South. In 1950 North Korea invaded South Korea in an attempt to unite the two regions, sparking a Cold War conflict: The USSR and China backed the North, and the USA supported the South. An armistice was signed in 1953. Kim il Sung was North Korea's leader from 1948 until his death in 1994 when his son Kim Jong-il took over the leadership.

North Korea's ongoing nuclear weapons programme has been condemned by the United States.

**South Korea
(Republic of
Korea)**
Area: 38,502
sq miles •
Population:
48,508,972 •
Capital: Seoul
• System of
government:
Republic

South Korea (Republic of Korea)

After independence from Japanese occupation, South Korea initially faced military regimes, but a democratic parliamentary system has functioned from 1987. Large industrial corporations such as Hyundai and Samsung have helped to make the country economically prosperous.

1948 Democratic People's Republic of Korea proclaimed in North; Republic of Korea founded in South Korea.
1950–53 Korean War, ends with armistice.
1955 Floods affect agriculture in North Korea.
1962 Sino-Mongolian border treaty signed.
1966 Mongolia and USSR sign treaty of trade and friendship; renewed 1986.
1986 Border between North and South Korea opened to allow family visits.

1994 Kim Il-sung of North Korea dies after 46 years in power; succeeded by his son Kim Jong-il.
1996–99 Famine in North Korea.
2000 North and South Korea sign agreement to improve relations, and work towards reunification.
2006 Han Myung-Sook becomes first woman prime minister in South Korea.
2009 North Korea refuses to curtail nuclear activities.
2010 Renewed tensions in Korea when the South accuses the North of sinking one of its warships.

Cambodia

Cambodia's recent history is dominated by the civil war in 1968–75 which saw the monarchy deposed, the rebel communist Khmer Rouge forces under Pol Pot unleashing a reign of terror, and the involvement of other nations such as Vietnam and the USA. Eventually in 1993 a constitutional monarchy was restored. Recent finds of offshore oil and gas could provide new sources of revenue.

Cambodia
Area: *69,898 sq miles* • Population: *14,494,293* • Capital: *Phnom Penh* • System of government: *Constitutional monarchy*

The Vietnamese communist leader, Ho Chi Minh.

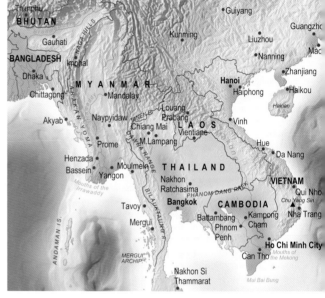

Laos
Area: *91,429 sq miles* • Population: *6,834,345* • Capital: *Vientiane (Viangchan)* • System of government: *Communism*

Laos

Laos, a mountainous and landlocked country, has a communist government, although the economy has recently been liberalized. During the Vietnam War the USA bombed Laos to destroy the "Ho Chih Minh trail," the North Vietnam supply route.

Milestone Events

111 BCE–939 China occupies northern part of Vietnam, naming it Annam.

9th–13th CENTURIES CE Khmer empire in Cambodia.

1044–1077 First unified state in Myanmar under King Anawrahta.

1350 Kingdom of Ayutthaya founded in region of present-day Thailand; becomes a dominant power.

1782 Chakri dynasty in Thailand changes name of state from Ayutthaya to Siam.

1802 Nguyen Anh of the Nguyen dynasty names his kingdom Vietnam.

1886 Britain occupies all of Burma; moves capital from Mandalay to Rangoon.

1887 France creates French Indochina from Vietnam and Cambodia; **1893** annexes Laos.

1939 Siam changes name to Thailand.

1945 Vietnam declares independence; **1948** Burma; **1952** Laos.

1953 Cambodia gains independence as kingdom.

Myanmar

Myanmar (Burma)
Area: *262,000 sq miles* •
Population: *48,137,741* •
Capital: *Naypyidaw (Rangoon until 2006)* •
System of government: *Military regime*

Formerly known as Burma, Myanmar is rich in resources but, under its military regime, remains poorly developed. Probably its most famous resident is Aung San Suu Kyi, a leader of the democracy movement, who is kept under house arrest.

Right: Aung San Suu Kyi.
Below: Traditional Thai dancers.

Thailand

Thailand
Area: *198,117 sq miles* •
Population: *65,998,436* •
Capital: *Bangkok* •
System of government: *Constitutional monarchy*

The only southeast Asian country that was not colonized by a European power, Thailand has recently faced several coups and popular demonstrations. Tourism is a major industry, and the country is known as the sex tourism capital of the world.

Vietnam

Vietnam
Area: *127,881 sq miles* •
Population: *88,576,758* •
Capital: *Hanoi* • System of government: *Communism*

In 1954 Vietnam divided into the communist North and non-communist South, experienced a vicious war that brought in Cold War rivals, and was reunited in 1975 as a communist "socialist republic."

1955–75 Vietnam War.
1960s Tourism in Thailand begins to develop.
1962 First of many military coups in Burma.
1968–75 Cambodian Civil War.
1975 Communists take control of the government in Laos.
1989 Name of Burma changed to Union of Myanmar.
2001 USA–Vietnam sign Bilateral Trade Agreement

2004 Norodom Sihamoni becomes king of Cambodia, succeeds father Norodom Sihanouk.
2006 Military coup ousts prime minister Thaksin of Thailand
• USA–Cambodia sign trade agreement.
2008 Cyclone Nargis strikes Myanmar, more than 80,000 dead, 50,000 injured.
2010 Thai Red Shirts protest movement broken up by military.

This region of southeast Asia largely comprises islands of the Malay archipelago.

Omar Ali Saifuddin Mosque, Brunei.

Brunei

The economy of Brunei, on the island of Borneo, is based on oil and natural gas. The sultan is one of the richest people in the world, and the government provides free education and health services.

Brunei
Area: 2,226 sq miles • Population: 388,190 • Capital: Bandar Seri Begawan • System of government: Constitutional monarchy

Indonesia
Area: 735,358 sq miles • Population: 240,271,522 • Capital: Jakarta • System of government: Republic

Indonesia

An archipelago of many thousands of islands (6000 are inhabited), Indonesia is now the third largest democracy in the world. The main islands are Sumatra, Java, Celebes (Sulawesi), and parts of New Guinea and Borneo, but there are several separatist movements.

Aceh, Sumatra, after the 2004 tsunami.

Milestone Events

500,000–30,000 YEARS AGO *Homo erectus* was in Indonesian islands.
500 BCE–400 CE Farming and trade settlements in the region.
1565 Spain begins to colonize the Philippines.
1670–1900 Indonesia comes under the Dutch.
1819 Singapore founded as a British colony.
1824 Dutch and British agree border between British Malaya and Dutch East Indies (later Indonesia).
1888 Brunei becomes British protectorate.

1898 Philippines transferred to USA from Spain.
1899–1902 Philippines revolt but lose war against USA; remain in American hands.
1945 Indonesia declares independence, Sukarno is president till **1967**.
1946 Philippines gains independence from U.S.
1957 Malaysia wins independence, forms federation.
1959 Singapore attains self-government.
1965 Ferdinand Marcos becomes president of Philippines; **1973** takes dictatorial powers.

Malaysia
Area: *127,355 sq miles* •
Population: *25,715,819*
• Capital: *Kuala Lumpur* •
System of government:
Constitutional monarchy

Malaysia

This stable federation of thirteen states and other territories was originally known as Malaya.

Philippines

There are eleven main islands out of the thousands that constitute the Philippines. Taken over by Spain during the 16th century, it was ceded to the U.S. in 1898 after the Spanish–American War. In 1935 the Philippines attained self-government, but was occupied by Japan in World War II, finally gaining independence in 1946.

Philippines
Area:
*115,831 sq
miles* •
Population:
97,976,603
• Capital:
Manila •
System of
government:
Republic

Ferdinand Marcos, president of the Philippines 1965–86, and his shoe-loving wife Imelda.

Singapore
Area: *269 sq miles*
• Population:
4,657,542 • Capital:
Singapore • System of
government: *Republic*

Singapore

Singapore, once under the British, joined the Malaysian federation but asserted its independence in 1965. A city-state, it is one of the most prosperous and well-organized nations of the world.

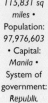

Timor-Leste (East Timor)
Area: *5,743 sq miles* •
Population: *1,131,612*
• Capital: *Dili* • System
of government:
Republic

Timor-Leste

After attaining independence in 1975 from Portugal, Timor-Leste or East Timor was occupied by Indonesia in 1976, and finally gained full independence only in 2002.

- Singapore becomes fully independent.
1967 General Suharto ousts Sukarno in Indonesia, becomes president for next 32 years.
1975 East Timor fights Indonesian occupation.
1984 Brunei becomes independent from Britain.
1986 Popular revolution ousts Marcos of Philippines.
1996 Bishop Carlos Felipe Ximenes Belo and Jose Ramos-Horta, of East Timor, win Nobel Peace

Prize for attempts to peacefully bring about East Timor's independence.
2002 Terrorist bomb in Bali kills more than 200.
- East Timor wins independence as Timor-Leste.
2004 Earthquake and tsunami off the coast of Sumatra leaves 200,000 dead in Indonesia.
- First direct Parliamentary elections in Indonesia.
2005 Indonesia reaches peace agreement with armed separatists in Aceh.
2007 Parliamentary elections held in Timor-Leste.

I ndia, Pakistan, and Bangladesh on the Indian subcontinent have a shared history. The whole region—home to an early urban civilization and great empires—was known as India up to 1947, when it gained independence from Britain. Then, two separate nations were created, India (mainly Hindu and Sikh), and Pakistan as a Muslim homeland.

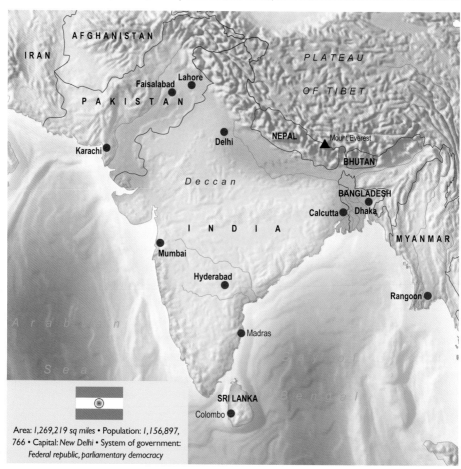

Area: 1,269,219 sq miles • Population: 1,156,897, 766 • Capital: New Delhi • System of government: Federal republic, parliamentary democracy

Milestone Events

250,000 BCE Stone Age settlements in the region.
7000 BCE Farming settlements in the northwest.
2500–1800 BCE Indus Civilization in northwest and west of the region.
1500-600 BCE Vedic texts, basis for later Hinduism, are composed.
6th–5th CENTURIES BCE Religions of Jainism and Buddhism are founded.
1469–1539 Life of Guru Nanak, founder of the Sikh religion.

1526–1857 Mughal dynasty in India.
1757 Battle of Plassey establishes British rule in India.
1913 Rabindranath Tagore (1861–1941) wins Nobel Prize for Literature.
1947 India attains independence from Britain; divided into India and Pakistan.
1948 Independence leader and pacifist Mahatma Gandhi assassinated in India.
1962 War between India and China.
1965 War between India and Pakistan.

Riots and massacres followed, leaving one million dead and 10 million fleeing desperately across the border.

Mahatma Gandhi (1869–1948), leader of India's non-violent freedom movement, is still revered today. In 1950 India became a republic—a secular democracy—and, on the basis of population, is the largest democracy in the world. The country's first prime minister, Jawaharlal Nehru (1889–1964), was a leader of the Non-Aligned Movement, countries that steered clear of the two Cold War camps.

India and Pakistan soon came into conflict over the northern Indian state of Kashmir, part of which is occupied by Pakistan. India also faced problems with China, particularly after sheltering the Dalai Lama and over 100,000

India's first female prime minister Indira Gandhi (1966–77, 1980–84) with her sons Sanjay and Rajiv.

refugees from Tibet. Terrorist attacks, insurgency in the northeast, a Maoist movement in central India, and a Sikh separatist movement in the 1980s all created instability.

From the 1990s economic reforms have transformed the country, now one of the fastest growing economies in the world, a center for information technology and with well-developed manufacturing and service sectors. To increase energy resources, India is developing nuclear energy for peaceful use. However, inequalities and poverty still exist.

India's culture is multi-lingual, multi-ethnic, and multi-religious, and its "Bollywood" film industry is one of the largest in the world.

Dancers in a typically extravagant Bollywood movie.

1972 Pakistan and India sign peace agreement.
1974 India conducts nuclear tests.
1984 Prime minister Indira Gandhi assassinated.
1985 South Asian Association for Regional Cooperation (SAARC) formed with seven South Asian countries.
1991 Former prime minister Rajiv Gandhi, Indira's son, assassinated.
1997 Arundhati Roy (b.1961) of India wins Booker Prize.

2005 Bus services begin between India and Pakistan across disputed Kashmir.
2008 India reaches the moon with an unmanned space probe.
• Terrorists kill nearly 200 people in Mumbai.
• Peace talks with Pakistan come to a halt.
2010 Eight Indian officials of Union Carbide given prison sentences for negligence causing world's worst industrial accident, the 1984 Bhopal gas plant leak.

Pakistan

Created as a homeland for Indian Muslims in 1947, Pakistan was wracked by riots at its formation. It has since faced wars with India, coups, periods of military rule, assassinations, and terrorist attacks.

Muhammad Ali Jinnah, first president of Pakistan.

Pakistan
Area: *307,373 sq miles* • Population: *174,578,558* • Capital: *Islamabad* • System of government: *Federal republic*

Bangladesh
Area: *55,597 sq miles* • Population: *1,58,050,883* • Capital: *Dhaka* • System of government: *Republic*

Bangladesh

Originally East Pakistan, the region felt dominated by West Pakistan, and after a struggle for independence, Bangladesh emerged as a separate nation in 1971. Dependent on agriculture, Bangladesh is prone to floods and cyclones, and is poorly developed.

Far left: Sheikh Mujib, considered the founding father of Bangladesh, signs the first Bangladeshi constitution.
Left: Sheikh Mujib.

Sri Lanka
Area: *33,069 sq miles* • Population: *21,324,791* • Capital: *Colombo* • System of government: *Republic*

Sri Lanka

Sri Lanka gained independence as Ceylon in 1948. In British times, Indian laborers were transported to the island, and in 1976 their descendants formed the Tamil Tigers separatist group. Civil war began in 1983, continuing intermittently until 2009 when the Sri Lanka government gained control of Tamil Tiger areas.

Milestone Events

7000 BCE Farming settlements in the northwest.
2500-1800 BCE Indus Civilization in northwest and west of the region.
1768 CE Nepal begins to unify, forms kingdom.
1907 Bhutan becomes unified kingdom.
1947 India attains independence from Britain; divided into two nations of India and Pakistan.
1948 Muhammad Ali Jinnah, founder of Pakistan, dies.
1951 Pakistani prime minister Liaquat Ali Khan assassinated.

1959 In Ceylon Srimavo Bandarnaike becomes first woman prime minister in the world.
1968 Maldives becomes republic.
1971 East Pakistan becomes independent as Bangladesh.
1972 Pakistan and India sign peace agreement.
• Ceylon changes name to Sri Lanka.
1974 Foreign tourists allowed to enter Bhutan.
1988 General Zia, president of Pakistan, and other top officials die in plane crash.

Nepal

Nepal, traditionly a Hindu kingdom, now has an elected government. A strong Maoist movement has contributed to recent internal turmoil.

Nepal
Area: *56,826 sq miles* • Population: *28,563,377* • Capital: *Kathmandu* • System of government: *Republic*

One of the former Living Goddesses of Nepal, young girls worshipped as the incarnation of a goddess.

Bhutan
Area: *14,824 sq miles* • Population: *691,141* • Capital: *Thimpu* • System of government: *Constitutional monarchy*

Bhutan

A tiny mountainous kingdom that was once closed to the outside world, Bhutan relies upon India for defense and foreign policy guidance.

Maldives

The Maldives consists of a group of about 1200 atolls in the Indian Ocean, many of which are uninhabited. Once a sultanate, it gained independence from Britain in 1965 and became a republic in 1968.

Maldives
Area: *115 sq miles* • Population: *396,334* • Capital: *Male* • System of government: *Republic*

A tourist resort in the Maldives, one of many giving the island a new source of income.

1990s After riots, Nepali speakers leave Bhutan, remain refugees in Nepal.

1998 In Bhutan, some powers ceded to National Assembly.

• Two-thirds of Bangladesh devastated by floods.

2001 In Nepal, King Birendra and relatives are shot dead by the crown prince.

2004 Forty five seats reserved for women in Bangladesh Parliament.

2005 Bus services begin between Pakistan and India across disputed Kashmir.

2006 Muhammad Yunus of Bangladesh, and his Grameen Bank providing micro-finance to the poor, receive Nobel Peace Prize.

2007 Benazir Bhutto, daughter of former Pakistani prime minister Zulfikar Ali Bhutto, assassinated.

2008 First multi-party presidential elections in Maldives; first parliamentary elections, Bhutan.

• Nepal becomes a republic.

O ften considered to be part of the Middle East, the Republic of Turkey spreads across two continents: Europe and Asia. Its strategic location has led to it playing a major role in history, and it is still a bridge between the continents.

As a secular democratic republic, Turkey came into being in 1923, after the decline of the Ottoman Empire and its defeat in World War I. Often called Turks, the Ottomans had ruled a huge area including southeastern Europe, West Asia, and North Africa. Turkey has a unicameral legislature. The prime minister is the leader of the majority party, while the president is selected by parliament. Turkey's economy has been reformed and improved, and the country is in discussions with the EU for membership.

The Ottoman Sultan Suleiman the Magnificent (r. 1520–66).

Once known as Anatolia, Turkey is home to the ancient city of Troy as well as Mt. Ararat, the traditional site of Noah's ark. The area was conquered or occupied by several

Milestone Events

7500–6000 BCE Town of Catal Hayak develops.
1250 BCE Trojan War fought at Troy.
547 BCE Cyrus of Persia conquers most of Anatolia.
129 BCE Anatolia comes under Roman empire.
330 CE Nicomedia (Constantinople) becomes new capital of Rome.
1071 Seljuk Turks win Battle of Manzikert, defeat Byzantines (Eastern Rome).

1243 Mongols conquer region.
1207–73 Life of Jalaluddin Rumi, great Sufi saint who lived in Seljuk Sultanate.
1326 Ottoman empire founded, flourishes for centuries before declining.
1453 Constantinople conquered by Ottomans.
1908 Young Turk revolution; reformists and nationalists restore parliament, demand constitution.

empires (Persia, that of Alexander the Great, Rome, Byzantium, the Seljuk Turks) before the rise of the Ottomans. During World War I Turkish authorities were involved in the mass killings of Armenians in Turkey, fearing that they were allying with Russia.

After the war Allied armies occupied much of the country. A Turkish national movement, led by Mustafa Kemal Pasha or Atatürk (1881–1938), a military commander, defeated the occupying armies in 1922 and founded the new Turkish republic.

Turkey today faces challenges to its secularism from Islamists. The country also has a large Kurdish minority, many of whom demand their own homeland. Recently, they have been granted more rights.

Area: 302,534 sq miles • Population: 76,805,524 • Capital: Ankara • System of government: Republic

Above: Mustafa Kemal Atatürk.
Top: The Topkapi Palace, Istanbul.

1914–18 Ottomans ally with Germany in World War I, are defeated; empire breaks up.
1919–23 Mustafa Kemal leads fight against Allied occupying armies; Turkish Republic proclaimed.
1923–38 As first president, Kemal Atatürk introduces reforms, modernizes Turkey.
1923 Constantinople renamed Istanbul.
1974 Turkey invades Cyprus.
1987 Turkey applies for full membership of the EEC; rejected for poor human rights record.

1993 Tansu Ciller becomes Turkey's first woman prime minister.
1999 Two earthquakes kill more than 17,000.
2002 Turkish women granted legal equality.
2006 Turkish writer Orhan Pamuk wins 2006 Nobel Prize in Literature.
2008 Parliament approves constitutional amendments which allow women to wear Islamic headscarves in university, changing Turkey's secular laws.

Eurasia: RUSSIA

Extending across Europe and Asia, with parts in both continents, Russia is the largest country in the world. Over the centuries Russia has gone through many changes, most recently emerging as a new federal nation in 1991 after the break up of the USSR. The central government is headed by a president who appoints the prime minister and cabinet, and has a bicameral federal assembly. Russia has nine federal districts which include 83 federal subjects, ranging from relatively autonomous republics to provinces and the federal cities of Moscow and St. Petersburg.

Initially the new state of Russia suffered a decline both economically and politically, but has rebuilt its economy and is again gradually gaining influence as a world power.

Area: 6,601,668 sq miles • Population: 140,041,247 • Capital: Moscow • System of government: Federation

THE PAST
Russia has been occupied from ancient days. Neanderthal remains have been found in the region, as well as some of the world's earliest structures.

Milestone Events

35,000–30,000 BCE Early occupation in the region.

16,000–10,000 BCE Early structures in region made using mammoth bones.

c. 2000–1600 BCE Sintashta culture in southern Urals; horse burials found.

7th–10th CENTURIES CE Khazars occupy part of the region.

989 Vladimir I of Kiev converts to Christianity, religion spreads.

1156 Moscow is founded.

1237–40 Mongols invade Russia; Mongol Golden Horde establishes rule in south Russia.

c. 1360–c. 1430 Life of Andrei Rublev, icon and fresco painter.

1480 Ivan III of Moscow defeats Mongol occupiers.

1552–56 Ivan the Terrible expands Russian rule.

1555–61 St. Basil's Cathedral constructed in Moscow.

1597 Serfdom legalized.

The Russian Steppes are perhaps the original homeland of the Indo-Europeans, and saw many nomadic peoples pass through. Slavic people probably settled in the region between the third and eighth centuries.

The name Russia comes from Rus, a term for a group of either Vikings or Slavs who settled in the northern region. In the thirteen century Mongols invaded, and by 1242 much of Russia was under the Khanate known as the Golden Horde, led

Empress Catherine the Great. Ivan the Terrible (Ivan IV, Grand Prince of Moscow).

by Batu Khan, grandson of Gengis Khan. Ivan III (ruled 1462–1505) of Moscow asserted independence from the Mongols, but Russia's initial expansion was followed by a period of chaos until the election in 1613 of Michael Fedorovitch Romanov, from an influential family, as tsar or king. He founded the Romanov dynasty which ruled Russia till 1917.

Peter I (the Great), tsar from 1682–1725, made Russia into a major European power. By this time Siberia had been conquered and Russia continued to expand. Russia's rising power in the Middle East was checked by the Crimean War (1853–56) but by 1884 much of Central Asia was conquered. By the time of World War I in 1914, Russia was a vast region.

St Petersburg

St. Petersburg was established by Peter I in 1703. Except for a brief four-year period, it was the capital of Russia from 1713 to 1918. It was renamed Petrograd (1914–24) and Leningrad (1924–91) before reverting to its old name. The city has beautiful architecture including palaces, churches, cathedrals, and museums. The homes of great musicians and writers who lived here have also been preserved.

1613 Michael Romanov becomes tsar (emperor); Romanovs rule till **1917**.

1667–70 Cossack and peasant uprising led by Stenka Razin.

1689 Russia and China sign treaty of Nerchinsk.

1703 Peter the Great founds city of St Petersburg.

1707–08 Astrakhan revolt in Russia led by Cossack Bulavin.

1708–09 King Charles XII of Sweden invades Russia; defeated in Battle of Poltava.

1757 Russian Academy of Arts founded.

1762–96 Catherine the Great is empress.

1772–1814 Russia conquers Crimea, parts of east Europe.

1799–1852 Life of Russian painter Karl Briullov.

1801–25 Tsar Alexander I rules Russia.

1809 Finland brought under Russian rule.

1812 Napoleon's invasion of Russia defeated.

1825–28 Iran–Russia War; Tabriz captured by Russia.

THE SOVIET ERA

The communist revolution of 1917 forced Russia to withdraw from World War I and was followed by civil war, but by the end of 1920 the communists had established their power and began to build a new country under Vladimir Lenin. Initially, four socialist republics were set up (Russia, Ukraine, Belarus, Transcaucasus), coming together in 1922 to form the Union of Soviet Socialist Republics (USSR), which other republics such as Georgia, Armenia, and Azerbaijan later joined.

Lenin died in 1924, and in 1929 Joseph Stalin assumed power, ruling till his death in 1953. During this time no dissent was allowed. Thousands were killed, exiled to the Central Asian republics, imprisoned, or sent to labor camps in Siberia.

The Cold War era began after World War

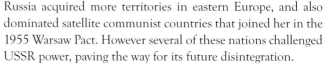

LENIN

Vladimir Ilyich Lenin (1870–1924) is considered the creator of the USSR and was the leader of its first government. He formulated and organized the revolution of 1917, and wrote extensively on Marxist theory and plans for the Soviet state; his works have been collected in 45 volumes. There are different views on his ideas and legacy but he was one of the greatest revolutionaries of the twentieth century.

II. During that war Russia acquired more territories in eastern Europe, and also dominated satellite communist countries that joined her in the 1955 Warsaw Pact. However several of these nations challenged USSR power, paving the way for its future disintegration.

The USSR had a planned economy, but gradually it had begun to decline. Mikhail Gorbachev, general secretary of the Communist Party from 1985 and later president of Russia, began to introduce market reforms and to allow more freedom with programs such as *glasnost* (openess) and *perestroika* (restructuring). Satellite states and USSR republics began to assert their independence and, by the end of 1991, the USSR had dissolved.

Joseph Stalin

Milestone Events

1828–1910 Life of Leo Tolstoy, author of *War and Peace*.
1830–31 Polish revolt against Russian rule suppressed.
1840–93 Life of composer Pyotr Ilyich Tchaikovsky.
1853–57 Crimean War.
1861 Serfdom abolished.
1867 Russia sells Alaska to the USA.
1873–1949 Life of Russian architect Alexey Shchusev, designs Kazan railway station, Lenin's mausoleum.
1877–78 Russo–Turkish war takes place.

1882 Tsar Alexander II assassinated.
1891–1953 Life of classical composer and musician Sergei Prokofiev.
1897 Revolutionary Social Democratic Party founded.
1903 Social Democratic Party splits into Bolsheviks (later communists) and Mensheviks.
1904–05 Russo-Japanese war, Russia is defeated.
1905 Revolution in Russia; Duma (parliament) established.
1906–75 Life of great composer Dmitri Shostakovitch.

USSR Culture

In its experiments as the first socialist state in the world, the USSR had several achievements despite its many failings. Free education increased the literacy rate from around 30 per cent to almost 100 per cent. Scientists were provided with the best facilities and made great strides, especially in nuclear energy and space research; in 1957 Sputnik was the first artificial satellite to orbit the earth, and in 1961 Yuri Gagarin was the first human in space.

Artists, writers, and painters were encouraged, but only if they did not challenge state policies. This led to a genre of dissident literature, known as samizdat, which was circulated secretly. In sports and games, including chess, the USSR also reached new heights.

Above: The first animal to orbit the earth, the Soviet space dog Laika was launched into orbit in *Sputnik II* in 1957.
Right: Writer Alexander Solzhenitsyn.
Far right: Leon Trotsky, a key figure in the revolution, was assassinated on Stalin's orders, and was fatally stabbed with an ice pick.

1914 Russia enters World War I.
1917 Russian revolution, tsar overthrown; Russia withdraws from war, loses Poland and other lands.
1918–22 Communists win civil war against non-communists (White Russians).
1921 Treaty of Nystadt between Sweden and Russia cedes Baltic provinces to Russia.
1922 Russia, Ukraine, Belarus, and Transcaucasus (later Georgia, Armenia, and Azerbaijan) join in Soviet union.

1925 City of Volgograd renamed Stalingrad.
1928 Collectivized farms established.
• First Five Year Plan for industrialization.
1933 USA recognizes Soviet Union.
1939 USSR and Germany agree Non-Aggression Pact, including secret plan to divide Poland.
1939–40 Russo-Finnish war, Russia acquires territory.
1939–45 World War II; USSR invades Poland 16 days after Germany does; **1941** Germany invades USSR and is eventually repulsed.

AFTER 1991

To maintain some sort of unity among the former parts of the USSR, Russia established the Commonwealth of Independent States (CIS), which was joined by most former states except for the Baltic countries. Meanwhile Chechnya, one of its provinces, declared independence.

Right: The battle of Stalingrad, 1942–43.
Below: A modern gas pipeline.

Milestone Events

1940 Leon Trotsky (b. 1879) Bolshevik leader, is assassinated in exile.
- Lithuania, Latvia, Estonia occupied; part of Romania ceded (became Moldavian Socialist Republic).

1945 Red Army marches towards Germany, enters Berlin.

1950 USSR and China sign fifty-year alliance.

1955 Warsaw Pact formed.

1956 USSR sends troops into Hungary.

1958 Nikita Krushchev becomes prime minister.

1961 City of Stalingrad reverts to name of Volgograd.

1968 Soviet and Warsaw pact countries suppress Czechoslovakia liberal movement.

1970 Alexander Solzhenitsyn (1981–2008) wins Nobel Prize for Literature.

1975 Andrei Sakharov (1921–89), human rights activist and dissident, awarded Nobel Peace Prize.

1979–88 USSR occupies Afghanistan.

1985 Mikhail Gorbachev becomes general secretary of Communist Party, introduces open and liberal glasnost and perestroika policies.

The early years of the new state were difficult and in 1991 there was an attempted coup against Gorbachev. Russia began to privatize industries, and a new wealthy elite developed. Oil and gas reserves helped revive the economy; Russia has the largest natural gas reserves in the world, and is second to Saudi Arabia in oil production. Its oil has been used as a political weapon to control former republics including Ukraine and Belarus.

Russia continues to battle separatists within the country and to interfere in the affairs of its former republics, however it has improved relations with the USA.

St. Basil's Cathedral, Moscow.

PUTIN

Vladimir Putin is credited with restoring Russia's economy and pride. Born in 1952 in Leningrad (St. Petersburg), he joined the KGB. He is a black belt in judo. After becoming president in 2000 he removed officials accused of corruption, but functioned in an authoritative style. He is now the prime minister of Russia.

1986 Accident in Chernobyl nuclear plant.
1988 Gorbachev becomes president of USSR.
1991 Boris Yeltsin becomes president.
- Soviet Union collapses; Commonwealth of Independent States is formed.
- Chechnya declares independence, **1994** Russia invades.
1992 Russia takes up USSR's seat in United Nations.
1993 MPs barricade themselves into parliament after dispute with Yeltsin; army breaks in.

1998 Financial collapse in Russia.
2000 Vladimir Putin is elected president; reelected **2004**; becomes prime minister **2008**.
- Nuclear submarine Kursk sinks; crew killed.
2002 Chechen rebels hold 800 hostages in Moscow theater; rebels and 120 people killed in rescue.
2004 Chechen terrorists hold children hostage in North Ossetia school, more than 300 killed.
2010 Suicide bombers kill 39 on Moscow Metro.
- Arms reduction treaty with USA.

EUROPE

Covering an area of 4,065,000 square miles, Europe forms the western part of the landmass known as Eurasia. Its northernmost point is in Norway, and its southernmost in Spain; the eastern boundary stretches from the Ural mountains to the Caucasus. Europe is thus not a separate continent, but is considered geographically and culturally distinct. Its highest point is Mt. Elbrus at 18,510 ft in the Caucasus mountains, and its longest river is the Volga (2,290 miles). Major mineral resources include coal and iron ore, with oil and natural gas in some areas.

One of Europe's great paintings, Leonardo da Vinci's *Mona Lisa*.

HISTORY

Early hominid occupation of Europe dates to at least one million years ago, and cave paintings were made by 28,000 BCE. Along the Mediterranean coast, cities were founded

by around 3000 BCE. Greece and Rome—the great early civilizations of Europe—formed the foundations on which later Western culture was based. Gradually the Roman empire began to dominate much of Europe, eventually spreading Christianity across Europe. Although the Western Roman empire declined in the fifth century, in the east the Byzantine empire continued until conquered by the Ottomans in 1453.

The Renaissance, beginning in the thirteenth and fourteenth centuries, was the

great age of European culture. From the fifteenth century Europeans began to explore the world, leading later to their great colonial empires. In the eighteenth century, the industrial revolution began in Britain, while France saw the new ideas and upheaval caused by the French Revolution. By the twentieth century Europe was industrialized and prosperous, but two world wars weakened the continent. The dissolution of Russia brought in many changes, particularly in Eastern Europe.

The Pope in Vatican City, Rome, heart of the Roman Catholic Church.

Finally, in the twenty-first century, the European Union has led to some common economic programmes and a movement towards further unity.

CULTURE

Even in this relatively small region a wide variety of languages are spoken, but many Europeans know more than one language, and are thus not culturally isolated. Though European colonies gained independence, European languages are also still spoken in former colonies.

Christianity is the dominant religion, although Islam is prominent in Turkey and Albania.

From the time of the Renaissance, Europe was the center of great scientists, artists, musicians, and writers, with trends often spreading across the continent.

Cuisine is diverse, but certain common aspects are the use of bread made of wheat, and a dependence on meat and dairy products.

Modern sports have largely originated in Europe, including discus, shot put, javelin, cricket, football, hockey, basketball, tennis, and golf.

The European Parliament Building in Strasbourg.

Scandinavia: NORWAY, SWEDEN

The countries of Northern Europe have a closely connected history, especially that of the Viking raiders and colonizers. Norway, Sweden, and Denmark also have similar languages.

These countries are economically well-developed with high living standards, combining free-market principles with welfare and social security systems.

Norway

Norway is headed by a prime minister with a unicameral parliament, which divides into two for specific purposes. The Sami people (Lapps) have a separate parliament with some autonomy.

Norway is prosperous due to its oil and gas deposits. There were around 29 small kingdoms in the eighth century, and the first united Norwegian kingdom was formed in the ninth century. Later, Norway came under Denmark, followed by Sweden, then gained independence in 1905. Norway was neutral during the world wars, but was occupied by Germany from 1940–45. The country has a rich literary tradition, including great writers Henrik Ibsen (1828–1906) and Knut Hamsun (1859–1952), who received the Nobel Prize for Literature in 1920. Edward Munch (1863–1944) is one of Norway's best known painters, and Edward Grieg (1843–1907) is one of its famous musicians. Norway awards the Nobel Peace Prize.

Norway is famous for its scenic fjords or mountain inlets.

Norway
Area: 125,020 sq miles •
Population: 4,660,539 •
Capital: Oslo
• System of government: Constitutional monarchy

Milestone Events

14,000–10,000 BCE First occupation of northern part of the region.

8th–10th CENTURIES CE Vikings raid and colonize other parts of Europe.

12th–19th CENTURIES Sweden takes over Finland.

1397 Union of Kalmar unites Denmark, Sweden, and Norway. Denmark becomes dominant.

1523 Sweden becomes independent under king Gustav I.

1660 Frontiers of Norway, Sweden, Denmark settled.

1814 Denmark cedes Norway to Sweden.

1849–1912 Life of Swedish writer August Strindberg.

1863–1944 Life of Norwegian painter Edvard Munch.

1867–86 Thousands migrate from Sweden to America because of food shortages.

1903 Norwegian Bjornstjerne Martinus Bjornsen (1832–1910) wins Nobel Prize for Literature.

1905 Union between Sweden and Norway peacefully dissolved.

Sweden

Sweden
Capital:
Stockholm •
Area: *173,859*
sq miles •
Population:
9,059,651
• System of
government:
Constitutional
monarchy

Sweden includes the islands of Gotland and Oland in the Baltic Sea as well as its mainland area. Although the country remained neutral during the two world wars and in later world affairs, Sweden was willing to shelter refugees and political dissenters. Prime minister Olaf Palme was an outspoken critic of the Vietnam War, the Soviet invasion of Afghanistan, nuclear weapons, and apartheid. He was assassinated in 1986.

The streamlined and stylized Swedish ceramics, glass, furniture, and steel products are popular around the world. Swedish chemist and industrialist Alfred Nobel funded four out of five Nobel prizes; a sixth, for economic science, awarded from 1968, is funded by the Bank of Sweden.

Right: The Oresund Bridge linking Sweden and Denmark.
Above right: Typical streamlined Swedish glassware.
Below: Alfred Nobel (1833–1896).

1911 Roald Amundsen of Norway is first to reach South Pole.

1918–2007 Life of Ingmar Bergman, Swedish film director.

1925 Ninth-century port of Kristiania renamed Oslo.

1940–45 World War II: Norway occupied by Germany; Vidkun Quisling declares himself head of government; 1945 executed for treason.

1952 Nordic Council founded to promote mutual interests of Scandinavian countries.

1960s Oil and gas deposits discovered in Norwegian sector of North Sea

1928 Norwegian Sigrid Undset (1882–1949) wins Nobel Prize for Literature.

1986 Olaf Palme (b. 1927), prime minister of Sweden, is assassinated.

1993 Norway mediates peace between Israel and PLO, leading to Oslo accords.

2000 Norway begins mediation between Sri Lanka government and Tamil separatists.

Denmark

A constitutional monarchy, the country is headed by a prime minister and has a unicameral parliament. Greenland and the Faroe Islands are self-governing territories.

Between the ninth and eleventh centuries the Danes invaded and ruled England. Later, Denmark was the dominant power in the union with Sweden and Norway.

The nineteenth century was Denmark's golden age, with composer Carl August Nielson (1865-1931); author of fairy tales Hans Christian Anderson (1805-75); the philosopher Soren Kierkegaard (1813-55); and writer Johannes Vilhelm Jensen (1873-1950), winner of the 1944 Nobel Prize for Literature

Above right: The statue of the Little Mermaid, Copenhagen, Denmark.

Denmark
Area: 16,383 sq miles (excluding Greenland and Faroe islands)
• Population: 5,500,510 •
Capital: Copenhagen • System of government: Constitutional monarchy

Milestone Events

14,000–10,000 BCE First occupation in the north.
8th–10th CENTURIES CE Vikings raid and colonize other parts of Europe.
c. 875 Vikings reach Iceland.
986 Eric the Red leads Icelandic settlers to Greenland.
11th CENTURY Leif Ericcson lands in Canada (Vinland).
12th–19th CENTURIES Finland comes under Sweden.
1380 Iceland enters a union with Denmark.
1397 Union of Kalmar unites Denmark, Sweden, and Norway; Denmark is dominant; **1523** Sweden leaves.

1445 Copenhagen becomes capital of Denmark.
1660 Frontiers of Denmark, Norway, Sweden settied.
1729 Greenland becomes Danish province.
1805–75 Life of Danish fairy-tale author Hans Christian Andersen.
1809 Finland taken by Russia, but becomes an autonomous grand duchy of Russia.
1814 Denmark cedes Norway to Sweden.
1849 Denmark becomes constitutional monarchy.
1906 All Finnish men and women get right to vote.

Finland
Area: *130,558 sq miles* •
Population: *5,250, 275* •
Capital: *Helsinki* • System of government: *Republic*

Greenland
Area: *836,330 sq miles* •
Population: *57,600* • Capital: *Nuuk (Godthab)* • System of government: *Parliamentary democracy (Danish dependency)*

Iceland
Area: *39,768 sq miles* •
Population: *306,694* • Capital: *Reykjavik* • System of government: *Republic*

Finland

Finland has an elected president. Occupied by Sweden and then by Russia, Finland gained independence in 1917; the country's greatest composer, Jean Sibelius (1867–1957) symbolized the nationalist struggle through his music. The Finnish company Nokia is a world leader in mobile phones.

The Viking Leif Ericson lands in Vinland (modern Canada) in the 11th century.

Greenland

Greenland enjoys considerable autonomy under Denmark. It is the largest island in the world, and almost totally ice-covered. Greenland's economy is primarily based on fishing

Iceland

Iceland became an independent republic in 1944. Its unicameral parliament is known as the Althing and is said to be the oldest in the world, functioning from 930. The country enjoys underground hot springs and geysers, but suffered deeply from major volcanic eruptions in 1783 and 1875, and recently in 2010.

Ash and debris are spewed into the atmosphere from Icelandic volcanoes.

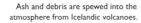

1917 Finland declares independence from Russia.
1940–45 World War II; Denmark occupied by Germany.
1943 Danish resistance helps nearly all the country's Jews escape to Sweden.
1944 Iceland declares independence from Denmark.
1948 Denmark grants self-government to the Faroe islands.
1952 Nordic Council founded to promote mutual interests of Scandinavian countries.
1979 Greenland granted home rule by Denmark.

1985 Iceland declares itself a nuclear-free zone.
1994–2000 Martti Ahtisaari is Finnish president.
2000 Oresund bridge is opened, the longest combined road and rail bridge, linking Denmark and Sweden.
• Tarja Halonen is first female president of Finland; 2006 reelected.
2008 Martti Ahtisaari wins Nobel Peace Prize for mediating in international conflicts eg. Kosovo.
2010 Ash from a volcanic explosion in Iceland halts air traffic across Europe.

Belgium

Belgium has a federal structure, with Dutch-speaking (Flemish) Flanders in the north; primarily French-speaking Wallonia in the south; and Brussels, a cosmopolitan city where both French and Dutch are official languages.

Initially occupied by Celtic tribes, Belgium spent centuries ruled by foreigners: Romans, Franks, the House of Burgundy, Spain, Austria, and France, before it was united with the Netherlands, from whom it split in 1830. Belgium itself colonized Rwanda, Burundi, and the Democratic Republic of Congo in Africa.

Belgium is known for its chocolate and wide variety of beers.

Belgium
Area: 11,787 sq miles •
Population: 10,414,336 •
Capital: *Brussels* • System of government: *Constitutional monarchy*

Traditional architecture in Ghent town center, Belgium.

The Atomium, Brussels, built for the 1958 World Fair.

Milestone Events

c. 5000 BCE Farming settlements in the region.
6th CENTURY BCE Celts occupy the region.
1st CENTURY BCE Roman empire conquers the region.
925 CE Netherlands or Low Countries comes under Holy Roman empire.
1060 Count Conrad founds House of Luxembourg.
1291 Swiss Confederation founded, initially with three cantons.

1437 Habsburg dynasty begins domination of Luxembourg.
c. 1466–1536 Life of Desiderius Erasmus, Dutch scholar and philosopher.
1499 Swiss Confederation gains independence from Holy Roman empire.
1515 Switzerland adopts policy of neutrality that it maintains through the centuries right up to World Wars I and II.
1568 Dutch revolt against Spanish Habsburg empire.

The Netherlands

International Courts of Justice, The Hague, the Netherlands.

Also known as Holland after its largest province, the Netherlands includes the self-governing Caribbean islands of Aruba and the Netherlands Antilles. About 20 per cent of its European mainland is water, and much of the land has been reclaimed from the North Sea, creating an extensive system of dykes.

Once dependent on her sea trade, today Netherlands has oil and gas reserves and several industries, and also exports agricultural produce and flowers. The International Court of Justice is based at The Hague, which is also the Dutch seat of government. The country is modern and liberal, tries to arrive at a consensus on all important matters, and is considered one of the most democratic nations in the world.

The Netherlands was ruled by the Habsburg dynasty for centuries, only winning independence in 1648 after an 80-year war of independence from Spain. In the sixteenth and seventeenth centuries, the Netherlands established colonies in several parts of the world. Known as the Netherlands' golden age, philosophers, scientists, and artists flourished at this time. Like many European countries, the Netherlands was conquered by France during its Revolutionary Wars, and was ruled by France from 1795 to 1815.

The Netherlands
Area: *16,040 sq miles* •
Population: *16,715,999* • Capital: *Amsterdam; seat of government: The Hague* • System of government: *Constitutional monarchy*

Anne Frank was killed in the Bergen-Belsen concentration camp at the age of 15. Her war-time diary, written while hiding in the Netherlands from the Nazis, is read around the world.

The timelines for Belgium, the Netherlands, Luxembourg, and Switzerland are shared on this and the next page.

1581 The northern Dutch United Provinces declare independence from Spain; **1648** Recognized in Peace of Munster; southern provinces stay with Spain.

1632–77 Life of Dutch philosopher Baruch Spinoza.

17th CENTURY Netherlands becomes a leading colonial power.

1795–1813 Netherlands occupied by France.

1798–1815 Switzerland occupied by French.

1815 Kingdom of the Netherlands formed, united with Belgium.

• Luxembourg becomes a grand duchy under the Netherlands.

1827–1901 Life of Swiss writer Johanna Spyri, author of the popular children's book, *Heidi*.

1830 Belgium secedes from Netherlands and forms separate kingdom.

1839 Luxembourg loses more than half its territory to Belgium, but gains more autonomy.

EUROPE

Luxembourg

Luxembourg is a tiny, landlocked country, whose history is linked with that of its neighbors. Prosperous and highly industrialized, its economy is now focused on banking and financial services, and people from neighboring Germany, Belgium, and France commute to Luxembourg every day for work.

Top right: Skiing at Zermatt, Switzerland.
Bottom right: Giselbert, Count of Luxembourg (1007–59).
Below: Notre Dame Cathedral, Luxembourg.

Luxembourg
Area: *998 sq miles* • Population: *491,775* •
Capital: *Luxembourg* • System of government:
Constitutional monarchy

Milestone Events

1848 Swiss constitution confirms federal system with centralized government.
1863 International Red Cross founded in Geneva.
1867 Luxembourg gains independence.
1912 Marie Adelade is first grand-duchess of Luxembourg.
1914–18 The Netherlands remains neutral in World War I.
1920 League of Nations headquarters established in Geneva.

1922 Dutch women get right to vote.
1930 Belgium passes law allowing Flanders and Wallonia to become single-language regions.
1940 World War II: Germany invades Belgium, Luxembourg, and Netherlands; Belgian, Netherlands governments function from London.
1944 Allied forces liberate the region.
1948 Benelux customs union established between Belgium, Netherlands, Luxembourg; 1958 Benelux Economic Union formed.

Switzerland

Switzerland
Area: *15,937 sq miles* •
Population: *7,604,467* •
Capital: *Bern*
• System of government: *Confederation*

Switzerland is a mountainous region, with a plateau between the two mountain ranges of the Alps. There are several lakes and rivers, and its scenic beauty is renowned. This small, neutral country is the headquarters of the United Nations. It has a very high standard of living and a developed, industrialized economy.

Switzerland's constitution dates back to 1874, though with several amendments since then. The Bundesrat (Federal Council) is elected by a bicameral legislature, which also elects the president, who serves for just one year. Important issues are decided through a referendum of all citizens.

In the Middle Ages Switzerland consisted of several small city states or cantons, who grouped together for mutual defence. Switzerland was recognized as an independent entity by the peace of Westphalia in 1648 that ended the Thirty Years' War. The country became a unified federal state in 1874.

Geneva, Switzerland.

1966 Princess Beatrix, heir to the throne of Netherlands marries German diplomat, after much controversy.

1971 Women in Switzerland gain right to vote in national elections.

1981 Switzerland grants equal rights to women.

1993 Belgian constitution changed; becomes federal state with three administrative regions.

1995 Flooding in the Netherlands causes evacuation of quarter of a million people.

1998 Swiss Dignitas clinic opens offering doctor-assisted suicide to terminally ill patients.

2000 Homosexuals gain equal legal rights in Netherlands; voluntary euthanasia legalized.

2002 Switzerland joins the UN.

2008 Luxembourg parliament restricts position of monarch to a purely ceremonial role.

2009 Switzerland relaxes its rules about banking secrecy rules to cooperate with international investigative organizations.

Frances has a republican system of government based on the constitution of 1958 (the fifth republic). The chief of state is an elected president, while the head of government is the prime minister. The legislature is bicameral. France is divided into 26 regions, including the island of Corsica and its overseas territories. These are further subdivided into 100 departments. In 2003 the constitution was amended, devolving more powers to the regions and departments.

Metropolitan or mainland France consists of plains, plateaux, mountain ranges in the Alps and the Jura, and the island of Corsica. European France is by far the largest and most populous part of the republic. Overseas France is the label for the overseas territories: French Guiana, Guadeloupe, Martinique, and Réunion.

France is an industrialized and well-developed country but agriculture is still important. It has rich mineral resources, fertile land, forests, and marine resources.

Area: 248,429 sq miles •
Population: 64,057,792 •
Capital: Paris
• System of government: Republic

THE PAST

France was occupied from the Stone Age, with cave paintings at Chauvet dating to around 30,000 BCE. Thousands of stone monuments, such as menhirs and dolmens, dating between 4000 and 2000 BCE, have been found in Brittany and elsewhere. By around 800 BCE France was occupied by Gauls, who gave their name to the land, and was conquered by the Romans between the second and first centuries BCE. With the decline

Milestone Events

1.8 MILLION YEARS AGO Early stone tools indicate occupation in the area.
80,000 YEARS AGO Neanderthals occupy the region.
30,000 BCE Chauvet cave paintings, many other cave paintings in the region.
5500–2500 BCE Farming cultures in the region.
51 BCE Julius Caesar conquers region for Rome.
741 Pepin the Short establishes Carolingian dynasty.
800 CE Charlemagne becomes Holy Roman emperor.
843 Empire partitioned by Treaty of Verdun.

910 Cluny monastery founded.
987 Hugh Capet founds Capetian dynasty in France.
1066 William of Normandy wins Battle of Hastings, conquers England.
1209 Albigensian crusade launched against Cathars, a sect accused of heresy.
1328–1589 House of Valois rules France.
1337–1443 Period of Hundred Years' War between France and England.

of the Western Roman empire in the fifth century CE, France was occupied by a Germanic tribe, the Franks. The Frankish Merovingian dynasty ruled till 751, followed by the Carolingians.

Meanwhile the Vikings invaded the region, establishing the territory of Normandy in northern France. The Carolingians ruled France till 987, followed by the Capetians and the Valois. France reached a height under the Bourbon kings, particularly Louis XIV. It had the largest population in Europe and was the center of new scientific discoveries and philosophical thought. It also began to acquire foreign colonies.

The French revolution of 1789 replaced the monarchy with a republic, and ushered in new ideas of equality and liberty. Though the republic was soon taken over by Napoleon (1799), its ideals influenced the whole world.

Depiction of Marianne based on a bust of actress Brigitte Bardot.

MARIANNE

A female figure depicted in different ways, Marianne is a symbol of France, seen on French euro coins and on postage stamps. The Marianne figure first appeared at the time of the French revolution of 1789, and recently real women have been depicted as Marianne, including the actress Brigitte Bardot (b.1934).

The Louvre Museum, France.

1562–98 Wars of Religion fought between Catholics and Protestants (Huguenots).
1608 French colonists found Québec in North America.
1614–1715 Reign of Louis XIV, the Sun King.
1642 Mathematician Blaise Pascal (1623–62) invents first calculator.
1682 French court moves to palace of Versailles.
1789 French Revolution, monarchy overthrown.
1792–1804 First Republic of France.

1793 Louis XVI executed.
1799 Napoleon Bonaparte takes control of France; 1804 proclaimed emperor (First Empire).
• French soldiers find Rosetta stone in Egypt.
1815 Napoleon defeated at Battle of Waterloo, sent into exile; monarchy restored.
1845–1924 Life of composer Gabriel Fauré.
1848 Revolution; Second Republic established.
1852 Second Empire founded.
1870–71 Franco–Prussian War, France defeated.

FRANCE AFTER THE WARS

After World War II many of France's colonies struggled for independence, particularly Indochina and Algeria. In 1958 the war hero General Charles de Gaulle brought in the Fifth Republic and gave the country a new direction, however, after student unrest and a general strike in 1968, de Gaulle resigned. Since then France has had mainly socialist governments, though in 2007 Nicholas Sarkozy of the conservative UMP won the presidential election.

General Charles de Gaulle.

CULTURE

French culture is among the richest in the world. Literature, music, philosophy, and art have flourished from medieval times, and modern French cinema offers innovative and experimental themes.

France is famous for its cuisine. It manufactures more than 250 cheeses and some of the best wines in the world. Among sports, the Tour de France is the greatest bicycle race in the world.

The Eiffel Tower, Paris.

Beaches at Cannes and other south of France seaside towns are attractive tourist destinations.

Milestone Events

1871–1940 Third Republic.
1874 The first Impressionist art exhibition, in Paris.
1889 Eiffel Tower is built in Paris.
1903 Prix Goncourt, French literary prize, awarded for the first time.
1914–18 World War I; France fights on Allied side; many battles take place in France with huge casualties.
1915–1963 Life of popular singer Edith Piaf.
1919 Treaty of Versailles; France regains Alsace-Lorraine.

1939–45 World War II; Germany occupies most of France; Vichy regime collaborates with Germany; General Charles de Gaulle leads government-in-exile.
1947–58 Fourth Republic.
1945–54 First Indochina War; Vietnam wins independence.
1954–62 Algerian War of Independence.
1956 France grants independence to Morocco and Tunisia.

Above: A vineyard in the Champagne region, where the famous wine is produced.
Right: The palace of Versailles.

CHARLES PERRAULT: THE FAIRY TALE WRITER

Using existing folk tales, Charles Perrault (1628–1703) wrote many of the stories now famous the world over, including Little Red Riding Hood, Puss in Boots, Cinderella, Sleeping Beauty, and Bluebeard.

1958 Fifth Republic under Charles de Gaulle.

1968 Student riots and national strikes.

1969 President de Gaulle resigns; Georges Pompidou elected president.

1974 Pompidou dies, succeeded by Giscard d'Estaing.

1981 Socialist candidate François Mitterrand elected president; reelected 1988.

1995 Jacques Chirac elected president, ending 14 years of Socialist Party; reelected 2002.

• France conducts nuclear tests in the Pacific.

2002–3, 2005, 2007 Widespread strikes protesting government cut-backs and pension changes.

2003 Constitution amended, gives more autonomy to regions and departments.

• Heatwave causes about 11,000 deaths.

2004 Religious symbols, including Islamic headscarf, banned from schools.

2007 Nicolas Sarkozy of conservative UMP party elected president.

2009 $33.1 billion package to rescue economy agreed.

Germany has plains, river valleys and plateaux in the center, with the Bavarian Alps in the south. Apart from the mainland area, its territory includes several islands.

Divided since 1945, East and West were reunified in 1990. Germany is an industrialized country with a high standard of living, but still faces problems of uneven development in the east and west.

Germany now has a federal republican system of government, and is divided into sixteen states. The president is the chief of state, but has a largely ceremonial role, while the chancellor is the head of government. There is a bicameral legislature. Each state has an elected assembly and some local powers.

Area: 137,847 sq miles •
Population: 82,839,758 •
Capital: Berlin
• System of government: Federal republic

THE PAST

Various Celtic and Germanic cultures were in the area when Rome invaded. In the fifth century Clovis I established a large kingdom that included part of Germany, but this kingdom broke up in 843 under the Carolingians,

The banks of the Rhine house many medieval and later castles.

Milestone Events

400,000–40,000 YEARS AGO Hunter-gatherers in Europe.

4500 BCE Farming settlements in the region.

2300 BCE Ancestors of Germanic people and Celts, probably Indo-Europeans, migrate to the region.

1800–400 BCE Iron Age cultures eg. Hallstatt, La Tene.

c.150 BCE Romans begin to influence the region.

9 CE Hermann (Arminius) forms a coalition of tribes and destroys Roman army at the

Teutoburg Forest; Romans later retaliate and draw frontier at the Rhine river.

c. 400 Romans begin to withdraw.

486 Frankish king Clovis establishes kingdom in the region.

800 Charlemagne, Frankish ruler of areas of present-day France and Germany, crowned Holy Roman emperor.

843 Carolingian empire divided into three, Germany emerges as a separate region.

Nazi leader Hitler (1889–1945).

and a separate country, East Francia, emerged in the region of modern Germany. East Francia consisted of a number of duchies, the most important being Franconia, Swabia, Bavaria, Saxony, and Lorraine. Otto I (936) of the Saxon line began creating a more centralized administration.

In later years Germany was part of the Holy Roman empire, ruled by the Habsburgs of Austria from 1438. In the sixteenth century the Protestant Reformation began, leading to a number of wars, partially based on religious differences. Peace was brought through the Treaty of Westphalia of 1648, and most of the German territories became independent. Gradually Prussia and Austria began to grow in power. Otto von Bismarck, chancellor of Prussia, was instrumental in strengthened his state and unifying Germany.

The unified country was a strong state with expansionist designs. In 1882 Germany was allied with Austria and Italy (Triple Alliance). Entering World War I as part of this alliance, Germany was defeated. Extreme nationalism, with the rise of Adolf Hitler and the Nazis, was part of Germany's efforts to regain its prominence in Europe. But World War II and the Nazi atrocities led to a ruined and defeated country, divided among the allied powers.

Ludwig van Beethoven (1770–1827).

MUSIC FESTIVALS

Home of the great musicians Johann Sebastian Bach, Ludwig van Beethoven, Johannes Brahms, and Richard Wagner, among others, Germany today hosts several music festivals including the Wagner festival at Bayreuth, and the Bach festivals at Ansbach and Leipzig.

The Berlin Wall.

962 German king Otto I becomes Holy Roman emperor; center of the empire is now Germany.

1138 Konrad III is first Hohenstaufen emperor.

1250 Death of Emperor Frederick II Hohenstaufen; empire disintegrates into small states.

1356 Golden Bull clarifies position of Holy Roman emperor or king of Germany: nobles and archbishops in German states elect king, who must then be crowned emperor by the pope.

1471–1528 Life of artist Albrecht Durer.

c.1497–1523 Life of Hans Holbein the Younger, painter and printmaker, known for his portraits.

1517 Protestant Reformation begins.

1525 Albrecht of Hohenzollern, grandmaster of the Teutonic knights, becomes Duke of Prussia.

1648 Thirty Years' War ends with Treaty of Westphalia.

1660 Frederick William, elector of Brandenburg, gains independence for Prussia through Peace of Oliva.

1687–1753 Life of architect Balthasar Neumann.

1724–1804 Life of philosopher Immanuel Kant.

GERMANY DIVIDED

Initially partitioned into four, and occupied by the USA, UK, France, and the Soviet Union, by 1949 Germany was in two halves. The city of Berlin was also divided into two. East Germany, or the German Democratic Republic, was recognized as a separate state by the USSR in 1954, while West Germany or the Federal Republic of Germany gained recognition as an independent state in 1955. By the 1980s it was a leading economic power in Europe.

Unification in 1990 dissolved the state of East Germany, making it a part of the Federal Republic in the west. After the

The Brandenburg Gate, Berlin, built in 1791 as a symbol of peace.

initial euphoria, Germany realized that unification brought many problems, as the west was more prosperous, while easterners had lived under conditions that guaranteed houses and jobs.

AFTER UNIFICATION

Housing and job shortages were accompanied by strikes and a recession that hit the country in 1993. Several industries in the east collapsed when faced with competition. However, the problems are gradually being resolved.

Chancellor Angela Merkel.

Milestone Events

1740 Frederick the Great becomes king of Prussia.
1749–1832 Life of writer Johann Wolfgang von Goethe.
1770–1831 Life of philosopher Friedrich Hegel.
1774–1840 Life of artist Caspar David Friedrich.
1791 Mozart's *Magic Flute* is considered the beginning of German opera; other great composers follow.
1806 Napoleon occupies Germany.
1815 German Confederation formed at the Congress of Vienna.
1844–1900 Life of philosopher Friedrich Nietzsche.

1848 Revolutions fail to achieve democratic union.
1871 Otto von Bismarck, prime minister of Prussia, unifies German states/principalites in new German empire (second reich).
1888 Kaiser (emperor) William II begins rule; focus on colonial expansion.
1890 Social Democratic Party of Germany (SPD), a workers' movement, is founded.
1914–18 Germany fights as part of Central Powers in World War I, defeated.

CULTURE

Germany is known for its scientific and technological achievements, and at the same time for its great philosophers, artists, musicians, and writers.

Left: Formula 1 racing champion Michael Schumacher.
Below: Enjoying the Munich Beer Festival.

1918–19 Conflict within Germany.
1919 Treaty of Versailles; Germany loses territory; foundation of Weimar Republic.
1933 Adolf Hitler becomes chancellor.
1934 Third Reich (empire) declared; single-party state, persecution of Jews.
1938 Austria and Sudetenland annexed.
1939–45 World War II; Germany is finally defeated and occupied by Allies.
1949 Division into east and west.

1961 Berlin Wall constructed.
1989 Berlin Wall falls.
1990 East and West Germany reunite.
1991 Berlin is the new capital.
2002 Dresden flooded by river Elbe after torrential rain.
2005 Angela Merkel of the Christian Democrats becomes first woman chancellor; 2009, reelected.
2009 Parliament agrees $63 billion rescue package to help stimulate the economy.

Italy includes several islands, among which are Sicily, Sardinia, and Elba, as well as Campione d'Italia, a small enclave in Switzerland. Within Italy, San Marino, and Vatican City are independent territories.

Italy became a democratic republic in 1948. The chief of state is the president, while the head of government is the prime minister, known in Italy as president of the council of ministers. The president is elected by both houses of parliament and 58 regional representatives for a seven-year term. The prime minister is appointed by the president and confirmed by parliament.

HISTORY

Italy was once the center of the vast Roman empire, whose capital was Rome. Roman culture, which had absorbed aspects of Greek civilization,

influenced many aspects of Western culture, even though the Western Roman empire ended in the fifth century.

In the early Middle Ages Italy came under several dynasties including the Carolingians and Hohenstaufens. Following this, independent city-states arose in the region. The Renaissance began

A sample of rock art from Valcamonica in the Lombardy plain, where petroglyphs were carved since prehistoric times.

Milestone Events

200,000 YEARS AGO Italy occupied by stone tool-using cultures.

8th AND 7th CENTURIES BCE Greek colonies in south and on Sicily.

c. 800 BCE Etruscan culture develops in Italy.

756 BCE City of Rome founded.

1st CENTURY BCE Roman empire founded.

285 CE Roman empire divides into Western and Eastern (Byzantine).

476 Germanic leader Odacer conquers Rome, Western Roman empire ends.

6th CENTURY Byzantine rule ends in Italy; small states formed.

800 Charlemagne crowned Roman emperor, lands include part of Italy.

c. 1170–c. 1240 Life of mathematician Leonardo Fibonacci.

1300s Italian city states flourish, Renaissance begins.

Area: 116,348 sq miles • Population: 58,126,212 • Capital: *Rome* • System of government: *Republic*

A detail of the creation of Adam from the ceiling of the Sistine Chapel, painted by Michelangelo between 1508 and 1512.

in these, particularly in the state of Florence. By the sixteenth century, Italy came under the Habsburgs, first the Spanish and then the Austrian branch.

Napoleon's conquests across Europe included north Italy, while republics were formed in the remaining area. After Napoleon's defeat, Italy was again in fragments, containing the Kingdom of Sardinia, the Kingdom of the two Sicilies, and the Papal States, along with Austrian duchies. The period of the Risorgimento followed, which included nationalist resistance to Austria. Secret societies emerged to organize resistance, among them the Carbonari of south Italy, and although revolutions took place in 1820, they were suppressed.

In 1831, Guiseppe Mazzini (1805–72) established the revolutionary Young Italy Society, which soon spread through Italy. Giuseppe Garibaldi (1807–82) and Conte Camillo Benso di Cavour (1810–61) were the other main leaders who unified Italy. Mazzini aimed to create a republic, but in the end a kingdom was created, proclaimed in 1861. Unification was completed in 1870. In 1871 Rome became the capital of the new kingdom of Italy.

Italy established colonies in Africa and began to modernize. In World War I Italy sided with the Allies. The economy suffered after the war, and in 1922 Benito Mussolini rose to power, gradually establishing a fascist dictatorship. In World War II Italy allied with Germany, but was defeated. Mussolini was killed in 1945, and in 1946 the king abdicated. In a referendum in 1946, Italy voted to become a republic, with its new constitution inaugurated on January 1, 1948.

1452–1519 Life of Leonardo da Vinci.

1475–1564 Life of artist Michaelangelo.

1494 France and Holy Roman Empire begin struggle for control of Italy.

1559 Most of Italy is under Spanish Habsburgs; **1700s** under Austrian Habsburgs.

1564–1642 Life of scientist Galileo Galilei.

1796 Napoleon conquers Northern Italy.

1814 Italy divides into many states, some controlled by foreigners.

1859 Several states unite with the powerful Italian kingdom of Sardinia.

1860 Giuseppe Garibaldi leads "Red Shirts," revolutionary Italian nationalists, liberates Sicily and Naples.

1861 Free Italian kingdoms unite as Kingdom of Italy under Sardinian king.

1871 Rome becomes capital of unified Italy.

1912 Italy occupies Libya after war with Ottoman empire.

THE REPUBLIC

Since 1948 Italy has had a number of short-lived governments. In the 1990s a movement to cleanse Italy of corruption began. Silvio Berlusconi, a controversial figure of the right-wing Forza Italia party, has been prime minister in 1994, from 2001–2006 and again from 2008. Italy has a diversified industrial economy, and a high per capita income, but has been severely affected by the global financial crisis of 2008.

Venice, city of canals.

Self-portrait by Leonardo da Vinci.

LEONARDO DA VINCI
(1452–1519)

Born in Vinci, Florence, Leonardo da Vinci was one of the greatest figures of the Renaissance. Multi-talented, he is primarily known for his art, particularly his paintings of the Mona Lisa and the Last Supper. In his journals he made sketches and provided details for a number of inventions, including a hang glider, a single-span bridge, a steam cannon, and musical instruments. Leonardo's drawing of the Vitruvian Man is reproduced on the euro.

Milestone Events

1915 Italy enters World War I.
1922 Benito Mussolini forms government.
1926 Grazia Deledda (1875–1936) from Sardinia wins Nobel Prize for Literature.
1929 Separate state of Vatican City created.
1935 Italy invades Ethiopia.
1936 Mussolini forms alliance with Germany.
1940 Italy joins World War II on German side.
1943 Peace with Allies, German occupation.

1944 Rome liberated by Allies.
1945 Mussolini is captured and shot.
1948 Italy becomes a republic.
1957 Italy is a founder member of the EU.
1972 Giulio Andreotti is elected prime minister; reelected 6 times in next 20 years.
1978 Former prime minister Aldo Moro is kidnapped and killed by Red Brigades.
1990S Nationwide investigation into political corruption, known as mani pulite (clean hands).

CULTURE

Italy, the center of the Renaissance, is known for great artists such as Michelangelo, Leonardo da Vinci, and Modigliani. The works of the poet Dante Alighieri formed the basis for the modern Italian language, and Vivaldi, Paganini, Rossini, Verdi, and Puccini are some of the great names in classical music. In popular culture, Italian pizza and pasta are now eaten throughout the world. However, Italy is also known for the criminal Mafia, who have influenced its politics and economy.

Right: Nationalist hero Giuseppe Garibaldi (1807–1882).
Below: Ruins of the Roman amphitheater, the Colosseum in Rome.

1994 Center-right Silvio Berlusconi is prime minister of coalition government.

1996 Center-left Romano Prodi elected prime minister; again **2006, 2008** resigns.

2001 Berlusconi elected prime minister again; also in **2008**.

2004 Berlusconi is found not guilty of corruption in previous business deals.

2006 Police capture Bernardo Provenzano, suspected mafia boss.

2008 Italy faces recession.

2008 Italy apologises to Libya for colonial years and agrees investment package as compensation.

2009 Earthquake hits Abruzzi region.

2009 Prime minister Silvio Berlusconi attacked at a rally in Milan, suffers broken nose.

2010 Violent outbursts against African migrant workers.

L ocated on the Iberian peninsula, Portugal and Spain are democratic nations which share aspects of their early history and culture. Iberians from Africa, Celts from France, Phoenicians, and Greeks all settled in the region, followed by the Romans, Visigoths, and Arabs. After this, though similarities continued to exist, the two countries developed in different ways.

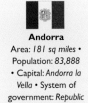

Andorra
Area: *181 sq miles* •
Population: *83,888*
• Capital: *Andorra la
Vella* • System of
government: *Republic*

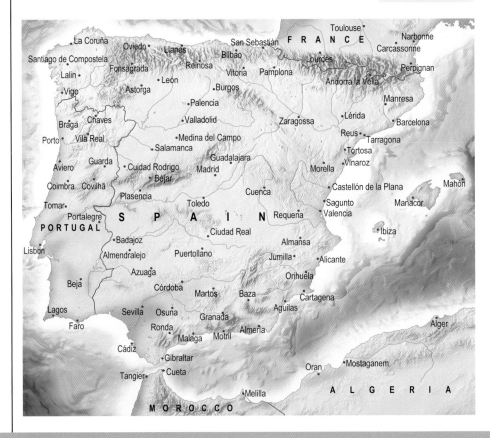

Milestone Events

1 MILLION YEARS AGO Region is occupied by early hominid species.

40,000 BCE Paleolithic cave paintings in Iberian peninsula.

5000 BCE Neolithic and Megalithic cultures.

3000 BCE Neolithic Almerian culture in southeast Spain.

1000 BCE Iberians, originally from North Africa, and Celts occupy the region.

1100–600 BCE Phoenicians settle in parts of region.

3rd CENTURY BCE Spain conquered by Carthage, city of Barcelona founded.

2nd CENTURY BCE Rome conquers Portugal and Spain.

5th–6th CENTURIES CE Visigoths occupy region.

711–18 Arabs conquer Spain, part of Portugal; Islam dominates.

997–1064 Northern Portugal reclaimed from Arabs.

11th–12th CENTURIES North African Berber dynasties Almoravids and Almohads rule part of Spain.

Antonio de Oliveira Salazar, Portuguese prime minister from 1932 to 1968.

Portugal

Portugal is a republic with an elected president. The administration is headed by the prime minister who is usually the leader of the majority party. The legislature is unicameral.

Portugal
Area: *35,556 sq miles (includes Azores and Madeira Islands)* • Population: *10,707,924* • Capital: *Lisbon* • System of government: *Republic*

THE PAST

The Arabs were expelled from Portugal in the thirteenth century. The fourteenth century is considered a golden age of art, when great religious sculptures were produced for the Church. During the following two centuries, Portugal became a world power, acquiring territories in South America, Asia, and Africa.

The Aviz dynasty ruled up to 1580, when an invasion by Spain brought the area under the Habsburgs of the Spanish line. In 1640 Portugal rebelled against Spain and reasserted its independence under the Braganza dynasty.

In 1750 Sebastiao de Melo, Marquis of Pombal, became chief minister, and introduced in economic reforms. In the nineteenth century Portugal began to decline, losing its largest territory of Brazil. Finally in 1910 the monarchy was overthrown and a republic established.

However, opposition to these changes led to a rapid succession of governments, more than 40 between 1910 and 1926, when a coup resulted in General Antonio Carmona becoming prime minister. His finance minister Antonio Salazar succeeded him, introducing measures which increased the wealth of the rich but made Portugal the poorest country in Europe.

By the early 1970s Portugal was seriously affected by revolts in the African colonies, which spurred a military coup in 1974 (known as Revolution of the Carnations). The colonies rapidly gained independence, and as Portuguese troops and settlers returned home from there, unemployment and economic problems increased.

Gradually the economy improved and political stability was maintained through a series of democratic elections.

The Algarve in southern Portugal is a favorite holiday destination.

The timelines for Spain, Portugal, and Andorra are shared on this and the next page.

1179 Pope recognizes Portugal as an independent state.
1248–1279 Arabs expelled from Portugal.
1278–1993 Andorra jointly ruled by French and Spanish figureheads.
1386 Portugal and England ally through Treaty of Windsor.
1478 Spanish Inquisition begins.
1479 States of Aragon and Castile rule Spain.
1492 Jews expelled from Spain.

• Christopher Columbus reaches Americas from Spain.
• Christians defeat the last Arab kingdom in Spain, Grenada.
1580 Portugal comes under Habsburgs of Spain.
1594 Portuguese Vasco da Gama reaches India.
1588 Spanish Armada defeated by England.
16th AND 17th CENTURIES Spain and Portugal gain colonies in America, Africa, Asia.
1714 Britain acquires Gibraltar from Spain.

Spain

Artist Pablo Picasso (1881–1973).

Spain is a constitutional monarchy with a bicameral legislature.

The Arab occupation of Spain from 711 left buildings such as the Alhambra palace and the Great Mosque of Cordoba. Islamic Spain was a center of art, science, and culture before Christian kingdoms reconquered the region.

In the sixteenth and seventeenth centuries Spain became an empire with overseas colonies in Africa and in the Americas, as well as extensive domains in Europe. The nation retained its overseas territories until the early nineteenth century.

The second Spanish Republic was founded in 1931, but right-wing military officers soon launched the Spanish Civil War. In the 1960s Spain became an industrialized economy, and its new democratic status was confirmed in the 1970s.

Spain
Area: 195,124 sq miles •
Population: 40,525,002 •
Capital: Madrid
• System of government: Constitutional monarchy

The Sagrada Familia, the Church of the Holy Family in Barcelona, is the masterpiece of architect Antoni Gaudi (1852–1926).

Milestone Events

1755 Lisbon devastated by earthquake.
1793–95 Spain fights war against France.
1807 Lisbon captured by France.
1808–13 Joseph Bonaparte, brother of Napoleon, becomes king of conquered Spain.
1810–25 Most Spanish American colonies win independence.
1822 Brazil gains independence from Portugal.
1898 Spanish–American war, Spain loses territories.
1908 Portuguese King Carlos assassinated.

1910 Revolution in Portugal establishes republic.
1916 Portugal enters World War I on side of Britain.
1923 General Primo de Rivera leads coup in Spain, made head of government by King Alfonso.
1931 Spain becomes republic.
1932–68 Antonio de Oliveira Salazar rules as dictator in Portugal.
1936–39 Spanish civil war; fascist leader General Franco gains power, rules as dictator.
1939 Spain and Portugal sign friendship pact.

The festival of the "Running of the Bulls" in Pamplona.

SPANISH AND PORTUGUESE CULTURE

Spanish and Portuguese cultures are closely related. Spanish dances, with their distinctive accompanying music, include the bolero and flamenco. Miguel de Cervantes (1547–1616), who created the character Don Quixote, is perhaps Spain's most famous author, and well-known artists include Pablo Picasso (1881–1973) and Salvador Dali (1904–89). Bull-fighting is a traditional sport, although in Portugal the bull is not killed in the ring.

1959 Basque separatist movement ETA founded.
1961 ETA begins violent campaign.
• Portuguese expelled from Goa, India.
1974 Military coup in Portugal.
1974–75 African territories gain independence from Portugal.
1975 Death of General Franco, King Juan Carlos succeeds in Spain.
1977 First democratic elections for 40 years in Spain.
1978 New constitution in Spain.

1982 Socialist government wins elections in Spain.
1993 Andorra becomes parliamentary democracy.
1999 Portuguese Macao transferred to China after 442 years.
2000 A new wave of violence from Basque separatists (ETA) in Spain.
2004 Islamic terrorists bomb trains in Madrid.
2006–07 Short-lived ETA ceasefire.
2010 Mass protests in Spain against government austerity measures.

This region of east Europe used to be either part of the USSR or was controlled by it. As the USSR began to disintegrate these states won freedom and independence in 1991.

Poland

In the seventeenth century, Poland was a center of culture and learning.

After World War II Poland became a Soviet satellite. From 1980, the trade union "Solidarity," led by Lech Walesa (b. 1943) opposed the Communist Party, and won the elections in 1989, the East European country to discard communism.

Lech Walesa.

Poland
Area:
120,728
sq miles •
Population:
38,482,919
• Capital:
Warsaw •
System of
government:
Republic

Milestone Events

1025 Kingdom of Poland formed.
1569 Poland forms commonwealth with Grand Duchy of Lithuania.
1645 Estonia occupied by Sweden; **1721** ceded to Russia.
1772–95 Poland partitioned between Austria, Prussia, and Russia.
1918 Poland gains independence.
1920 Baltic states Estonia, Latvia, Lithuania, formerly part of Russia, gain independence.

1921 Belarus split between Poland and USSR.
1921–22, 1932–33, Famine in Ukraine.
1939–45 World War II; German invasion of Poland is trigger for war. East Europe occupied by Nazis, then by Soviet Union in its advance on Germany.
1943 Jews in the Warsaw ghetto fight Nazis.
1944 Stalin deports 200,000 Tatars from Crimea region of Ukraine.
1940s Baltic states annexed by USSR.
1947 Poland becomes communist.

The Bratislava city museum, Slovakia, founded in 1868.

The Charles Bridge in Prague, Czech Republic.

Czech Republic and Slovakia

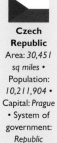

Alexander Dubcek.

O nce a united nation, the Czech Republic and Slovakia separated in 1993. Both countries introduced market reforms and have growing and relatively stable economies. German demands for the Sudetenland in southern Czechoslovakia were a partial cause of World War II. During the war the Czech government in exile turned to the USSR for help.

In 1968, during the "Prague Spring," Alexander Dubcek's (1921–92) democracy movement was suppressed by a Soviet-led invasion. When the USSR began to crumble, the peaceful "Velvet" or "Gentle" Revolution of 1989 led to democratic elections in 1990.

Later there was a "Velvet divorce," with two separate nations being created.

Czech Republic
Area: *30,451 sq miles* •
Population: *10,211,904* •
Capital: *Prague*
• System of government: *Republic*

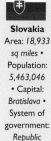

Slovakia
Area: *18,933 sq miles* •
Population: *5,463,046*
• Capital: *Bratislava* •
System of government: *Republic*

The timelines for Poland, the Czech Republic, Slovakia, Belarus, Estonia, Latvia, Lithuania, and Ukraine are shared on this and the next page.

1948 Czechoslovakia becomes communist.
1955 Czechoslovakia and Poland are founder members of the defensive Warsaw Pact.
1968 Alexander Dubcek becomes head of Czechoslovak Communist Party, launches "socialism with a human face," liberal reforms known as Prague Spring; USSR leads Warsaw Pact forces to overturn changes.
1970 Riots in Gdansk, Poland over food prices; hundreds killed.

1980 Trade union Solidarity formed in Poland.
1986 Accident at Chernobyl power plant in Ukraine.
1988 Latvia People's Front formed to lead independence struggle.
1989 Peaceful 'Velvet' revolution in Czechoslovakia; Dubcek elected speaker in new non-communist parliament.
• Writer Vaclav Havel (b. 1936) elected president in Czechoslovakia; reelected **1998**.

Lithuania

Lithuania
Area: *25,212 sq miles* •
Population: *3,555,179* •
Capital: *Vilnius*
• System of government: *Republic*

Lithuania was a reluctant Soviet republic from 1944 to 1991, when it gained independence.

Latvia

Latvia
Area: *24,938 sq miles* •
Population: *2,231,503* •
Capital: *Riga*
• System of government: *Republic*

Latvian people probably reached the area in the ninth century, but the region was ruled by other countries, most recently the USSR, until 1991.

Right: Costumed stilt walkers in one of Lithuania's many traditional festivals.
Below: Lake Voistre in Estonia.

Milestone Events

- Lithuanian Communist Party supports independence.
- Poland forms Third Polish republic.
- **1990s** Thousands of Tatars return to Ukraine.
- **1990** Lech Walesa of Solidarity trade union becomes president of Poland.
- **1991** Break up of the Soviet Union: Estonia, Latvia, Lithuania, Ukraine become independent from USSR.

- **1993** "Velvet divorce" in Czechoslovakia: divides peacefully into two independent countries, Czech Republic and Slovakia.
- Havel elected president of Czech Republic; reelected **1998**.
- Constitution of 1922 restored in Latvia.
- **1994** Aleksandr Lukashenko elected president of Belarus, creates authoritarian government.
- **1999** Belarus and Russia sign treaty aiming at further integration.

Bison in the Belavezha National Park, located
partly in Belarus and partly in Poland.

Estonia
Area:
17,462
sq miles •
Population:
1,299,371
• Capital:
Tallinn •
System of
government:
Republic

Estonia

On the eastern shores of the Baltic Sea, Estonia has taken cultural influences from its past rulers: Russia, Denmark, Germany, Sweden, and Poland.

Belarus
Area: 80,155
sq miles •
Population:
9,648,533 •
Capital: Minsk
• System of
government:
Republic
(authoritarian)

Belarus

Belarus still has several restrictions on personal freedom.

Ukraine
Area: 233,032
sq miles •
Population:
45,700,395 •
Capital: Kiev
• System of
government:
Republic

Ukraine

The second largest country in Europe after Russia, Ukraine supplied a large part of the USSR's agrarian produce.

St. Michael's Cathedral in Kiev, Ukraine.

The timelines for Belarus, Estonia, Latvia, Lithuania, Ukraine, Czech Republic, Poland, and Slovakia are shared on this and the preceding page.

- Vaira Vike-Freiberga of Latvia is first woman president in East Europe; reelected **2003**.
- **2001** Ukraine and Russia re-link electricity grids.
- **2002** Floods in Prague, in Czech Republic.
- **2004** Orange Revolution in Ukraine leads to democratic elections; Victor Yuschenko elected.
- Poland, Czech Republic, Slovakia, Estonia, Latvia, Lithuania join European Union.
- **2006** A dispute over price rises leads to Russia temporarily cutting gas supplies to Ukraine.

- **2007** In dispute with Belarus Russia cuts oil pipeline.
- **2009** Slovakia joins Euro zone.
- Russia again stops gas supply to Ukraine until agreement reached on prices.
- Ukraine and Russia reach agreement on oil transit, allowing through supply to western Europe.
- **2010** Belarus forms Customs Union with Russia and Kazakhstan.
- President of Poland Lech Kaczinsky and other officials die in plane crash.

Albania

Albania has a poor infrastructure but is introducing market reforms to improve the economy.

Albania
Area: *11,100 sq miles* • Population: *3,639,453* • Capital: *Tirana* • System of government: *Republic*

Bulgaria
Area: *42,811 sq miles* • Population: *7,204,687* • Capital: *Sofia* • System of government: *Republic*

Bulgaria

Bulgaria held the first multiparty elections of the Soviet era, which turned it into a democracy in 1989.

Cyprus

Conflicts between Greek and Turkish Cypriots revived in 1963.

Cyprus
Area: *3,572 sq miles* • Population: *1,084,748* • Capital: *Nicosia (Lefkosia)* • System of government: *Republic*

The spectacular Belogradchik rocks, Bulgaria.

Milestone Events

5th–4th CENTURIES BCE Classical Greek civilization flourishes.
c. 200 BCE–C.1400 CE Roman/Byzantine rule.
1453 Ottomans begin to conquer whole region.
1829 Greece, Romania (**1878**), Bulgaria (**1908**), Albania (**1912**) win independence from Ottomans.
1914 Britain annexes Cyprus.
1940 World War II: Greece invaded by Italy.
• USSR creates Moldavian Soviet Socialist Republic.

1941–44 Greece occupied by Germany.
1944 Albanian communists resist Germans; Enver Hoxha becomes head of state till 1985.
1945–46 Romania, Bulgaria become communist.
1946–49 Civil war in Greece: royalists defeat communists.
1960 Cyprus becomes independent of Britain.
1965 Nicolae Ceausescu takes over in Romania.
1967 Military coup in Greece.
1974 Turkey occupies north Cyprus.

The Acropolis, Athens.

Greece

Moldova
Area: *13,070
sq miles* •
Population:
4,320,748 •
Capital: *Chisinau
(Kishinev)* •
System of
government:
Republic

Known for its great ancient civilization, Greece is a highly developed nation. After World War II there was a civil war between communists and non-communists and in 1974 the monarchy was overthrown. In 2010 Greece suffered a financial crisis which had the potential to affect the whole European Union.

Greece
Area: *50,949
sq miles* •
Population:
10,737,428 •
Capital: *Athens*
• System of
government:
Republic

Moldova

Once part of Romania, Moldova came under the Soviet Union in 1940. Its poor economy has encouraged illegal emigration and people trafficking.

Romania
Area: *92,043
sq miles* •
Population:
22,215,421
• Capital:
Bucharest •
System of
government:
Republic

Romania

Nicolae Ceausescu came to power in 1965 but lost popularity. In 1989 he was overthrown and executed.

Bran Castle, Romania.

1989 Uprising in Romania; Ceausescu shot.
1989–90 Free elections in Bulgaria.
1991 Moldova declares independence.
• Albania holds first multi-party elections.
1996 Non-communist government in Romania.
1997 Albanian rioters raid army stores for weapons.
2000 Cyanide-contaminated water escapes dam in Romania, reaches Yugoslavia and Hungary.
2004 Cyprus joins the EU but is still divided.
2005 Angry protests over labor laws in Greece.

2007 Bulgaria and Romania join the EU.
2008 Negotiations to unite Cyprus begin.
• Riots by young people in Greece.
• EU halts aid to Bulgaria because of lack of government action over corruption and organized crime.
2009 Greece's debt crisis threatens other European nations; EU offers a rescue package.
2010 Turkish and Greek Cypriots leaders fail to reach agreement on reunification.

These nations once formed the country of Yugoslavia, a separate monarchy from 1918 to 1991, and a liberal communist regime under President Tito after World War II.

Tito died in 1980, but the death blow for Yugoslavia was the collapse of communism in 1989, leaving a vacuum that power-hungry nationalists rushed to fill.

After free elections in 1990–91 Croatia, Slovenia, and Macedonia proclaimed their independence, followed in 1992 by Bosnia and Herzegovina, while Serbia and Montenegro became the new Federal Republic of Yugoslavia (FRY).

Serbian president Slobodan Milosevic's call for Serbian expansion was a major factor in the wars that followed.

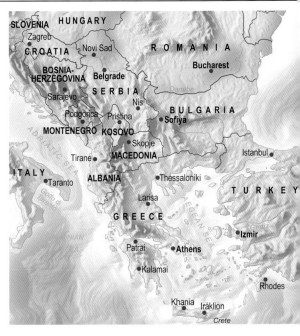

Bosnia–Herzegovina

First Serbs and then Croats turned on the Bosniak Muslim population. In December 1995 peace was agreed by creating a semi-autonomous Serbian territory within Bosnia–Herzegovina.

Bosnia and Herzegovina
Area: 19,767 sq miles •
Population: 4,613,414 •
Capital: Sarajevo
• System of government: Federal republic

Croatia

After Croatia declared independence from Yugoslavia in 1991, four years of fighting between Serbs and Croats followed.

Croatia
Area: 21,851 sq miles •
Population: 4,489,409 •
Capital: Zagreb
• System of government: Republic

Milestone Events

c. 8000–2000 BCE Farming cultures in the region.
15th–17th CENTURIES Region comes under Ottoman empire.
18th CENTURY Austria–Hungary controls part of the region.
1878 Serbia, Montenegro gain independence.
1913 Turks driven out of Kosovo and Macedonia by Balkan allies.
1914 Archduke Franz Ferdinand of Austria–Hungary killed in Sarajevo; triggers World War I.

1918 Kingdom of Serbs, Croats, Slovenes formed;
1929 Renamed Yugoslavia.
1941 World War II: Germany invades, communist resistance led by Josip Tito.
1945 Tito declares communist republic; **1946** creates six republics within federal Yugoslavia.
1980 Tito dies.
1990–91 After the collapse of communism, nationalist parties win elections in every republic.
1991 Slovenia, Croatia, Macedonia break away.

Kosovo

Kosovo, with an Albanian majority, declared independence from Serbia in 2008. This is not accepted by Serbia, but more than 60 countries have recognized it.

Kosovo
Area: *4,203 sq miles* •
Population: *1,804,838* •
Capital: *Pristina*
• System of government: *Republic*

Macedonia

After Macedonia gained independence, Greece objected to its Hellenic name, and in 1993 the country took the formal name the Former Yugoslav Republic of Macedonia when it joined the UN.

Gathering firewood during the siege of Sarajevo, 1992–96.

Montenegro

In 2006 Montenegro split from Serbia

Macedonia
Area: *9,928 sq miles* •
Population: *2,066,718* •
Capital: *Skopje*
• System of government: *Republic*

Montenegro
Area: *5,333 sq miles* •
Population: *672,180* •
Capital: *Podgorica*
• System of government: *Republic*

Serbia

After the violence and attempt at "ethnic cleansing" during the civil war, Serbia brutally suppressed the demands for independence by the Albanian majority in Kosovo.

Serbia
Area: *29,913 sq miles* •
Population: *7,379,339* •
Capital: *Belgrade*
• System of government: *Republic*

Slovenia
Area: *7,827 sq miles* •
Population: *2,005,692* •
Capital: *Ljubljana*
• System of government: *Republic*

Slovenia

After independence Slovenia had to repel attacks by the Serb-run Yugoslav army, but is now a stable economy and a functioning democracy.

* Serb-run Yugoslav army fails to conquer Slovenia; helps take Serb-inhabited land in Croatia.
1992 Bosnia declares independence; Bosnian Serbs begin ethnic cleansing.
1992–92 Bosnian Serbs besiege Sarajevo.
1995 8000 Bosnians massacred at Srebrenica.
* Dayton Peace Accords signed by Bosnia, Serbia, Croatia, end Bosnian war.
1997 Serb nationalist Slobodan Milosevic becomes president of Yugoslavia.

1999 Kosovo becomes UN protectorate.
2000 General strike in Yugoslavia; Milosevic resigns; Vojislav Kostunica becomes president.
2003 Federal Republic of Yugoslavia renamed Serbia and Montenegro.
2004 Ethnic violence in Kosovo.
* Slovenia joins NATO and EU.
2006 Montenegro separates from Serbia.
* Under trial for war crimes, Slobodan Milosevic dies in prison in The Hague.

Austria
Area: *32,383
sq miles* •
Population:
8,210,281 •
Capital: *Vienna*
• System of
government:
Federal republic

Austria

Austria is a prosperous democracy with a long history as a great empire. The chief of state is a president, while the chancellor is the head of government.

The vast Austro–Hungarian empire dissolved after its defeat in World War I. With many Nazi sympathizers, the new, small nation of Austria was annexed by Germany in 1938. After World War II Austria was occupied by the Allies, regaining sovereignty in 1955.

Vienna's popular attraction, the Spanish Riding School.

CULTURE

Austria has a rich musical heritage. Wolfgang Amadeus Mozart (1756–91) is perhaps its best-known composer, though there were many others such as Joseph Haydn (1732–1809), Franz Schubert (1797–1828) and Gustav Mahler (1860–1911). In the world of ideas Sigmund Freud (1856–1939) laid the foundations of psychoanalysis, while Ludwig Wittgenstein (1889–1951) was one of the world's great philosophers.

Wolfgang Amadeus Mozart.

Milestone Events

1000 BCE Celtic people live in the region.
15 BCE Roman empire controls part of the region.
c. 895 Magyars dominate Hungary.
955 Otto I, Holy Roman emperor, defeats Magyars in Hungary.
1001 Stephen I founds kingdom of Hungary.
1526 Hungary defeated by Ottomans in Battle of Mohacs, becomes part of Ottoman empire.
1683 Turkish siege of Vienna defeated; Austria pursues Ottoman army and gains Hungary.

1815–48 Prince Metternich, chancellor of Austria, dominates European politics.
1849 Hungary proclaims independence, Austria reasserts control with Russian help.
1866 Liechtenstein becomes independent of Germany.
1867 Dual monarchy of Austria–Hungary established.
1914 Archduke Franz Ferdinand assassinated in Serbia, trigger for World War I.
1918 Austro–Hungarian empire dissolved.
1920 Austria becomes a republic.

Hungary
Area: *35,918 sq miles* • Population: *9,905,596* • Capital: *Budapest* • System of government: *Republic*.

Liechtenstein
Area: *62 sq miles* • Population: *34,761* • Capital: *Vaduz* • System of government: *Constitutional monarchy*

Hungary

After World War II Hungary became a communist state. In 1956 its attempt to break free of USSR control was suppressed by Soviet troops, but it remained liberal, and after elections in 1989 it became a democratic republic.

Right: Hungarian leader Imre Nagy (1896–1958) was executed by the USSR for his part in the 1956 uprising.
Below: A panoramic view of the Hungarian capital, Budapest.

1938 "Anschluss" (union); Austria unites with Germany.
1945 After World War II Austria occupied by Allies.
1949 Hungarian People's Republic formed, in association with USSR.
1956 Soviet troops crush Hungarian uprising.
1989 Hungary opens its border with Austria, allowing East Europeans to reach the West.
• Communists give up power, Republic of Hungary formed.

1990 Democratic Forum wins elections in Hungary.
1995 Austria joins EU.
2000 Ecological disaster in Hungary, as cyanide-polluted water flows in rivers.
• EU imposes diplomatic sanctions on Austria after far-right Freedom Party joins coalition government.
2004 Hungary joins EU.
2009 Far-right Hungarian Jobbik party wins 15 per cent of the vote in European Elections.

United Kingdom

The United Kingdom comprises England, Wales, Scotland, and Northern Ireland, as well as some outlying territories. England, Wales, Scotland are parts of the island of Great Britain, while Northern Ireland is part of the island of Ireland.

Separated from Europe, Britain is only 22 miles from France and is now linked by a tunnel under the English Channel. The chief of state is a hereditary monarch, whose role is ceremonial, and the government is headed by a prime minister. The legislature is bicameral: the elected House of Commons and the House of Lords.

HISTORY

The islands experienced several migrations and invasions, including by the Celts and Romans. After the withdrawal of Rome in the fifth century, England fragmented into small states, some of which employed mercenaries from Germany to defend their kingdoms from the northern Picts and Scots. By the seventh century these mercenaries, collectively known as Anglo-Saxons, settled in the south and east, displacing earlier rulers and providing much that became known as "English."

Danes and Vikings also conquered parts of Britain, and the last invasion was the Norman Conquest in 1066.

Milestone Events

c. 500,000 YEARS AGO Islands are first occupied.
8000–6000 BCE As ice caps recede and seas rise, land bridge to continental Europe is submerged.
c. 3100 First phase of building Stonehenge.
c. 650 BCE Celtic culture reaches British Isles.
43–409 CE Roman conquest and occupation of Britain.
c. 250 Scots, possibly from Iberia, settle in Ulster.
449 Anglo-Saxon invasions begin.
496 Legend says King Arthur defeats the Saxons.
c. 500 Scotland invaded by Celts from Ireland.

c. 790 Danish raids and settlement begins.
843–78, 889–1040 House of Alpin rules Scotland.
871 Alfred the Great of Wessex defeats Danes.
1002 Brian Boru becomes chief king of Ireland.
1066 Norman conquest of England.
1215 King John accepts Magna Carta.
1216 Llewellyn founds principality of Wales.
1337–1453 Hundred Years' War with France.
1343–1400 Life of Geoffrey Chaucer, whose *Canterbury Tales* is first work in vernacular English.

GVLIELMVS · CONQISTER ·

William the Conqueror.

The English kingdoms began to unite in the 10th century. England's union with Wales began in 1284 and was formalized by an Act of Union in 1536. In 1707, England and Scotland united as Great Britain; Great Britain and Ireland united in 1801. However, southern Ireland separated in 1921–22. England has dominated British history, but Scotland, Wales, and Northern Ireland have recently received more local powers.

Meanwhile, from the seventeenth century onwards, England began to expand her territories overseas in North America, Australia, Asia, and Africa. The first country to industrialize, Britain became the greatest power in the world, with the largest empire. However, in the eighteenth century, it lost its North American territories that became the USA.

At the beginning of the twentieth century Britain still had a huge empire. Britain suffered economically during World War I, but by the Paris Peace treaties of 1919, gained further colonies—those of Germany in Africa, and Turkish territories in the Middle East.

The Second World War placed new economic burdens on Britain, and the cost of suppressing freedom movements in the colonies seemed too high. The post-war Labour government was also more inclined to grant independence,

UK
Area: 94,058 sq miles •
Population: 61,113,205 •
Capital: London
• System of government: Constitutional monarchy

so, beginning with India and Pakistan in 1947, most of the colonies gained autonomy over the next two decades. British culture, including its tradition of parliamentary democracy, had an impact on its former territories.

Despite the loss of most of its overseas territories, in the twenty-first century the UK is still a political and economic power.

War-time prime minister Sir Winston Churchill.

1455–85 Civil war, Wars of the Roses.
1532 Tudor King Henry VIII breaks with Catholic Church, forms Protestant Church of England.
1536 First Act of Union between England and Wales; English conquest of Ireland begins.
1558–1603 Reign of Elizabeth I.
1564–1616 Life of playwright William Shakespeare.
1588 Spanish invasion fleet, the Armada, defeated.
LATE 16th CENTURY Britain begins colonizing foreign nations.

1603–25 James VI of Scotland rules as James I of England, uniting the two crowns.
1642–46, 1648–49 Civil War in England and Scotland, ends with execution of Charles I, founding of Commonwealth under Oliver Cromwell.
1660 Restoration of the monarchy.
1661 Charles II is crowned king.
1689 Parliament passes Bill of Rights.
1721–42 Sir Robert Walpole is leader of House of Commons, considered Britain's first prime minister.

249

ENGLAND

England is highly developed and technologically advanced. The capital, London is considered one of the greatest cultural cities in the world. Though English is the main language, England is multicultural.

William Shakespeare (1564–1616) is perhaps the most famous English writer, though Charles Dickens (1812–70) and the Romantic poets are also particularly well known.

Classical musicians include Henry Purcell (c.1659–95), Edward

The Beatles.

Elgar (1857–1934), and Benjamin Britten (1913–76), while rock and pop music has been prominent since the 1960s, the time of the Beatles and the Rolling Stones. Great scientists have included Isaac Newton (1642–1727) and Charles Darwin (1809–82).

Above: The Tower of London.
Left: William Shakespeare.

Milestone Events

c.1750 Industrial revolution begins; Britain becomes advanced, leading power in world.
1752 Britain accepts use of Gregorian calendar.
1837–1901 Reign of queen Victoria.
1840s Potato famine in Ireland, thousands emigrate.
1851 Great exhibition opens at Crystal Palace, London.
1871 Universities Tests Act allows any man, no matter what his religion, to get higher degrees and hold office.
1899–1902 Anglo-Boer war in South Africa.

1905 Sinn Fein nationalist party founded in Ireland.
1907 Triple Entente signed by Britain, France, Russia.
1914–18 UK enters World War I.
1916 Irish nationalists' Easter uprising; proclaim Irish Republic, but movement crushed.
1918 Right to vote granted to women over 30.
1921 Irish Free State founded as a Dominion of UK.
1922 The British empire covers about one quarter of the world's area and population.
1924 Labour Party first comes to power.

Caernarfon Castle, Wales.

WALES

Wales has its own culture and language, though most of the population speaks English. Its National Assembly meets in its capital, Cardiff. Literature in Welsh has its own traditions, and dates back to the sixth century. Dafydd ap Gwilym of the fourteenth century is generally considered the greatest Welsh poet of all time.

DEPENDENT TERRITORIES OF THE UK

The UK still has a number of territories which are self-governing but dependent on the UK for defense and foreign affairs.

These include Bermuda, British Antarctic Territory, Cayman Islands, Falkland Islands, Gibraltar.

The Isle of Man and Channel Islands are not part of the UK, but are direct dependencies of the British Crown.

1926 Widespread strikes.
1927 The name The United Kingdom of Great Britain and Northern Ireland is adopted.
1931 Unemployment increases after world economic depression.
• British Commonwealth founded.
1936 King Edward VIII abdicates in order to marry an American divorcee, Wallis Simpson.
1937 Irish Free State becomes Republic of Ireland, a fully independent state.

1939–45 World War II, UK fights against Germany.
1940 Winston Churchill becomes prime minister.
1947 First Edinburgh International Festival held.
• Britain grants independence to India, then to other colonies in later years.
1948 National Health Service founded.
• Immigration from the Caribbean and other Commonwealth countries begins in earnest.
1949 UK is a founder member of NATO.

SCOTLAND

Scotland now has its own parliament, and has always had its own legal system. Glasgow, the largest city in Scotland, was once a great industrial and cultural center, while its capital, Edinburgh, is home to important annual festivals. In the eighteenth century Scotland had 75 per cent literacy, the highest in Europe. Great thinkers, philosophers, scientists, and poets belong to this time, including David Hume (1711–76), Adam Smith (1723–90), and Robert Burns (1759–96), Scotland's national poet.

Eilean Donan Castle, Loch Duich, Scotland.

NORTHERN IRELAND

Northern Ireland to the northeast of the Republic of Ireland is part of the UK. It has faced bitter conflicts between the mainly Roman Catholic nationalists who wanted to unite with the Irish Republic, and the mainly Protestant unionists who wished to remain with UK. After 1998 a degree of peace was established and it now has its own legislature and executive.

Milestone Events

1953 Elizabeth II is crowned queen.

1969 "The Troubles" in Northern Ireland: British troops keep order; separatist Irish Republican Army (IRA) attack police, troops, Protestants.

1970 Sinn Fein, political party in Northern Ireland, splits.

1973 UK and Ireland join EEC.

1979 Conservative Margaret Thatcher becomes first woman prime minister, reelected 1983, 1987.

1982 Falklands War with Argentina.

1984 The IRA bomb the hotel in Brighton hosting the Conservative Party conference; five killed.

1986 The Conservative government begins program of privatization of major industries.

1990 Poll Tax riots in London oppose new local poll (head) tax.

1992 The Channel Tunnel opens linking UK to France.

Republic of Ireland

The Giant's Causeway, Northern Ireland.

Ireland became divided in 1921–22, with 26 counties gaining independence and six remaining with the UK as Northern Ireland. There was civil war in 1922–23 between those who supported the Irish Free State, and those who felt it betrayed their aspirations for a united, independent Ireland. The country became a sovereign state in 1937, and a republic in 1949.

Ireland
Area: *27,133 sq miles* • Population: *4,203,200* • Capital: *Dublin* • System of government: *Republic*

Between 1995 and 2000 Ireland's high economic growth rates led to the nickname the "Celtic Tiger," before the economy declined.

The Temple Bar district of Dublin has a reputation for great night life and drinking spots.

- Church of England agrees to accept women priests.
- **1997** Labour Party led by Tony Blair wins election; second term in **2001**; third, **2005**.
- Diana, princess of Wales, killed in Paris car crash.
- **1998** Devolution: Scottish Parliament, Welsh Assembly, Northern Ireland Assembly created.
- **2001** The Eden Project, artificial biomes, opens in Cornwall.
- **2001** Britain joins USA's war in Afghanistan.

- **2003** UK joins in USA's war against Iraq.
- **2005** Islamic terrorists bomb London.
- IRA formally ends armed struggle against UK.
- **2008** Women bishops allowed in Church of England.
- Financial crisis in UK.
- **2010** Coalition government led by David Cameron of Conservative Party (with Liberal Democrats).

Australia is a small continent, but a large country. It consists mainly of flat plains and low plateaux, apart from the mountainous region of the Great Dividing Range, and is on the whole a dry region. Along the east coast is the Great Barrier Reef, a long chain of coral reefs. The Commonwealth of Australia has six states, two territories, and several dependencies, and has a federal government. The British monarch is also the monarch of Australia, and is represented by a governor-general, while the prime minister is the administrative head. Australia has rich mineral resources, as well as sources for renewable energy, and some unique animals particularly the koala and the kangaroo.

Australia
Area: 2,988,902 sq miles • Population: 21,262,641 • Capital: *Canberra* • System of government: *Constitutional monarchy with federal parliamentary democracy*

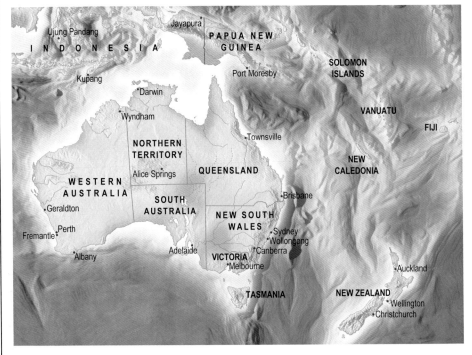

Milestone Events

60,000–40,000 BCE First humans arrive in Australia, probably from southeast Asia.

20,000 Aborigines spread south to Tasmania.

600–1400 CE Polynesians reach New Zealand.

1640 Abel Tasman, Dutch explorer reaches New Zealand; names Tasmania Van Dieman's Land.

1770 Captain James Cook claims territory of Australia for Britain.

1788 British penal settlement of 800 convicts established at Sydney, New South Wales, Australia.

1790s Individual settlers arrive in New Zealand.

1828–32 Black War in Van Dieman's Land: white settlers are encouraged to capture aborigines; genocide follows and most native survivors are transported to Bass Strait Islands.

1829 Colony established in West Australia, at Perth; **1836** colony founded in South Australia.

Uluru (Ayers Rock) in Australia's Northern Territory.

Australia was possibly first occupied around 40,000 BCE or even earlier. Population was sparse across the vast region until Europeans began to settle here in the eighteenth century. The existing indigenous population declined after their arrival. The first British settlement, consisting of convicts along with officials to guard them and administer the region, was founded in 1788, and named Sydney. Later, immigrants from Britain came by choice, particularly after gold was discovered in the region. The early settlers were largely cut off from their home country; letters could take one year to arrive by sea.

In 1901 Australia became a federation. Agriculture and mining were the mainstay of its economy, and Australia is still one of the largest exporters of coal and wool. It is an industrialized and highly developed economy, and has begun to recognize the rights of the indigenous people.

Australian aboriginal culture includes use of body paints and the unique musical instrument, the didgeridoo.

CULTURE
Aboriginal art began with rock paintings, typified by those in Arnhem Land in the Northern Territory. From the late nineteenth century, Australian painters of European origin began to depict typically Australian scenes. Aboriginal literature was initially oral, consisting of myths, legends, and sacred tales. Much of it has now been recorded in English. Other literature is not merely written by Europeans, but also by later Asian immigrants. Aboriginal music has the unique didgeridoo instrument.

1840 Treaty of Waitangi, indigenous New Zealand Maori chiefs cede sovereignty to Queen Victoria, but retain rights to territory.

1845–72 Land Wars; Maoris resist British incursion in New Zealand, defeated.

1848–50 Formal colonies established in New Zealand.

1850s Gold discovered in Australia, a series of gold rushes follow.

1851 European population in New Zealand is estimated to be 26,707.

1852 Constitution Act in New Zealand creates general assembly and two chambers.

1856 Australia is first country in the world to have secret ballots in elections.

1861 Gold discovered in Otago, New Zealand.

1893 New Zealand gives women right to vote, first country to do so, but not the right to stand for election.

1896 Truganini, the last full-blood Tasmanian aboriginal still on the island, dies.

AUSTRALIA

New Zealand in the Pacific Ocean consists of two large islands, North and South, as well as smaller islands and overseas territories. The country is a parliamentary democracy although the British monarch is the head of state, represented by a governor-general.

With mountains, highlands, rivers, and waterfalls, New Zealand has considerable hydroelectric power, as well as coal and natural gas.

The islands were probably settled by Polynesians from around 600 CE onwards. Abel Tasman and James Cook were the first European visitors to the islands, which were later annexed by Britain.

New Zealand became the first country in the world to give women the right to vote, in 1893.

New Zealand
Area: 103,363 sq miles •
Population: 4,213,418
• Capital: Wellington
• System of government: Constitutional monarchy with parliamentary democracy

The New Zealand economy is based on agriculture, manufacturing, and tourism. The economy suffered in the late nineties from the Asian economic crisis.

Above: A Maori man displaying traditional tattoos.
Left: Koala bears are unique to Australia and will not survive in other countries.

1995 to 2010

1901 Federal Commonwealth of Australia formed.
1902 Australia grants women, except Aborigines, right to vote and run for election.
1907 New Zealand becomes dominion of Britain.
1911 Canberra becomes capital of Australia.
1915 Australia and New Zealand suffer severe losses in Gallipoli campaign of World War I.
1939–41 World War II: Anzac forces fight with Britain; the U.S. sites its supreme command for the Pacific campaign on Australian territory.

1947 New Zealand becomes independent from UK.
1948 Australia encourages immigration from Europe.
1951 New Zealand, Australia, USA, sign Anzus Pacific Security Treaty.
1973 New Zealand exports suffer when UK joins the EC.
1984 New Zealand bars nuclear-armed ships from her ports.

OCEANIA ISLAND TERRITORIES

There are a large number of island countries in Oceania: Fiji, Kiribati, Marshall Islands, Nauru, Palau, Papua New Guinea, Samoa, Solomon Islands, Tonga, Tuvalu, Vanuatu, and the Federated State of Micronesia.

Above: Tongan dancers.
Left: The ancient culture of Papua New Guinea survives today.
Below: The islands of Oceania can offer unspoilt tropical beaches, such as this one on Fiji.

1986 Australian law becomes independent from that of Britain.

1993 Native Title Act passed to grant land rights to Aborigines in Australia.

1995 New Zealand government agrees to return to Maoris lands that were illegally seized in the 19th century, and to pay compensation.

1999 In a referendum, 55 per cent of Australians vote to keep the UK monarch as head of state rather than have a president.

2006 Australia and East Timor agree to share revenues from oil and gas finds in the Timor Sea.

• Maori queen Dame Te Ata dies in New Zealand after reign of 40 years.

2008 Australia apologizes to aborigines for abuses.

• New Zealand is the first western nation to sign a free trade pact with China.

• Quentin Bryce is the first female governor-general of Australia.

2009 180 people die in bushfires in Victoria.

INDEX

272